GIVING UP THE GHOST

GIVING UP THE GHOST

A STORY ABOUT FRIENDSHIP, 80S ROCK,
A LOST SCRAP OF PAPER,
AND WHAT IT MEANS
TO BE HAUNTED

ERIC NUZUM

Dial Press Trade Paperbacks 🦁 New York

A Dial Press Trade Paperback Original

Published in the United States by Dial Press Trade Paperbacks,
an imprint of The Random House Publishing Group,
a division of Random House, Inc., New York.

DIAL PRESS is a registered trademark of Random House, Inc.,
and the colophon is a trademark of Random House, Inc.

Library of Congress Cataloging-in-Publication Data

Nuzum, Eric.
Giving up the ghost: a story about friendship, 80s rock, a lost scrap of paper,
and what it means to be haunted / Eric Nuzum.
p.   cm.
ISBN 978-0-385-34243-8 (pbk.)—ISBN 978-0-345-53468-2 (eBook)
1. Nuzum, Eric—Psychology. 2. Nuzum, Eric—Friends and associates.
3. Ghosts—Psychological aspects. I. Title.
BF1471.N89 2012
133.1092—dc23
[B]
2012006290

Printed in the United States of America

www.dialpress.com

2 4 6 8 9 7 5 3 1

Book design by Elizabeth A. D. Eno

All people are like this when they are dead. . . .
The soul flits away as though it were a dream.
—Homer, *The Odyssey*

I would like, if I may, to take you on a strange journey.
—Criminologist, *The Rocky Horror Picture Show*

This is a story about a boy. A boy who became very lost.

It's a story about the girl who helped him find his way. Then she left him on his own. Then she died.

It's a story about spending twenty years trying to forget one year of your life.

It's a story about eventually turning to the thing you fear most to help you remember.

It's a story about ghosts.

It's a story about being trapped in time.

It's a story about what it means to be haunted.

GIVING UP THE GHOST

PROLOGUE

There are many kinds of ghost stories. Here's one.

One night in June 1984, I took a girl from my high school named Laura to meet my friend Jimmy at a local miniature-golf course, the Putt-O-Links.

Putt-O-Links was located at the end of a long strip of abandoned industrial buildings outside of Canton, Ohio. Canton was once a blue-collar Mecca devoted to making vacuum cleaners, ball bearings, and steel. During the 1980s, Canton, like the entire Midwest Rust Belt, was in absolute denial that its way of life was dying right before its eyes. I don't think *globalization* was even a word then, but places like Canton were already experiencing it firsthand.

Each spring the world around Putt-O-Links got smaller and smaller. One by one the nearby factories closed. Next, the car dealerships down the street moved. After that, the diner closed. Eventually, the Putt-O-Links and the ice cream stand next door were the only signs of life for half a mile in any direction. Then, that spring, the Putt-O-Links didn't open either. Neither did the ice cream stand. There were no GOING OUT OF BUSINESS or THANKS FOR THIRTY GREAT YEARS signs, just tall weeds and a fallen rusty chain that had once closed off the parking lot. It looked almost as if the owners had just forgotten that summer was coming and it was time to open again.

My friend Jimmy didn't let Putt-O-Links's change of fortune slow him down; he still went golfing there at least three times a week just like he had every summer. Every time I was with him, highlights of his mini-golf exploits were always part of the conversation. He shared his secret for getting his little pink ball exactly up the middle of the big clown's tongue and explained how the now stationary windmill blades always screwed up his hitting par on the twelfth hole. So when I told him I wanted us to hang out with Laura, a girl I'd only recently started spending time with, he immediately suggested meeting up at Putt-O-Links.

Jimmy had been designated as the drummer in my budding quasi-fictional rock band, Ritzo Forte, a group that largely existed in order to impress girls with the claim that I was in a rock band. I'd seen Jimmy sit behind his drum kit and play for about three and a half seconds one time when we were doing bong hits in his basement. That was good enough for me. I was to be Ritzo Forte's singer, songwriter, and principal stylist. I owned a Radio Shack microphone and a mike stand on which to put said microphone. Ritzo Forte had a name, a list of influences, even some song lyrics and titles. The only things missing were bandmates, equipment, complete songs, rehearsals, and actual performances.

However, I had put a great deal of thought into this band and its potential awesomeness. It was just a matter of time until everything fell into place. I was trying to impress Laura with my seriousness and determination, so I thought it would be good for us to go out with Jimmy.

It was almost dark by the time we got to Putt-O-Links. Introductions weren't necessary. They weren't that kind of people. Laura knew who Jimmy was; he knew her. Jimmy had been briefed for the occasion. I reminded him of all the cool bands he was supposed to like, drilled him on the titles and lyrics of the songs we hadn't written yet, and confirmed our plan to buy matching knee-length leather coats for all Ritzo Forte members.

Jimmy and I had gone to school together for six years but were never really tight until our senior year, when it became increasingly apparent that we were both going to be "Left Behinds." Left Behinds were those kids who weren't visiting many college campuses or filling out a lot of admission applications. It just seemed like a waste of time. It was obvious that we weren't going anywhere. Jimmy and I bonded because we both knew that when all our other friends left for school that fall, we'd be pretty much all we had left.

"Someone broke into the storeroom and stole all the putters," Jimmy said, pulling a decrepit set of clubs from the trunk of his car when we arrived. "But they left all the balls. I don't get that. I mean, you could think of a lot of stuff to do with buckets of golf balls, but what could you do with all those clubs?"

I should have pointed out the hundreds of other potential uses for a golf club but decided to roll with Jimmy's line of thought.

"What could you do with buckets of golf balls?" I asked, handing out beers.

"Umm, like, throw them at stuff," Jimmy said with a hint of indignation. "A golf ball could even be used as a lethal weapon. It's just like we learn in jujutsu training."

When Jimmy wasn't talking about mini-golf, drums, or pot, he was often talking about jujutsu. He had signed up for a twelve-week beginner's course at the YMCA, attended four classes, then dropped out because it interfered with watching *Monday Night Football*. He had been plotting his triumphant return for eight months, claiming to practice on his own almost daily.

"A jujutsu student learns that almost anything can be used as a weapon when necessary," he explained as he handed out clubs and we got set up at the first hole.

Jimmy gestured for Laura to go first. She picked a ball, lined it up, then stood frozen.

"I can't see the hole," she said.

"What do you mean?" I asked.

"I mean, it's completely dark out here and I have no idea what I'm aiming at."

"Fuck that," Jimmy said, taking a swooping step toward the tee, swinging his club grandly and swiftly at the colored balls, sending one firing toward the side of a miniature church. The ball ricocheted off the building and buzzed past my head almost instantly, causing me to duck out of its way.

"It's Beer Golf. Just swing and see what happens," he said.

I should explain that Beer Golf wasn't really a game. The name suggests some kind of wacky rule-heavy drinking game with madcap arcanery requiring players to swig every time they miss par or set their ball down without touching their elbows or something. Beer Golf was no such thing. Rather than modifying each other, the words simply described the two primary simultaneous activities. When not doing one, you did the other. It probably should have been called Beer and Golf, but Jimmy, as its originator, got to name it as well as determine the rules. Not that there were any rules to speak of, besides that Jimmy got to be master of ceremonies and determine who did what when, and who bought the beer (it was never Jimmy).

We continued through the next six or seven holes without

incident. Laura was very focused on the golf part of the evening, Jimmy and I on the beer part. We played in the moonlight, laughed a lot, made fun of one another at every possible opportunity, and worked through a twelve-pack of disgustingly cheap Wiedemann beer without much effort. Jimmy was instructing us how to navigate around an empty water hazard when headlights panned across the course. They were from a car entering the parking lot. Specifically, a sheriff's patrol car.

Outside of instinctively putting down our beers, we stood completely still as we saw an officer get out of the car, put on a wide-brimmed hat, and walk toward us, shining a flashlight in our faces.

"I'd like some ID and a reasonable explanation of what you're doing out here," the deputy said.

"Oh, we just look after the place and play sometimes," Jimmy said.

"Shut up," I snapped, trying to keep my voice quiet enough that the deputy wouldn't hear me.

"We just make sure that everything's okay and nothing is busted or gets broken."

"Jimmy," I whispered.

"You know, some people will come in here and vandalize the place. We just make sure people know someone is out here watching it," he continued.

"So the owners asked you to be here?" the deputy asked.

"Well, not exactly," Jimmy replied.

"Do you even know the owners?"

"Yeah, sure. Not by name, but I came here for years," Jimmy replied.

"So you have no consent or permission to be here, but you say you are taking care of the place," she said. "Tell me how that works."

Jimmy yammered on about civic duty and Good Samaritan-ism. After telling Jimmy to be quiet and collecting our IDs, the deputy instructed us to sit on a bench while she radioed in our info. We were told that if we got up for any reason, we would be stopped. Assuming that that involved a gun, we sat there quietly while she was in the car.

"Okay, you guys are clean," she said on returning. "But that doesn't mean we don't have a serious problem."

"Serious like what?" I asked.

"Serious like trespassing," she said. "And theft . . . and open container . . . and destruction of property."

"Wait," interrupted Jimmy. "We didn't—"

"You are playing with stolen equipment, aren't you?" the deputy cut in. "We can tack on something else if you like."

"Look, Officer, we obviously put no thought into what we were doing here," Jimmy said. "It was a mistake to come here, I understand that now. I really did like the owners of this place. They used to let me clean up balls out of the hoppers to earn free games. They let me play an extra round when it wasn't busy. I've spent days and days here every summer since I could walk. They were good to me. I would never do anything to disrespect that."

The deputy inhaled deeply.

"I guess what I'm saying is that I'm sorry . . . we're sorry. These guys just came here because I asked them to; they have nothing to do with this."

"You certainly haven't done much to show your respect," the deputy said.

"I didn't break into that storeroom. That was someone else," Jimmy said. "Really, we didn't mean any harm. I guess I just come out here because it's fun and I miss it. I don't want to let it go."

"I can't just let you off," the deputy said.

Even in the darkness, I could see a tiny sparkle in Jimmy's eyes.

"I'll tell you what," Jimmy said. "How about a friendly way to settle this?" He reached into his pocket, pulled out a light blue ball, and dropped it down in front of the tee. "Let's say I take one shot right from where that ball sits," he said. "If I miss the hole, you can take me in and charge me with whatever you want. But if I make it in one shot, then you let us go and we promise never to come back here again."

The deputy stared at Jimmy. Then she looked at the hole, illuminated by the headlights of her patrol car. There were two empty water hazards with a ten-inch strip of loose Astroturf between them, then a slope down to the green, which had a small cement ditch surrounding the edges. The ball was way off to the side of the rail next to the tee. It would be difficult, if not impossible, in daylight, sober, and without the threat of prosecution hanging over his head.

"One shot?" she said.

"One shot," Jimmy replied.

"What the hay," the deputy said. "Let's see you give it a try."

"So we have a deal?" Jimmy asked.

"You don't have nothing if you don't hit a hole in one," she replied.

Jimmy nodded to the deputy and got into position behind the ball. He broke his concentration once to ask me to move out of the light. He moved his head and eyes back and forth down the fairway several times, exhaled loudly, then slowly and fluidly swung his club forward.

The ball rolled precisely down the middle of the two water hazards, swooped down the slope, took a slight hop as it entered the putting green, and landed directly in the cup with a deliberate and distinct plastic *plop*.

"Fucking hell," I said, letting out a bit of a laugh before I realized that none of the others were making any noise. We just stood there for a moment staring at one another.

"Would you like to try, Officer?" Jimmy asked.

We all stood there staring at the deputy; she was looking Jimmy right in the eye.

"I'm going to go down to Maggiore's to get a can of iced tea," she said. "I'm going to be gone for about ten minutes. When I come back, there will be no sign of you or of you ever even being here. Anything you took or moved will be put back where it belongs. If you are here when I get back, I will charge you with everything I can think of. And if I ever drive by this place, which I do several times a week, and I see you here, there won't be any more golfing contests. You will go to jail. Do you hear me?"

"Yes, Officer," Jimmy said. "Thank you."

"Okay then, get out of here," she said, turning back to her patrol car.

As we saw the car's taillights head down the road, I dropped to the ground and screamed, Laura started jumping up and down, and Jimmy just stood there smiling.

"Hey, Nuzum, why don't you toss me some of that piss swill you always buy."

"Jimmy, how the fuck did you do that?!?" I yelled.

"Dude, I golf here three times a week. I can't remember the last time I *didn't* get a hole in one on that hole. Now get me a beer before I steal your wallet and your girlfriend and go buy some more."

"I'm not his—"

"Yeah right, whatever," Jimmy interrupted. "Beer. Now."

We were so excited by Jimmy's amazing performance that we stood around drinking and talking for probably another half hour, almost forgetting that we had to leave before the deputy came back. Then we rushed through our goodbyes and headed off into the night.

Here's the thing about the story I just shared, the thing that makes it feel like a ghost story.

I'm the only one left to tell it.

I often warn people about being my friend, for two reasons. First, I'm a lousy friend. I forget people's birthdays. I can't remember their kids' names. I don't recall where they just went on vacation or what my friends' husbands/wives/lovers do for a living.

The second reason is that a lot of my friends end up dead. I have seen a disproportionately large number of my friends die at young ages. Steve and Scott died of AIDS. Tim, Connor, and another guy named Tim all from various forms of cancer. Drugs took Dan, Monica, and a third guy named Tim. Brad, Meghan, Jim, and Sherry all died in auto accidents. My friend Doug destroyed his liver and died. I don't even want to think about the ones who died from suicide. You name a path to an early grave, and I'm sure I have some young formerly alive friend who followed it. I've even had a few friends who died with no one quite certain how or why, they just did. Regardless, I've seen more than my fair share of untimely deaths. It's left me with a lot of questions. I wonder about what happened to all of them after life. I worry about who will remember their experiences and stories, right their wrongs, and carry on what was important to them. I think about how their lives and deaths are supposed to affect and change me. An unfortunate consequence of this high body count is that when I look back at the friends who've had the most influence on who I've become, I realize that most of them are gone.

One in particular: Laura. Most of this book is the story of my friendship with Laura and what happened to each of us before and after our evening of Beer Golf.

When I started writing about this time in my life, particularly my friendship with Laura, I wanted to look up Jimmy, to see what he was up to. After a small amount of digging, I found out that Jimmy had died a few years earlier, a heart attack at age thirty-nine. He left behind a wife and kid.

The sheriff's deputy possibly aside, that means I am the only one who is here to remember that night at the Putt-O-Links.

I once heard an interview with Rev. Billy Kyles, who was standing on the balcony at the Lorraine Motel in Memphis when Dr. Martin Luther King, Jr., was shot dead in 1968. He said he'd come to peace with his role in history: "God unfolded to me that I was there to bear witness. Events need witnesses, those with some degree of clarity, so people can say what they saw."

When I first heard him say that, I was surprised by the idea of accepting what, to me, felt like an unextraordinary life, simply being there to witness the action of others. I think most people would aspire to be history makers, not history watchers. But now sometimes I wonder if I'm supposed to be a dumbass lowbrow version of the same thing—if my purpose in life is simply to remember stupid shit like Beer Golf.

For me, it's almost impossible to recall these old stories without experiencing the pain of losing those who are no longer around to tell them themselves. I think of Laura and Jimmy and I miss them.

They are some of my ghosts.

I have a lot of them—ghosts, that is.

That's not even counting my "real" ghost.

Assuming, of course, that my real ghost was actually real.

Here's another ghost story.

Twenty-odd years later, I'm sitting in an Italian restaurant on Seventeenth Street in Washington, D.C. It's just a big, mostly empty yellow room with generic tables and chairs and generic artwork, completely lacking in anything distinctive. However, it's easy to find, never busy, and away from the areas where tourists lurk, which is why I often use it as a meeting spot.

Across the table is my friend Matt.

Matt used to be my best friend. But Matt and I haven't really spoken in years. Since back when *all that* happened.

I look down at my plate and notice some chunks of zucchini.

I hate zucchini.

I mean, I *really* hate zucchini.

It isn't that I hate the taste of zucchini. I have no recollection of what zucchini tastes like at this point.

There was a time in my life, back when Matt and I were close friends, when the sight of zucchini would cause me to stop eating, as I would refuse to eat not only zucchini but anything that had touched zucchini.

I've mellowed as I've aged. Now I simply flip it off to the side.

My feelings about zucchini are one of a collection of things that my friends refer to as "Ericisms": things I passionately do or refuse to do for what appears to be no apparent, rational, or cogent reason. It isn't like these are debilitating compulsions or anything. In my own way, I have sound reasons for them all.

The zucchini thing started one summer when I was nine or ten years old. My parents had decided to put six zucchini plants in their garden. By the end of that summer, my dad would come back into the house every evening with armfuls of ripe zucchini. My mom made zucchini everything: zucchini bread, zucchini pasta, zucchini salad, zucchini parmigiana, and at least three different zucchini casseroles. No matter what she made, our house was still filled with fresh zucchini. They tried taking bags of zucchini into work and offering it to their friends. I think they even started leaving zucchinis on our neighbors' porches at night. After I told my mom that I couldn't eat any more zucchini, she started hiding it in our food and taking a degree of pleasure in telling me, after we'd eaten, how many of the things I'd just consumed had, in fact, contained zucchini. That's when I said I would never, ever again eat a zucchini, or anything that contained zucchini or even touched zucchini. A promise I've largely kept.

Now, see, that isn't a crazy story. It (almost) makes sense. It isn't like I once looked at a zucchini and saw a face that suddenly began speaking to me, begging me not to eat it or any of its squash brethren.

My friends, though, don't really care why I won't eat zucchini. They just think I'm trying to be funny or difficult or contrarian. To them, it's just another Ericism. Like when I refuse to use pens with blue ink, won't wear clothing with logos or writing on it, swear off pork for a year, or touch the door frame of airplanes when I'm about to board.

Or like when I insist on opening any closed doors inside my house.

My wife suffers from this one all the time. She closes doors to the guest room or office or other rooms we aren't using. Then I come around sometime later and open them again. She closes. I open.

She thinks I'm doing it just to annoy her. Whenever she gets irritated to the point of mentioning it to me, she always gets the same response.

"I *hate* closed doors."

She closes. I open.

This has been going on for sixteen years.

Recently, after a rapid-fire bout of openings and closings of our guest room door (or perhaps it was a few rounds with the laundry room door), she—for the first time—asked if there was a particular reason *why* I hated closed doors.

"Of course there is," I replied. I had always assumed the answer was obvious.

She raised her eyebrows slightly, as if to reluctantly invite me to expand my answer.

"Because there could be a ghost on the other side," I answered.

I don't have a problem with *all* closed doors—just the ones that might have ghosts hiding behind them. The problem is when I look at a door and can *feel* something on the other side. Something that shouldn't be there. I'll look at a closed door and instantly become overwhelmed with dread—a heavy, thick feeling in my chest that sends cold waves of fear throughout my body.

That's how I know.

So how have I dealt with these occurrences? I just make sure I'm around as few closed doors as possible. No closed door, no feeling of dread. No feeling of dread, no ghost.

Have I ever seen a ghost emerge from behind a closed door? No.

But that doesn't mean one isn't there.

After pushing my zucchini to one side, Matt and I spend the rest of our reunion dinner talking about our lives and our work. But we don't talk much about the past. You'd think we would, as we have a lot in common. Growing up in Canton, we went to the same school and church youth group, did stuff together on weekends. But we rarely wade into that history, especially *that time*. *That time* is why we were best friends for almost two decades, then absolute strangers for two more.

At the end of the meal, though, Matt looks me straight in the eye and says, "So, do you still see ghosts of little girls in blue dresses?"

I just about choke on a piece of garlic bread.

"How do you know about that?" I ask.

At first, Matt says nothing. "Know about it? You were obsessed with it," he eventually says, now a bit uncomfortable that the conversation topic had stuck. "You talked about it all the time. You don't remember?"

I can count on one hand the people I remember ever telling about the Little Girl. Matt is not one of them. I have told bits to a few people here and there during late-night drunken conversations. Even my wife has never heard the whole story.

Over the course of several years during my late teens, I slowly became unhinged, disillusioned, and depressed. I started losing touch with the distinction between what was real and what wasn't. What started off with a curious noise coming from my parents' attic ended in the belief, forged in my dreams, that I was haunted by a ghost who wanted to harm me—or at least warn me of harm to come.

The dreams were all more or less the same.

I'm in a forest at night walking among a thick crop of trees. Then I stumble into a clearing with high grass made bright with moonlight. There's a picnic table.

As I walk toward it, I can see three or four people sitting there. They stop their conversation to look up and stare at me as I approach.

There is always a man sitting at the far end of the table wearing a cheap matted wolf costume, complete with a loose-fitting mask that makes him look sort of like Batman, except with tall ears and a long, bent snout. He slowly points toward another path at the opposite side of the clearing. He doesn't say anything; he doesn't need to. I know exactly where he wants me to go, why he wants me to go there, and what's waiting for me.

As I enter the path, I can see Her outline in the moonlight. I step closer and start to see detail.

A Little Girl in a Blue Dress.

She's wet, like She's been in water.

She's staring right at me, eyes wide, cold, and dark.

When I'm only a few steps from Her, She starts yelling at me. It sounds like gibberish. She never moves, never takes Her eyes away from mine. As I come closer, She seems more and more irritated and frantic.

When She is at the point of screaming so loud that She's shaking, I wake up.

The dreams weren't always that complete; most times I just experienced moments, sometimes just a few scenes mashed to-gether or in a different order. In the beginning, often all I'd experience was the very end. Her standing there, outline illu-minated by moonlight, then the gibberish. Sometimes I'd go months without having these dreams, then I'd have several in a week. I eventually started putting the pieces together in my head. The Little Girl in the dreams was making the strange noises that I heard in my parents' attic. It was Her I felt on the other side of a closed door.

Coupled with a deluge of substances calling out "Drink me," "Swallow me," and "Smoke me," the dreams contributed to my losing touch with everyone and everything around me. I ended up strung out and on suicide watch in the mental ward of a local hospital.

Very few people in my life stuck with me through all this. One who did was Laura. It was Laura who really helped me get on my feet again, who put me back together, while I was in denial, the whole time, that I was very much in love with her.

A few months later she left for college.

Not long after that, she was in the wrong place at the wrong time and was killed.

She saved me from my imaginary ghost but became one herself.

One that continues to haunt me today.

"You don't still believe that little ghost girl lived in your attic, do you?" Matt asks.

I just give him a polite smile.

I have no idea what really happened.

"Oh, come on," he says. "That was all chemically induced."

I just shake my head.

"Do you remember inviting Thérèse and me to your little exorcism?"

As he tells me the story, details slowly start coming back to me. Details I buried twenty years ago. What Matt describes as an exorcism was actually more like a séance—a séance to communicate with and get rid of Little Girl. I'd photocopied some ritual from some book at the library, then tried to get Matt and his girlfriend to read it with me.

I was so high at the time that I was drooling while I tried to read. When I started having trouble saying the words, I picked up a marker and started writing random images and words on the walls of my bedroom.

And that's about all I remember—forgotten for two decades until suddenly shaken loose over a plate of shitty zucchini-laced pasta.

Matt notices the time. He has to go.

A few weeks after our meal I write to Matt, asking him to tell me more about that night upstairs in the attic. The ritual. The writing. The talk about the Little Girl. I need someone's help to move beyond the fragments that I've retained from that time, refugees of my repeated attempts to forget. Matt agrees, saying he'd be happy to help later.

"Later" turns into later still, as Matt is too busy with work, travel, and his family to go over what he remembers. Eventually, it becomes clear to me that he isn't interested in going back there. This isn't his journey.

Not long afterward I'm visiting my friends David and Gina. We are sitting in their driveway drinking beer and watching their night-blooming cereus do its thing. Most of the year, the night-blooming cereus is probably the world's ugliest plant. It is huge, with strange twisted woody branches. When I first saw this thing in their living room, I assumed it was dead. But one night, only once a year, after the sun sets, the night-blooming cereus opens its huge white blossom, emitting a pleasant perfume. The flower wilts and dies off by the following morning.

Typically a night-blooming cereus produces only one or two blossoms for its one magical night each year, but this year David and Gina's has somehow managed close to twenty. On the night all the blossoms are set to open, people come and go from their house all evening, simply to stand in their driveway and watch all these flowers slowly open. At some point in the evening, one of our fellow night-blooming cereus watchers asks David which window of their house "was the one with the ghost."

As part of a series of newspaper columns David had written about buying and renovating their house, they'd brought in a psychic to tell them about their new home's spiritual energy. The psychic had told them that there was a concentration of energy in the summer bedroom, which is on the second floor, directly above where the night-blooming cereus is currently performing its annual show.

After the conversation moves to other topics, David asks why I visibly shuddered when he pointed the ghost-inhabited room out to the fellow blossom watcher.

While I don't talk about Little Girl, I've always been quick to tell people a simpler truth: that I'm scared of ghosts. I offer it to explain why I'll walk across a street to avoid some supposedly haunted location or close my eyes and plug my ears whenever a ghost-themed movie trailer comes on in the theater. I will audibly gasp and walk out of a room when some innocent channel surfing lands on a broadcast of *The Sixth Sense* on HBO. People just assume these are more Ericisms. No one ever thinks I'm all that serious about my fear.

When I tell people that I'm scared of ghosts, they all have the same reaction: They want to tell me a ghost story. I've always found this particularly odd. I'm sure they don't intend to be mean, but that's pretty similar to saying you're an alcoholic and having your friend reply, "Oh man, let's do a shot of Jäger-meister! Don't you love that smack of licorice that kicks in as it burns down the back of your throat?"

It happens every single time.

Most of the stories are third-person. The teller's mother, aunt, best friend, or trusted co-worker heard a sound coming from an empty room, witnessed a gravy boat move across a table, or saw a disembodied head hovering outside a bedroom window.

Whenever someone tells a ghost story, they do so without a drop of the skepticism they apply to anything else. Why is that? Why do people have a near compulsion to tell and believe ghost stories? Especially since, after centuries of encounters, no one has put forth a single shred of conclusive evidence that these stories are anything other than pure bullshit. People from all walks of life, well-educated people, religious people, old, young, and even those who appear to believe in nothing else whatsoever are willing to entertain the possibility that some unexplainable experience might be the work of an apparition.

Including me.

My own reluctance to share my experience has always been a litmus test for me when it comes to judging ghost stories told by others. To my ears, those who are quick to share first-person encounters with the dead are usually mistaken, lying, exagger-ating, or just looking for some easy attention. I put much more stock in those who would rather not talk about what they've experienced. Their encounters with ghosts are confusing, even embarrassing and somewhat humiliating. The things they ex-perience don't make a lot of sense or flow together in a tidy little narrative.

"I don't know if I've ever told you this before," I say. "But I'm really scared of ghosts."

"Why's that?" Gina asks.

While the night-blooming cereus is working its magic, I tell them the whole story. Starting with the noises in the attic, the Little Girl in a Blue Dress, my depression, Laura, everything. It is probably the first time in half my life that I've told anyone the whole story. I mean, I know all the pieces, I've just never realized how they all fit together.

Telling the story, I realize how tired I am of dragging around the memories and feelings and fears of that time in my life. I don't want to be scared anymore, and the key to not being scared is starting to confront and unravel the thing I fear even more than ghosts: my past.

Shortly after the night-blooming cereus bloomfest, I put a sticky note next to my computer monitor and start a list, a list of haunted places. I plan to force myself to visit some of them, if for no other reason than to see what will happen. I'm thinking that if I can see their ghosts, it can help me understand my own.

How are the two things connected? The only way I can describe it is to compare it to synesthesia, the neurological condition where people get their senses cross-wired. They smell loud sounds or see colors when they bite into something sour or sweet. People with synesthesia often correlate words and numbers with color and will talk about how music "looks" to them—kind of like tripping on acid.

When I see a trailer for a ghost movie, all I can think about is my past desire to end my life. When I see someone doing drugs, all I can think about is a Little Girl in a Blue Dress. When someone talks about a haunted building, I think of Laura. My memories and fears are all twisted and knotted together, impossible to separate neatly. In order to remember and make sense of them, I'm going to have to scare each last detail out of myself.

I realize that if I want peace with my past, I have to enlist the help of the one remaining vestige of that time in my younger life.

Ghosts.

NOW

"Where are the ghosts, Eric?"

"We aren't looking for ghosts right now, Curry. We're looking for mutant wild animals."

Pause.

"Where are the mutant wild animals, Eric?"

Neither my friends Curry and Joe nor I honestly expect to find any mutant wild animals. But you never know. It only takes one tale to be true for us to end up shredded, eaten, or running for our lives.

In 1972 Warner Brothers decided to break in to the theme-park business by opening Jungle Habitat, a combo zoo, drive-through safari, and entertainment complex located in rural Passaic County, just outside of West Milford, New Jersey. It was once home to more than fifteen hundred animals, including lions, giraffes, rhinoceroses, tigers, camels, monkeys, and even a few dolphins. Almost from the beginning, things started going terribly wrong. Within its first month of operation, an Israeli tourist was mauled to death by two lions. A woman was grabbed and bitten by a baby elephant. Rhinoceroses slammed into automobiles. Animals began preying on other animals in front of carloads of children. Tons of animal waste started to leak into the town's water supply. Several creatures escaped into the surrounding communities.

After operating Jungle Habitat for four years, Warner Brothers had had enough. Ticket sales were down and the problems inherent with combining humans and wild animals in a contained area weren't getting any better. So they came up with what they thought was a perfect solution: Make it even bigger. They wanted to add roller-coasters, a log flume, a merry-go-round, and other rides to make it more like a traditional amusement park. The township residents were tired of dealing with Jungle Habitat and voted down the expansion. Warner Brothers took that as its cue and finally shut things down for good.

That's when the rumors started.

There were stories that some of the animals were too old and/or sick to be moved, so the Jungle Habitat staff just left them there. According to the tales, some survived, crossbred, and moved with their mutant offspring into the surrounding woods. There they wait by the roadside for some poor schlub to wander by. There may be some truth to these stories. After the Jungle Habitat people split, a large number of carcasses were found on the property, including that of a dead elephant. They remained out in the open for eight months before someone bothered to bury them. And people routinely spot exotic birds that should not be seen in rural New Jersey.

Today, all that remains of Jungle Habitat is a few ramshackle buildings, overgrown roads, broken fences, and the occasional piece of equipment. We find a few rusted cages and piles of wood, but most everything else is picked clean. Vandals long ago carted away anything that could be carried out of the park, so all the missing signage turns the place into a daunting maze: twenty-nine miles of twisting and intersecting road. Most of the pavement is in surprisingly good condition for having sat here untended for more than thirty years, but weeds sprout through the many cracks and the surrounding woods creep in from the sides, giving the illusion that former two-lane roads are now only four-foot-wide paths. What was once a three-thousand-car parking lot is now just a sea of broken asphalt and knee-high weeds.

However, Jungle Habitat is just the opening act to our real destination, on the other side of the mutant-creature-infested woods: Clinton Road.

Clinton Road is an otherwise unremarkable ten-mile stretch of patched asphalt and sand about an hour north of Newark, New Jersey. It's also ground zero for almost every back-road urban legend in America. Think of any preposterous and im-plausible story that involves a dark and lonely stretch of pave-ment, and there's a Clinton Road version of it. There have been terrible stories about ghosts, witches, mysterious deaths, mutants of nature, and occult happenings on Clinton Road going back to the early eighteenth century.

Our task there is a simple one: to do everything that you are never supposed to do on Clinton Road.

We intend to provoke the area's rumored ghosts and other paranormal creatures while avoiding the also-rumored cults, escaped lunatics, Satanists, hitchhikers, crazy inbreeds, KKK groups, cannibals, and other Clinton Road lurkers who pur-portedly want to kill, rape, dismember, haunt, torture, or oth-erwise bother us. This doesn't even take into consideration the other very real threats along rural Clinton Road: poisonous snakes, black bears, and fields of poison ivy everywhere you look. Oh, and it's wild-turkey hunting season to boot, so we have to be careful that we don't get shot by a hunter who mistakenly thinks he wants to serve us to his family for Thanksgiving.

It always amazes me how when you discover something you've never heard of or encountered before, it suddenly finds its way into your life and you can't avoid it. It's kind of like when you buy a new car. You had no idea there were so many silver Honda CRVs in the world until you bought a silver Honda CRV. Then, suddenly, you notice them everywhere. You pass them every day and wonder, "Where did all these silver Honda CRVs come from?"

Clinton Road is like that.

I was in a bookstore during a vacation on Long Beach Island in New Jersey when a magazine caught my eye. It was an issue of *Weird N.J.* The issue was entirely devoted to Clinton Road stories. Readers had written in to share their own experiences and those they'd heard. There were hundreds of them. Like many things you buy on impulse, the magazine sat there unread for a long time. Of course, realizing that it was filled with *ghost stories* didn't encourage me to get to it any earlier. Then, shortly after my dinner with Matt, I saw a segment on TV about Devil's Alley, a now abandoned housing development located along Clinton Road. After fishing out my copy of *Weird N.J.,* I found thousands of webpages and postings sharing stories of bizarre goings-on along Clinton Road. Some were first-person stories, others were passing along dire tales that "honestly actually happened" to the teller's cousin, neighbor, or grandmother, or a kid at school. To me, the most incredible part of the Clinton Road mythos is that there is absolutely no explanation as to why all this legendary horribleness should happen *there*. Nothing important ever happened along Clinton Road. Few people have ever lived in the area. It isn't particularly beautiful, or ugly, or otherwise notable. Yet it seems every New Jersey resident I meet has something to say about this long stretch of nowhere.

To make things easier for us, I went through every Clinton Road legend I'd come across and put together a master list of all the recurring moral warnings for Clinton Road travelers:

• Do not pick up hitchhikers.

• Do not flip off passing cars.

• Do not mention a car accident involving a blue 1988 Chevy Camaro.

• Do not discuss area ghosts or hauntings while on Clinton Road.

• Do not pick up shiny objects, step inside a circle of rocks, assist stranded motorists, investigate lights or glowing objects in the woods, acknowledge any drivers who blink their headlights at you, assist a bride in need of a ride to her wedding chapel, walk or drive down unpaved roads or paths, touch or pick up discarded items of clothing (especially those that move on their own), taunt any unknown sources of noise coming from the woods, or explore origins of any tapping, knocking, or thunking sounds coming from the exterior of the car.

• Do not attempt to move, drive around, or investigate trees that fall in the roadway.

• Do not stand on the edge of the reservoir bridge or throw coins off the bridge.

• Do not eat bagels.

• Avoid all animals, fires, local residents, disembodied hands, fellow travelers, men with no arms, midgets, UFOs, large groups of suspicious characters, horses, anyone shouting seemingly random numbers, black pickup trucks, miniature ponies, dogs that appear to be floating on air, nudists, and albinos.

Violate any of these rules, and terrible, awful things will happen.

Whenever I share this list with my friends, everyone trips up on the same item.

"Why can't you eat bagels?"

"Well, it really isn't that you can't eat *any* bagels," I reply. "You just can't eat bagels that you find on the side of the road."

"Who would want to eat bagels sitting on the side of the road?"

"Well, obviously someone," I explain. "Or the Clinton Road Satanists wouldn't have anyone to sacrifice."

Over the years several travelers on Clinton Road have reported seeing large piles of bagels by the side of the road— hundreds of them, just sitting there. *Naturally,* these people assumed this had to be the handiwork of the Devil. It's said that the satanic cults hiding along Clinton Road will leave stacks of bagels sitting around to lure in passersby. When the unknowing bagel eaters start munching, the Satanists snag them, then cart them off to some awful demise.

Despite the distraction of demonic baked goods and mutant creatures, we have one specific goal here on Clinton Road: to find ghosts. Clinton Road is supposedly filled with hundreds of them. We only need to prove the existence of one.

The outlandishness of almost any story associated with Clinton Road is exactly why I decide to make this my first stop on my ghost-seeking journeys. In some way, the sheer nuttiness of Clinton Road lore makes it seem more accessible, albeit still quite frightening. Goofy danger is still danger.

After Jungle Habitat, we stop at an Italian restaurant near the southern tip of Clinton Road to eat before heading out to ghost hunt. We tell the waitress what we're doing. She tells us we're crazy. A few minutes later she returns to inform us that the entire kitchen staff agrees that what we're doing is terribly unwise. After filling up on pasta and garlic bread, we drive a mile or so around the woods to reach Clinton Road itself. Just before the final turn, we pass a small three-shop strip mall that includes a store called U.S. Bagel.

"Oh, man," says Curry. "I wonder if that's where the Satanists get their bagels."

"That would be very convenient," Joe replies.

"And very patriotic," I add.

To be honest, Joe and Curry aren't exactly my first choices to accompany me on my trip to Clinton Road. They are goofballs. I know they will never do what I ask, will make fun of me endlessly, and will follow every possible tangent like someone waving a set of keys in front of a toddler. Before asking them, I went through several other friends, all of whom turned me down, saying things like "That sounds like torture," "You know this just provides my wife with more evidence that you are a bad influence on me," and "So you want me to sit around with you in dark, scary places waiting to be attacked. Why can't we just go out for beers like normal friends?" Joe and Curry are here because they're my only friends who said yes.

Shortly before we left, I had made a rental-car reservation.

"Oh, I almost forgot to ask," said the agent on the phone in the midst of gathering reams of useless data about me. "Are you interested in any of our supplemental coverage for the car? For only . . ." As she rattled off all the benefits of this über coverage, my mind was focused on the master list of Clinton Road legends I'd just finished assembling that morning.

"I would like every type of insurance coverage you offer," I interrupted. "I don't care what it costs, just add it on."

I think I blew her mind—or helped her fill her bonus quota for the month or something. All I know for sure is that by the time I'd gotten off the phone, she was very excited and I was paying twice as much money to insure the car as I was to rent it. I could have brought that thing back in three hundred pieces on the back of a flatbed truck and wouldn't have had to pay a dime or answer a single question.

It's just a little past 10 P.M. when we finally turn onto Clinton Road. Our plan is to simply drive up and down the road over and over again until we see something.

Even though it's only forty miles from Times Square, Clinton Road is, quite seriously, in the middle of nowhere. We can't even get our cell phones to work. While there are some houses at either end, once you are a half mile in there is nothing except road and a lot of trees. The forest is dense and pushes itself right up to the edge of the road, occasionally causing an errant branch to come within a few inches of the side of the car.

Clinton Road's supposed wickedness doesn't stop with the outright bizarre and outlandish. Even the few artifacts of real life along Clinton Road have been given nefarious alternative backstories. An imposing and crumbling furnace left over from an eighteenth-century iron smelter is rumored by Clinton Road enthusiasts to be part of the ruins of a Druidic temple where human sacrifices and rituals were conducted. In 1905, a man named Richard Cross built a castlelike mansion on some high land overlooking the reservoir. It eventually fell into disrepair and burned down. Its partial shell has been rumored to be the remains of a satanic castle where more rituals and sacrifices take place. Most of the traffic signs along Clinton Road are spray painted with pentagrams, skulls, and words like *fear*, *rape*, and *death*, complete with arrows pointing the way down some footpath toward their suggested awfulness.

For all our goofing off, all three of us are completely silent as we head up Clinton Road for the first time. From photographs taken during the daytime, Clinton Road just seems like an unassuming, unremarkable, and more than slightly undermaintained country back road. But at night it feels cloistered, dark, and suffocatingly empty. The moonlessness of the night doesn't make it any more welcoming. It feels unfinished, like it was abandoned. I find myself resisting going above twenty-five miles per hour. It's like we're traveling down a stranger's driveway rather than along a public road.

We're on the road no more than ten minutes before Curry, jumping up from the backseat, slams his hand into my headrest.

"Oh my God, there's a frog!" he screams. "Stop the car so I can chase it."

"I am not stopping the car so you can chase a frog," I say.

"Tell me again, why are we coming here to chase things if you are too scared to actually get out of the car and chase things?"

We drive up and down the entire ten-mile length of Clinton Road eight times. Our evening's tally is embarrassingly slim: Cop cars: 6; bags of trash: 5; deer: 3; frogs: 1. Satanists, mutants, albinos, and ghosts: 0. Before leaving we make one last stop: the reservoir bridge, approximately halfway down the road. This will be our real moment of truth, as a lot of Clinton Road's suggested nonsense takes place close to the reservoir bridge, where the long-gone original town of Clinton once stood in what's now a thin clearing in the trees between the road and water. There are differing legends about a boy who died on the bridge. According to most versions, a boy was struck by a car and thrown into the water. Supposedly if you stand by the edge of the bridge, the ghost of the boy will materialize and push you in.

We find an old trailhead just north of the bridge and stash the car there. Almost as soon as Curry is out of the car, he takes off into the darkness.

"Let's run down the path. We aren't supposed to do that, right?" he says from ten yards down, before even looking back to see if we're following.

"No way," I say.

"Why not?"

"He's scared," says Joe.

Of course I'm scared.

"Have you been ignoring everything I've told you about this place? You have no idea what or who is down there."

"I thought the point of this trip was to do things we shouldn't be doing," Curry replies.

"He's got a point," says Joe, joining Curry farther along the path. No map. No idea where they're going. No means to find their way back.

I wave my flashlight down the path, illuminating huge patches of poison ivy dotting its entire length. "If you get stuck, don't expect me to come rescue you."

"Okay, Eric," Curry replies as he and Joe start to fade into the woods. "You stay right there . . . by yourself . . . alone in the dark. Maybe the ghost boy will show up and keep you company."

They're quickly out of sight and I'm there alone.

Am I scared?

Well, it's more like terrified. An adrenaline knot in my stomach keeps growing and growing as I realize how intensely and amazingly dark it is. Unless you've been out in the country on a dark night, it is almost impossible to imagine how oppressive and complete darkness can be. It's like being blind, but worse. Blindness means you can see nothing. However, being out on Clinton Road at night means sensing just enough form and motion around you to wonder what's causing it and why, yet having no way to figure it out. A flashlight makes it worse. While it illuminates part of your surroundings, it renders everything else around you pitch-black.

I can hear myself breathing and feel my heart beating in my throat.

While I stand there, in the dark, listening to Curry and Joe fade away into the distance, I make myself shut my eyes. *I'm going to close my eyes,* I say to myself. *And if there is a ghost here, I will see it when I open them again.*

Since I started repeating these words to myself as a child, I've always referred to this as "calling out." I bargain with the ghosts, offering a simple proposition: If you exist, I'll see you when I open my eyes. Even though it is probably complete nonsense, calling out always gives me a weird sense of relief, as if I've proven to myself that it's safe to walk around, sleep, or do whatever. I've done this hundreds, probably thousands of times in my life, and I've never seen a ghost. You could take this as evidence that ghosts don't exist—or you could take it as evidence that the ghosts are simply not interested in taking up my proposition.

Before Clinton Road, the last time I remember calling out was a few years ago at my parents' lake house.

A few days before I arrived, a bunch of kids had decided to go on a late-night boat ride for some moonlit waterskiing. Except there was no moon. And the boat didn't have any lights on it. And the first dude on the skis didn't even know how to swim. And both he and the boat driver were drunk.

I'm sure I don't need to give too many details, but the boat hadn't even made a single loop around the lake before the boaters realized that the drunken novice skier wasn't there anymore. They circled around to pick him up.

No sign.

They kept looking for hours and didn't bother to call the cops until the morning.

The police searched and searched.

Nothing.

When I arrived at the lake and found out what all the activity was about, I started making light of the apparent Darwinism at play. I stopped joking when I noticed the boy's father sitting in a picnic shelter near the shore every day watching the increasingly desperate search effort for his son. He just sat there, day in and day out, waiting.

They started out with divers and quickly moved on to large hooks. After a few days they took cadaver-sniffing dogs out in rowboats. Then came additional divers with more-expensive-looking equipment. There was even talk of using explosive charges.

I couldn't stop thinking about the boy, especially at night when the searchers went away and the moon reflected off the still lake, with the boy's body hidden somewhere underneath.

At bedtime on the first night I was there, an image came into my head, an image of a dead boy, dripping wet, standing outside the patio door. I imagined his jellied, waterlogged white skin, his dilated eyes. His face stuck somewhere between desperation and anger. In my mind, I saw him just standing there, shaking. Every night before I lay down in bed to not sleep, I'd see the image in my mind. I'd just lie there or toss and turn all night, waiting for the drowned drunk nonswimmer to show up. I eventually was so freaked out and tired that on the last night I was there, I got up and walked out onto the patio at 3 A.M. and called him out.

I'm going to close my eyes. And if there is a ghost here, I will see it when I open them again.

Nothing.

I went back inside and fell asleep.

After three weeks, long after my visit had ended, they found the boy, almost directly across from my parents' house, tangled in some sunken branches deep under the surface.

I stand there at the head of that trail near the Clinton Road reservoir, in the dark, listening to Curry and Joe fade away into the distance.

I'm going to close my eyes. And if there is a ghost here, I will see it when I open them again.

When I open my eyes, all I can see through the darkness is the bridge itself.

The only thing I can really see is the graffiti on the Jersey barriers mounted on top of the bridge. According to stories, the ghost boy's name is written on the bridge's guardrails. I conclude that unless the dead kid's name is Alice or I Love Weed, we can immediately write off this part of the story. One of the few legible things written on top of one of the barriers is "All the fairytales of Clinton Road . . . never prove true."

Curry and Joe's voices are getting louder; they're heading back up the trail toward me. They tell me that they'd made it about forty yards before Joe thought he heard and saw a pack of approaching bears, then announced he would go no farther and headed back to the road. After reuniting, we line up along the guardrail.

There is a part of the reservoir bridge legend that is Clinton Road's best-known ghost story. It says that if you stand on this bridge and throw a coin into the water, the dead boy will throw it back to you. This is the story that most drew me to Clinton Road in the first place. It's a pretty cut-and-dry legend. Either the coin comes back, or it doesn't. Sometimes the coin hits you, sometimes you see it land on the ground, and other times you might find it in your car or clothes the next day. Some versions call for pennies, others quarters. We have brought both, each covered with our initials in red fingernail polish.

"Which way are we supposed to face?" asks Joe.

"What do you mean?"

"Are we supposed to face the road . . . or the water?"

"I don't know," I answer. "I hadn't thought of that."

"I'm facing the road," Curry interjects. "If this ghost kid is going to knock me in, I want to see him coming."

"I thought you didn't believe in any of this."

"Well, fuck you guys then. He'll push you in first."

The thing I'll remember most about the moment that follows is how quiet it is. No breeze, no insect or animal sounds, and none of the chatter you associate with being out in the woods at night. Nothing. It is absolutely and completely still

and silent. It's as if someone suddenly has pressed a Pause button and life has simply stopped.

Then Joe whispers that he sees someone in the woods coming toward us.

"Look over in the trees. Someone's shining a flashlight up
the path."

Curry and I swing our heads over, and then we see it too.
It's like a lightning flash inside the forest, and then it's gone.

I think to myself: Who would be walking down a dark path
in the woods in the middle of the night? The trails around the
reservoir simply run in giant loops going nowhere. There are
no houses or parked cars for at least four miles in either direction. Anyone or anything out on that path probably has even
less of a reasonable excuse for being there than we do.

A few seconds later we see it again—a bright light swinging
in our direction, then gone. It's maybe thirty yards down the
bank of the reservoir.

"Oh, shit," Curry states flatly.

"What do we do?" asks Joe.

"You can start by keeping your voice down."

"Oh, shit," Curry repeats softly.

We see two flashlights pointing toward us, then back toward
the lake.

Then we realize that they aren't flashlights at all but headlights. Headlights from a car winding along Clinton Road,
going very fast and heading directly for us.

My first thought is that the car would come around the
hairpin curve, see three sketchy-looking dudes standing on the
bridge, freak out, go out of control, and slam through the barriers, thus taking its passengers, us, and whatever else is lurking
around that bridge straight into a watery grave.

"What do we do?" Joe repeats.

"I don't know," I offer. The car's less than twenty yards from turning onto the bridge and isn't slowing down.

"How about we duck?" Curry suggests.

"Duck?"

"Yeah."

"Now?"

"Yeah."

"Okay. Three . . . two . . . one, duck!"

With that, we all slam against the ground behind the Jersey barrier, just as the car skids around the corner, tears up and over the bridge, and then speeds away into the night.

"Man, I can't believe we hid," I say, brushing little bits of Clinton Road from the front of my shirt and pants a minute later. "We're lucky it didn't lose control."

"Let's try the coins."

"Eric should go first," Curry says.

I should. The three of us have traveled here so that I can do just that.

As I raise my hand, I can feel a heavy rush in my chest. I would have expected that I'd feel scared, but this time it isn't fear. It feels more like sadness. Or maybe it's just a sudden memory of sadness.

You see, this is less a story about ghosts than it is a story about what it means to be haunted.

As much as I want to encounter the boy at the bridge, or a haunted Camaro, or any of the hundreds of other horrible things that we're supposed to stumble across up and down Clinton Road, I know no coins are ever going to come back. But I'm still scared. I'm scared to begin facing the truth. Not the truth of Clinton Road, but the truth of me.

You might think that standing there on the reservoir bridge, with no idea where this journey will take me, I'd want to throw the coin hard, to heave it into the lake in a way that reflected all the weight attached to it.

Instead, I simply open my hand and bend it slightly, letting the coin slowly slide off my fingers, down past the guardrail, and quietly into the darkness. The hushed *plop* of a single coin sinking into the still water marks the beginning of my quest.

I just close my eyes, hold my breath, and wait.

THEN

"Eric!" my dad shouted from downstairs. "Phone!"

It was about seven or eight at night, in June. A year before things got really bad.

My room was in the attic of our house on Thirty-fourth Street in Canton, Ohio.

The closest phone was in the den one floor below.

I'd spent the evening before raiding my pill stash and washing it down with a warm twelve-pack of Wiedemann, drooling for a while, and then throwing the bottles over the neighbor's roof. I hadn't left my room at all that day, mostly because I couldn't work up the courage. Leaving meant walking by the door to the spare room. My family rarely went in there, except to get Christmas decorations, wrapping paper, or whatever else was stored in its closets and crawlspaces. The door was always closed. It was always dark in there, and terribly hot in summer. Of course, my room was the same way, just on the opposite side of the hall. But it wasn't the heat or the dinginess I minded.

The spare room was where She was.

Usually, when I could tell She was there, I'd summon the strength to run by the door before She could realize I was just an arm's length away. This morning I wondered if She could simply reach out and grab me as I ran by. I'd never thought of that before. Therefore, I just sat there, too scared to find out the answer to my new question.

Earlier that day, I'd thought I heard Her moving around on the other side of the door. I had slowly walked out of my room into the hallway, barely breathing so that I could hear any other telltale noise. I told myself that I was going to walk right up to the door, call Her out, swing the door open suddenly, and have this over with. But of course, I never did. Instead, I used the phone call as an excuse to chicken-shit out and run past the door and down the stairs. Nothing reached out and grabbed me. Despite the fact that my fear had kept me captive for more than twelve hours, pissing in empty soda bottles to avoid having to go downstairs to a bathroom, as I rounded the landing to head downstairs, I'd already forgotten all about it.

I was surprised that my father was even willing to speak to me to let me know I had a phone call. My parents and I had just had a big fight over my "unacceptable behavior" at a cook-out they'd hosted. At some point during the gathering, some-one had pulled out a camera to take a few photos. I leapt up and asked them to stop taking my picture.

I'd noticed my parents immediately start to squirm. I'd pre-viously announced to my family that I did not want any pho-tographs taken of me. I had read somewhere that American Indians did not like having their photographs taken because they felt the process stole part of their soul. At the time, I needed every bit of my soul I could hold on to. So every time a camera appeared, I disappeared or asked that whoever was holding it not take my picture.

Not that I was really much you'd want to photograph.

I'd fallen in love with thrift stores before I was old enough to drive myself to them. I bought as many old suits, hats, and coats as I could get with the lawn-mowing money I had left over after buying records. Even though I had no idea how to sew things together, I routinely tried to alter my clothing by cutting pieces off collars, sleeves, pockets. Eventually I graduated to saving up money for the annual rummage sale in the prop and costume department of the local community theater, which allowed me to expand into pirate gear and military uniforms. I loved vintage clothes but hated ironing, so most of what I bought eventually ended up looking like it had spent the previous three decades stuffed in a shoe box.

For most of my teens, I wore my hair long to hide from my parents a variety of piercings. (In the days before it was routine for men to have *any* earrings, I had no idea there were such things as starter or piercing earrings, so I gave myself multiple piercings by pushing regular earring posts through my earlobes.) I'd taken to cutting out sections of my hair in order to make it spike up straighter, so all my piercings were eventually discovered. Then I discovered hair dye. Then I discovered how to make your own hair dye with Kool-Aid mix and bleach.

Whenever "Punk Day" or the impossibly politically incorrect "Hobo Day" would pop up during Homecoming Week, someone would invariably compliment my costume even though I was just wearing my normal clothes.

Even my parents would have to admit that by graduation I'd started to tone down my look considerably. Rather than wanting to be instantly recognizable as an individual, by then I simply wanted to disappear.

"Hello," I said into the phone as I plopped down on the den couch, slightly out of breath from my run down from the attic.

It was my friend Cassandra. She was a "friend" the way that former "girlfriends" become "friends," especially when the "girlfriend" is the one who would rather just be your "friend." Honestly, Cassandra was never really my girlfriend, just someone I openly and repeatedly tried to trick into being my girlfriend. A few dates. A few hand-holding incidents at football games. I'm not sure there was ever even a kiss involved in the torrid affair I had tried to create.

As in most of my friendships lately, there was strain. It had been a while since I'd spoken to Cassandra.

There was a time when my friends found my antics charming, maybe even exciting. They thought I was a fun person to be around because I seemed to have so few boundaries and was always "acting wacky." To me there was nothing particularly wild about suddenly speaking in gibberish or wearing a Halloween costume to the grocery store in the middle of summer. If it was eccentric, it was the most tepid, safe form of eccentricity imaginable.

But at a certain point, as I felt less and less connected to the world around me, those mild antics stopped feeling like enough to express myself. I just kept pushing. I used my behavior as a smokescreen, worried that if I wasn't being wacky, people might see me as I felt I really was. The more cut off I felt, the more desperate and outrageous I felt I had to be. My friends grew less and less enthused about spending time with me when I started throwing food or stuffing tree leaves into my mouth or flipping over drinks on a restaurant table or forcing myself to vomit in public or lighting bags of garbage on fire. My antics weren't so funny anymore.

I was just about to make something up in order to get off the phone when Cassandra blurted out, "There's someone here who wants to say hello."

Fumbling phone noise.

"Hey," announced a girl's voice.

I had no idea who it was.

"It's me."

Still clueless.

"I just got back last week, and we were wondering what you were doing."

"Oh . . . I'm just . . . umm," I answered.

"You don't know who I am, do you?"

"Sure I do," I lied.

"It's Laura," she said.

"Laura," I replied, as if saying the word out loud would pluck the connection out of the haze for me.

"Laura Patterson," she said, getting a little testy. "Did you even know I was gone?"

"Sure I did," I said, telling the truth this time. I knew she had been on some exchange program to some foreign country and had been gone the whole school year.

I had met Laura in junior high, where she was a year behind me. At the time, she was "going with" my friend Timmy. Outside of note passing and the occasional tight-lipped kiss after school events, "going together" in seventh grade was pretty meaningless. You couldn't drive, had nowhere to go, and either weren't allowed or couldn't afford to do anything. It was kind of like being an old married couple, except you could control your bowels and stay awake past 8 P.M.

Even with these limited expectations, Timmy wasn't really up to the task. He even had me break up with Laura on his behalf. It had been a crisp spring morning in front of Walter C. Crenshaw Junior High School.

"Hey, Patterson," I yelled as I walked past her before school one morning. "I just talked to your boyfriend Timmy yesterday."

"Oh yeah?" she replied.

"Yeah . . . See, that's the thing . . . He said he doesn't want to go with you anymore."

Laura looked like a tomboyish pixie: short hair, small features, and big dark eyes. At that moment, she looked like a tomboyish pixie who was about to cry.

"It's no big deal," I consoled her. "He really didn't like you that much anyhow."

It seemed like a comforting thing to say at the time.

She ran away and didn't speak to me for a year or so.

We ended up at the same high school and exchanged occasional hallway greetings, which sometimes had a tendency to linger for a bit. We'd catch each other's glance at pep rallies or assemblies. However, I didn't make much of an effort to get to know her until she started dating this guy named James, who I really hated.

Some friends and I had pulled off an amazing prank against our assistant principal, which I won't discuss here because of Ohio's liberal statute of limitations. James and his friends spread rumors that *they* had been the real perps. I figured the best way to get him back was to flirt openly with his new girlfriend.

Laura and I had study hall at the same time. This was the perfect opportunity to make my move. By this time Laura had grown into the perfect little fresh-faced A student. She wore cute sweaters, Docksiders, and peg-legged jeans.

After we started talking at study hall, I was surprised at how witty she was. Previously, she'd come across as quiet, almost painfully shy. But the more time I spent around her, the more brightness emerged. She was funnier than me (not a high mark, but I was still impressed), she was way smarter (again, not a tough standard), she knew more about music and books than I did (which really got to me), and she had a comeback

for every smart remark I volleyed in her direction. Eventually we were sitting together every day and talking about everything: politics, religion, the twisted imbecile logic of people, whatever. James was pissed, but that stopped being the point, and he'd soon be out of the picture anyhow.

I never seriously thought of her as anyone I would date or see outside of school; she was just someone fun to pass time with. The summer after her sophomore year she left to spend her junior year abroad, and since I knew I'd graduate before she got back, I figured that was the end of it. There are times when injecting even the smallest amount of separation into a friendship makes reconnecting uncomfortable.

I fumbled with the phone to buy a second or two to think of something to say.

"So how was . . ."

"Finland?" she replied.

"Yeah, how was Finland?"

"Finland was fine," she said. "I spent a lot of time traveling. I visited eleven countries."

"Eleven, huh?" I said, trying not to sound impressed. Outside of one summer in Jamaica and a trip to the Canadian side of Niagara Falls, I'd never been outside the United States. I hadn't even visited my fifth state yet.

"In Europe they have tons of music festivals, so I saw a lot of bands. Incredible bands."

While I was drinking, masturbating, and being haunted by the Little Girl, Laura was widening her lead on cool music. I needed to instantly juice my cred.

"Yeah, well, I'm in a band now."

This, technically, was not a lie. Jimmy and I had put an ad in the local record store looking for bandmates. Despite a list of "influences" that clearly set out that we were destined for punk-rock greatness, the only calls we'd gotten were from heavy-metal wannabes. What we wanted were punk-rock wannabes, but we were patient.

"Oh really? What's it called?"

"Ritzo Forte."

"Really?"

"*Forte* means loud," I explained. Having been to eleven European countries, I assumed she would know that. "*Ritzo* just sounds good with *forte*."

"So, when you aren't rocking out, what do you do with yourself?"

"Now that school is over?" I asked.

"Yeah."

"I have a shit job as a janitor at T.J. Maxx."

"Is it really a shit job? Do you have to clean up shit?"

I could hear some giggling in the background from Cassandra and no doubt some other girls who had egged Laura into talking to me in the first place.

"Actually, I do. The other day I got a call from the women's fitting room. A woman had gone into the back stall and, well, you know."

"And you had to clean it up?"

"Well, first I went into the actual bathroom, which was twenty yards away, if she had even asked, and threw up. Then I went back and cleaned it up."

"Do they pay you extra for that?"

"What? For cleaning up human waste in a fitting room or because I puked?"

"No, the cleaning."

"No, that's included in the $3.35 an hour they pay me."

After a few more minutes of back and forth, we decided to get together the next afternoon. I was given some very clear instructions about picking her up. I was to drive to her parents' house and wait. I was not to get out of the car, approach the house, or knock on the door—just show up when I was sup- posed to and sit there.

I got there a little early. Laura's house was small—really small—maybe three or four rooms. Even if the attic had been finished, I couldn't quite get my head around how Laura, her two parents, and her two brothers could fit into that space. Her house sat in a neighborhood that looked like it had been built all at once during the 1950s. The homes had rarely been updated since. There wasn't a lot of landscaping or trees. In our study-hall conversations before she went to Finland, it was obvious that Laura cared about her family, but she equally went out of her way to avoid talking about them. She only shared what she wanted to share, which was little. Her mom was a social worker and her dad did some kind of construction work that often had him away from home for long stretches. I also knew that she had a large extended family that had lived in the area for generations. But even that took some prodding.

I also knew Laura had gone to a special grade school for gifted students. The gifted kids came from two extremes of the spectrum: affluent families, who expected their kids to excel, and poor families, where the kids stuck out so much that they ended up in the gifted program. To kids like Laura, the program was a way out, not an expectation.

I put the seat back and shoved a tape into the deck: The Smiths, *Meat Is Murder.* It seemed like a good choice to demonstrate my coolness. I found three warm beers in the backseat and started on one. I'd begun to doze off when I heard the door open quickly and slam shut. I looked over and was shocked out of my light buzz by this smiling thing in my passenger seat.

Her hair was jet black, lying dead flat in some areas, wildly askew in others. It was cut to different lengths, looking like she had trimmed it herself without a mirror (which, I'd soon learn, was the truth). It hung over her face, completely covering one of her eyes, which were underscored with thick black eyeliner. She wore a ratty white T-shirt that had things written on it in Magic Marker that I couldn't read, despite a preponderance of exclamation marks next to the words. Her black jeans looked like they'd been put through a tree mulcher, then taped and pinned back together. But she still wore the Docksiders I remembered her for.

She looked as if someone had brined her in a vat of punk rock, then forgotten to rinse her off afterward. It was a metamorphosis. I didn't want her to know how mesmerized I was.

"Looks like you had an interesting year" was the only thing I could think to say.

"What makes you think so?"

"Come on," I challenged. "Who are you? I mean, I almost thought you were a homeless person about to steal my car."

"I'm just me. Maybe you never noticed before."

"Fine. Where are we going?" I asked.

"Wherever."

"That's very helpful."

"Why don't we go someplace you want to go?" she offered.

We rolled down the windows and started off. We just drove.

Once we pulled away from the curb, I can't remember a single word we said to each other for the rest of the day. I don't even remember enough to reconstruct what might have been said. Even if I could remember, how do you describe a moment like that? A moment that simply stuns you. A moment when everything seems to suddenly freeze and explode. Perhaps you just discovered the best friend you'll ever have, or perhaps you just fell in love, or perhaps everything you thought you knew suddenly changed.

We left her house as minor-league acquaintances and returned several hours later as best friends. Even though I remember a lot of other times with her, that day has been put somewhere where I'm not allowed to access it. It's like my memory wanted me to simply keep a few images of that day and that's all.

I remember that it was sunny and warm and the sky was blue.

I remember her hair flapping in the wind.

I remember noticing, for the first time, that she had very small teeth.

I remember that the roar through all the windows meant we had to yell our entire conversation.

I remember that I kept making jokes and she laughed a lot.

I remember that she'd always try to push her hair behind her ears whenever she was about to make a point.

I remember fumbling a lot with the tape player.

I remember that she punched my arm at least three times for making smartass comments.

I remember that I didn't think once about getting high or about the Little Girl in a Blue Dress.

I remember that when I dropped her off at home, we exchanged tapes. She gave me a dub of Killing Joke's *Fire Dances*, and I gave her my copy of Brian Eno's *Music for Airports*.

I remember knowing, even then, that I'd remember that day for the rest of my life.

．．

"Eric?"
"What?"
"Spider."
Giggling.

What if others could see you for what you really are? Not what
you think you are. Not how others perceive you. Not what you
want to be. But the truth.

The dead can do that. I believed it as a child, and I still believe it now. Whenever I'm asked to explain what about ghosts
makes me so afraid, I always point to *A Christmas Carol.* I have
a very Dickensian view of the dead. I believe the dead see
clearly—they know the truth of our past, present, and future. I
think that when we die, all our questions are answered and all
mysteries are revealed. If you believe that ghosts are dead souls
trapped here for various unknown reasons, that means a ghost
knows all. A ghost may know more about you than you do.

"Michael?"
"What?"

"Spider."

More giggling.

Like any kid, I spent my early childhood desperately wanting to fit in, but I really didn't have a lot to build on. Some kids dressed funny, acted like geeks, had crooked teeth, sucked at athletics, weren't popular, wore glasses, were generally awkward, or did poorly in class. I was a perfect storm of all these, a tsunami of dork. Early on, I resigned myself to being "the weird kid"—a mantle that, while not ideal, gave me some kind of anchor in the world, a place, a role to fill.

In many ways, I grew up a pretty typical kid. Specifically, a pretty typical boy. Young boys are creatures of intense, loyal, and deep passion. When I was a young child, I was passionate about exactly four things: the TV series *The Six Million Dollar Man,* Kiss, *Star Wars,* and writing to elected officials.

To the other kids at school, I was just a fairly unremarkable kid who was occasionally funny but did and said a lot of weird stuff. Even though I loved to learn, school ended up becoming a bum deal for me before I'd even hit the third grade, squeaking by with just enough C's to keep from being held back. Whenever I was interested in or curious about something, I had an ability to quickly learn and absorb everything about it. The problem was, I was rarely interested in or curious about my classmates or the things they were learning in school. So I'd sneak my way into drawing or writing or daydreaming—or phase out entirely.

From an early age I was an expert at pushing boundaries without actually crossing them—almost constantly on the verge of getting into trouble. My teachers tried everything, isolating my desk behind a divider, sending me to counselors, and even humiliating me in front of my classmates. Nothing worked. At my parents' insistence, I went through a regime of tutoring, testing, and specialists. At one point I was sent to a neurologist who thought I was hyperactive and put me on large doses of Ritalin. None of it really made much of a difference. I'd already made the decision, conscious or not, that it might be a better strategy to give up. It felt like it was futile to care. I'd already resigned myself to being a square peg. I wasn't meant to be part of things, I thought. I didn't like the same things others liked. I didn't care about the things they cared about. I didn't find the same things funny. Perhaps it can be romanticized in hindsight: that I was independent or that I was a unique personality—whatever. Those rationalizations would be great if they weren't driven by always feeling like a sojourner, a visitor in my own world.

The letter writing to elected officials started, more or less, as something to do with an old manual typewriter I'd found in my grandparents' basement. I was really drawn to this thing, to the idea of legitimizing my thoughts and ideas by typing them on paper. Problem was, at ten years old, I really didn't have many thoughts to legitimize. After a few sessions of staring at the keys or typing my name and address over and over again, I just started writing letters. I really didn't have anyone to write to—or write about—so I started writing to politicians. I did it out of curiosity, to see if I would ever hear anything back. I would watch the evening news with my parents, notice something in the fourteen seconds I would spend looking at the non-comics part of the newspaper, or hear adults talking about some important issue. Then I would sit down in front of the typewriter, write a letter expressing my view on the subject, and send it off. A while later, I'd receive a reply, thanking me for sharing my opinion. After the first few exchanges, I came to the quick conclusion that my letters were an important contribution to democracy and society.

My congressman, Ralph Regula, was a patient man, or at least his staff was, as he often answered four or five letters per month from me on topics ranging from military-weapons programs to relations with the Soviet Union to the federal budget. I wrote him routinely for years and received a thorough reply to each letter, which I kept in a folder along with answers to all the other letters I wrote—to city council members, local police and fire chiefs, United States senators, and even, on several occasions, the president of the United States.

I saved my opinions on the big issues—about the rising price of oil or inflation—for President Carter. Letters to the president are often answered, if they are answered at all, by a generic postcard thanking the writer for taking the time and assuring him that his opinion matters to the president. But on one occasion I received a letter from some suit at the Office of Management and Budget, thanking me for the list that I'd sent to President Carter of federal programs I felt should be cut or reduced. Little did this guy realize that he was writing to a preteen who'd just learned what deficit spending meant a few weeks earlier in civics class.

One morning I was summoned to the vice principal's office. When I got there, I saw a uniformed police officer sitting there, apparently waiting for me. My mind immediately ran through any potential felonious hijinks I may have participated in that would result in a *cop* coming after me *at school*. The only thing that came to mind was an egg I threw at Jim Galapaco's house because he'd tried to steal my bicycle seat.

It turned out that the officer had been dispatched by the police chief to pass along his personal thanks for my recent letter offering my thoughts concerning his public-safety initiatives I'd read about in the paper. The visiting cop told me I seemed like a model citizen and invited me to join some kind of Nazi Youth–like junior police group.

"You'll get a badge and a certificate," he offered.

I politely declined. I felt I was most productive working outside the system, I told him.

Kiss was the soundtrack to my life. Even though they sold millions of records, I kind of felt like they belonged to me exclusively. It may have been that not many other kids at my school had discovered Kiss, or perhaps it was because they seemed so excitingly foreign to the rest of the world I'd experienced so far, but it almost felt as if they had existed in obscurity until I became a fan—an obsessed fan. By that time, I already listened to a lot of pop music, but Kiss was different. Kiss was weird. I was weird. In my mind, we were a perfect match.

While I longed to play electric guitar or bass, my parents had decided that piano lessons were a better option. After practicing "Für Elise" for the nine thousandth time, I would peck out the melody lines of Kiss songs. Eventually, I came to see my keyboard skills as a potential asset. If, someday, Kiss decided to add a piano player, I would be ready to step in. I even had a character/persona picked out. I could be "the Viper" and stand behind my piano with a costume and makeup to morph me into something vaguely snakelike, in a Kiss kind of way. I had notebook pages filled with potential costume and makeup designs, complete with plans for how we could outfit our family's baby grand piano with rhinestones, reptile-like leather demon heads, and claws (even though vipers don't have claws). I also had a character/instrument-related gimmick ready to go. At the appropriate point in the song, I could press a button with my seven-inch leather heels and the top would explode off my piano in a mushroom cloud of smoke and fire, revealing a large mechanical snake. The viper would continue to rise up and up out of the piano, presenting itself to the crowd's amazement and cheers. Then, when it came time for my Big Piano Solo (placed in between the Big Guitar Solo and the Big Drum Solo), I would drop a little "Für Elise" into the middle of "Hotter Than Hell" and *blow people's minds.*

Kiss was something that adults hated, which was fantastic. But the real attraction to me was freedom. People expected Kiss to be outlandish, so they could pretty much get away with anything they wanted to do, say, and wear—as long as it was over-the-top. It would never be odd if Kiss wore black tights and codpieces—it would be odd if they didn't. To a young boy just about to enter his teens, who was already beginning to feel like an outcast because of what he did, wore, and said, the idea that people would accept this kind of behavior, let alone encourage it, was an absolute magnet.

Along with a few other kids who drew Kiss-related art in notebooks and on our blue jeans, I decided to create the ultimate tribute to my heroes: a band.

After a significant amount of debate, we eventually decided on a name: Kiss Junior.

The ensemble consisted of my friend Terry on guitar and vocals, his sister Tammy (who I had a terrible crush on) on tambourine, and me on electric organ. I had come into a small tabletop organ and—seeing that it was more portable than the family baby grand—took it to Terry and Tammy's house for band practice. It had a half-sized keyboard and one four-inch speaker mounted on the side of the cabinet.

Terry had no idea how to play guitar; he didn't even know

how to tune it. He had received a cheap guitar-and-amp combo for Christmas. After noodling with it for about half an hour he'd figured out how to make it give feedback. That was where his guitar self-instruction ended. Further, Terry was completely tone-deaf, and even his feedback was arrhythmic. His playing and singing amounted to screaming lyrics and beating his guitar quickly during fast passages, then screaming lyrics and beating his guitar slowly during softer moments.

Our repertoire consisted entirely of Kiss songs. This complicated matters, because no Kiss songs contained arrangements for electric organ, tambourine, and untuned guitar. However, despite our handicaps, we fully intended to rock.

Whenever we'd get the chance, we'd gather in Terry and Tammy's basement in front of an old bedsheet that Terry had decorated with a Kiss logo with a "Junior" slapped underneath it.

Terry would put a Kiss record on the turntable and drop the needle, and we'd flail away. We did this almost every afternoon for the entire summer. To us, Kiss Junior wasn't just a salute to our favorite band—Kiss Junior was our preteen version of pure joy.

We had one fan, a slightly retarded boy who lived next door, Brian, who always smelled like pee and had an obsession with blowing up fruit and vegetables with firecrackers. Brian would come by whenever he heard us practicing and sit watching on the stairs with his mouth wide open.

We only performed for others once, at Tammy's birthday party. Tammy had about eight girls from school over for cake, presents, screaming, and giggling. Banned from the house, Terry and I hung out in the backyard with a few friends, pretending not to care yet desperate to know what was going on inside.

At one point we were allowed in to get some leftover pizza and Terry saw an opportunity to impress the gaggle.

"You know, we have a rock band," he offered. "And Tammy is in it."

They stared at Terry, then at Tammy.

"You have to play for us," one girl suggested.

Bait taken.

Tammy wanted nothing to do with it and tried to talk us and her friends out of it. But Terry was already corraling everyone into the basement and ordered me to set up our equipment. Before I knew what was happening, he dropped the needle during the crowd roar before the live version of "God of Thunder," and we were off.

The hi-fi started belching out thumpy noise, Terry started screaming and banging his guitar, I hit tiny organ keys, and Tammy just stood there with her eyes fixed on the floor. Our assembled audience seemed somewhat frozen, occasionally wincing at the noise and wondering what they were supposed to make of this. After a minute or so, someone giggled, then a few others started laughing.

Tammy threw down her tambourine and ran upstairs crying. I stood there unsure if I was supposed to go comfort one bandmate or stay and perform with the other. My first thought was to run after Tammy. In my mind, just as I'd catch up with her, the next song would start, I'd belt out an impassioned rendition of "Beth," and Tammy would fall into my arms.

But, as much as I ached to comfort Tammy, I knew Terry would either kick my ass for leaving or make fun of me for eternity because I had the hots for his sister. So I stayed. The show had to go on, I rationalized. Despite missing one-third of our band, Terry had no intention of stopping. After each song, he'd make his guitar feed back, throw his hands in the air, repeatedly yell, "Thank you" to the assembled children, and then get ready for the next song. No one applauded. No one did anything.

One by one, the kids quietly left the basement and went upstairs. By the end of the album side, it was down to just Terry and me, plus Brian.

Terry and I were not deterred; we were hell-bent on rocking, ferociously.

A few days later, Terry observed that while we had played Kiss music, we lacked any Kiss-related costumes or makeup. Since painting our faces would be a lot easier than finding seven-inch leather boots with skulls on them (especially in a size four), we decided to invest in some cheap Halloween makeup. We found our opportunity one evening while Terry's family had gone out to a movie.

We were about halfway finished with Kiss-inspired makeup when we heard his family pull in the driveway. We panicked. Terry started to run water in the bathtub and told me to scrub my face. Of course, the cheap greasepaint wouldn't come off and our efforts to clean it off just spread it further over our faces.

Eventually, we were discovered.

"What are you two doing in there?" Terry's mother asked.

"We're taking a bath," Terry quickly offered.

"Together?" she asked.

"Yeah, we're almost finished," Terry said, hoping that it would placate his mother long enough for him to clean off the makeup.

As soon as we stepped out of the bathroom, Terry's parents called us downstairs. We sat nonchalantly on the couch with a look of confused-yet-politely-inquisitive wonder on our faces, as if we were worried what possibly could be wrong.

"What were you doing taking a bath together?" Terry's mother asked.

"When no one else is home," his father added.

In the middle of Terry's rambling answer, Terry's father looked at me and squinted.

"What's that around your eyes?" he asked.

I paused for a moment, then answered: "Makeup."

Terry placed his head in his hands and sighed.

I could see Terry's father starting to boil.

"Are you guys gay?" he asked, containing his obvious anger and trying to maintain an air of sincere concern.

I was sent home and Terry was grounded.

The incident drove a permanent wedge in Kiss Junior—the band broke up the next day.

Afterward, Terry and I grew apart, as young kids do. Terry was two years older than me, which started to make a difference as we became teens. I lost track of him after high school, though I knew he was playing in a heavy-metal band and was pretty serious about it (and, obviously, he had finally learned to play his guitar).

One evening last year, I was lazily scrolling through Facebook when I saw a link an old classmate had shared. It was an article about a guitarist who had been killed by a punch from one of his own bandmates. The dead guitarist was Terry.

Terry had gone on to live a pretty extraordinary life. He played in a number of metal bands, cut two albums, and started a business focused on bringing rock bands to play for overseas troops. With his own band, he played USO shows in more than thirty countries. He even taught guitar to troops stationed in Korea for a few years.

Following a gig in his adopted hometown of Colorado Springs, two of his bandmates got into a fight over carrying equipment out of the club. Terry stepped in to break it up and took a punch to the back of the head. He spent twelve days in a coma, then died.

He left behind a young daughter.

Kiss Junior was not listed on his resume.

"Eric?"

"What?"

"Spider."

Giggling.

I'm not sure how that spider joke started. I'm not even sure it counts as a joke. It was just one of those things between brothers that's kind of funny the first time it happens. It was probably a practical joke—saying "spider" to someone (implying that there's a spider on or near him), then watching him go into a freak-out spasm, brushing and swatting to get rid of the nonexistent spider. Since so few things that little boys say are legitimately funny, you work with the material you have, repeating it over and over again, laughing even though you aren't sure why it's funny anymore.

In addition to "spider," my brother and I regularly cracked each other up with other comedy gold mines, like farting in the sleeping dog's face, imitating Mr. Hendler next door, and pretending to be scared by the noises coming from the attic.

We'd notice them every few weeks. Basically, it was just a loud thud coming from upstairs. Whenever we'd hear one, we'd look at each other with mock terror.

"Michael?"

"What?"

"It's a ghost!"

Then we'd both put our hands up to our faces and pretend to scream.

Hilarious.

We noticed the thuds shortly after we moved into the house and never gave them much thought. It was an old house; it made lots of noises. At first, we assumed it was our cat, who loved to climb on top of tall furniture, then leap to the floor and run away. Eventually I started noticing the thuds occurring when the cat was sitting in the same room with us.

Around that time, I started taking the bus back and forth to junior high. Our bus driver always liked to keep us guessing. He seemed to change his route and stop order almost daily. We'd never be certain from which direction he'd arrive or at what time.

This resulted in a lot of downtime, during which I would stand with an assortment of kids from my neighborhood, trying to guess when our shifty bus driver would arrive. The inevitable boredom of standing around waiting usually resulted in one of two things happening: (a) some of the kids would start teasing me about something; or (b) I would make some kind of desperate attempt to entertain them in order to divert their attention. This was a lot of pressure—always having some conversation topics or jokes ready to go and having no idea when the bus would arrive to keep them from turning on me. Sometimes I even brought candy or some show-and-tell-type item.

One morning a kid named Jason walked up to me and asked if I was retarded.

"Pardon me?"

"Are you a retard?" he asked. Some of the other kids were starting to gather around us. I gritted my teeth. I knew what was coming.

"No, I'm not retarded," I said.

"Well, you look like a retard," countered Jason. "You act like a retard, too."

I already knew the futility of trying to argue about subjects like suggested retardation. It was just impossible to win.

"I guess I'm whatever you want to see," I said. "I guess I'm like a TV."

"What are you talking about?"

"I guess I'm like a TV," I repeated. "You can see whatever you want on TV. If you don't like it, you can just change the channel."

"Only a retard would think they were a TV," Jason offered.

"No, here," I said, placing my hand in front of him, palm upward. "Here is my remote control," I said, gesturing to my empty hand.

"You *are* retarded!" Jason exclaimed.

"No, here," I said, pantomiming reaching for an invisible remote and then offering it to Jason with my other hand. "Here, take it," I said.

Jason cautiously put his hand forward to receive my invisible remote.

"Now press the channel button," I said.

Jason just huffed as the other kids silently watched.

"Press the channel button," I repeated.

Jason made an unnecessarily dramatic pressing gesture with his finger. I jerked forward and pretended to be a newscaster delivering news.

Jason pressed it again.

I changed into a sportscaster announcing a baseball game.

Jason pressed again.

I was a soldier fighting to save his buddies on the battle-field.

Jason kept clicking and I kept changing.

In my mind, the other kids would bust out laughing and find every character more hilarious than the last. But none of them laughed. Actually, none of them did anything. They just stood there, mouths open, watching me. I prayed that the bus would finally show up and save me from this. It seemed like it was never coming. Jason just kept clicking and I kept changing: Mork from Ork, then a damsel crying over a fallen lover, then Fred Astaire dancing and singing in the rain.

"Hey, man, see if it has a Pause button," one kid shouted.

"Sure it does," Jason said. "Right here."

He pantomimed one final button press—and I froze.

And stayed frozen.

The kids started laughing.

I could hear the bus pulling up behind me. The kids lost interest in me and started to line up. I stayed frozen.

After all the other kids got on the bus, the driver looked down at me and squinted.

"Hey, quit jerking around and get on," he called out.

I stood frozen. I was in pause.

Even though I could feel everyone staring at me and hear them giggle and laugh, being frozen felt good. It felt like there was a barrier between me and them. It was like I had a protective shell between my feelings and the things that hurt them.

I guess the right thing to do would have been to listen to the driver and get on the bus, but being frozen felt so peaceful. I knew I'd never hear the end of it, but I just kept standing there.

"If you don't get on this bus this minute, I'm going to leave you here, I swear," the bus driver yelled. The kids on the bus grew silent.

I just stood there.

"Fine, I'm sure they'll send Mr. Barnes down here for you when they hear about this."

With that, he drove away.

I continued to stand frozen for some time after the bus left. I knew the school would never send Mr. Barnes out for me. They had a schoolful of other things to worry about. After a few cars drove by and asked me if I needed any help—then quickly drove away when I didn't move—I got tired of being there and started walking home. I eventually called my mom at work and told her I threw up on the way to the bus stop and needed to stay home sick. I spent the day sitting in my room, periodically picking up an invisible remote control, pointing it at myself, and going into pause for a while.

It was around this time that my grandmother died; I was just past my thirteenth birthday. We always called my mother's mother Bobalu. She was the anchor of our family. Despite a sometimes difficult life, she was a happy person. She could have a conversation with just about anyone. She also smoked like a chimney, suffering through a few heart attacks and lung cancer before she died at sixty-two.

I'd never experienced anyone dying before. When we first got word that she'd passed away, I wasn't immediately sad or in shock or even that upset. I was curious. The rituals of death and funerals and mourning were foreign to me, and fascinating. Everyone in my family, which was normally so happy together, was suddenly sad and crying. I asked tons of questions and wanted to know everything. What would her coffin be made of? Where were they keeping her body? Would she look different dead than she did when she was alive?

When the day of her calling hours arrived, I walked into the funeral parlor, took one look at Bobalu's casket, and completely lost it. The casket was closed, so it wasn't like I saw her remains. I saw a box. On the inside of that box was my grandmother's body. Her death suddenly stopped being a curiosity and smacked me right in the gut.

In the following days and weeks, I became obsessed with thinking about what happened to Bobalu when she died. I came to believe that she went to heaven because she was such a good person. When she got there, God answered all her questions about her life. As a result, Bobalu no longer knew me as the bright, near-flawless grandson with unlimited potential. She saw me as I really was. She now knew the frustrations and disappointments. She also knew about my growing disconnection from the world. In death, Bobalu knew everything. She knew the truth.

One night a few months after the funeral, I was sitting in my bedroom when I heard one of the thuds. Not a distant thud, like something outside the house. It sounded close, like something heavy and thick hitting the attic floor directly above me.

I ran out of my room and up the attic stairs at the end of the hallway. When I got to the top, I could see moonlight coming through the windows of our playroom, one of the two attic rooms. While it was normal for toys to be strewn over the room, nothing seemed particularly out of place. There was nothing big on the shelves, so nothing could have fallen to make the noise I heard.

Without turning on any lights, I turned toward the door to

the room in the back of the attic. As soon as I looked at the door, I was overwhelmed with panic. I felt like I was stuck underwater and couldn't breathe. We'd lived in that house for a few years by that point, and I'd never given that door or that room a second thought. Now the sight of it left me unable to move or even consider turning on a light, let alone try to find out what was on the other side. It just felt like something was present in that room that had never been there before. Something I wanted nothing to do with.

Then I started to wonder if whatever was in that room had come over into the playroom and pounded on the floor, summoning me, knowing that I was right underneath, knowing I would come upstairs to investigate. Now it was in the room across the hall, waiting for me to come to it, or to come after me.

I stood there in the dark, not sure what to do. Going back downstairs meant walking right by that door, easily within arm's length of whatever was on the other side. Eventually I mustered up the courage to run back downstairs to my room and sit with my heart pounding in my throat. For the rest of that night, any noise I heard was evidence that whoever or whatever was up there might be coming downstairs.

For a long time afterward, I would do anything to avoid going up there. I'd swap chores with Michael, find an alternative to whatever was stored up there, not play with certain toys. Anything to not be in the attic, especially at night.

Eventually, I had to go up for some reason or another. I was nervous but felt nothing even remotely similar to what I experienced that first night. In fact, it felt so confusingly unscary that I ended up exploring the entire attic—each room, closet, and crawlspace. I was fine.

But every so often I'd be up there and I'd get that feeling.

It was like being surrounded by something you felt sure was there but wasn't. I could feel all the warmth drain out of the room, then an abrupt and extreme sense of danger. My heart and mind would both race, I'd start to hyperventilate, and everything would suddenly go out of control. It always happened when I was looking at the closed door to the spare room, and always when I was alone. I would be overcome with fear, drop whatever I was doing, and run.

I can't tell you when the dreams started exactly. Or why they started. Around the time I entered my teens, they just suddenly became part of my life.

Standing in the woods. Then the clearing. Then the picnic table. Then the people, including the guy in the cheap wolf costume pointing to the other side. Then the second path.

Then Her.

She is probably eight to ten years old. She has straight blond hair that goes a few inches past Her shoulders. She wears a simple powder-blue dress with no ornamentation or frills. She is dripping wet. Her cheeks are a little hollow, but otherwise She looks perfectly fine. Our eyes lock as soon as I see Her. She doesn't look sick or dead or particularly stressed about anything—until I get close.

Then She starts talking in something that sounds like gibberish or an evangelist's prayer tongue. The closer I get, the louder and more agitated She becomes. It's like She's scared of me; She doesn't look angry. It's almost like She thinks our time together is running out and She becomes more and more desperate to connect, for me to understand what She's saying. Except for Her eyes—empty, dark, and still. Then, when I'm close enough that I could almost reach out and touch Her, She starts to shout at me.

Then it's over.

I'd wake up in an absolute panic. My heart was racing and about to push itself out of my chest. I'd bolt up and scan the dark room for any sign of Her. Then I'd spend hours trying to calm myself down to the point where I could sleep again. I'd tell myself anything, just to feel safe closing my eyes, even for a moment.

Sometimes the dreams would occur in the standard order. Sometimes the scenes were mixed up or I'd just see a few fragments and not the whole thing. I remember a few occasions when I'd only see an image—the wolf guy, or Her standing there speaking Her gibberish. Regardless, they all ended exactly the same way—with me sitting upright in bed, breathing hard and fast, disoriented, scanning the darkness for Her, convinced She had finally come for me.

Those who've heard the story of these dreams have all asked the same question: What is so scary about a little girl?

You see, that's always been the rub. There is nothing inherently scary about a little girl.

Which is exactly why She was so terrifying to me.

It wasn't what I knew about Her or the dreams that frightened me; it was what I didn't know.

The unknowns about the Little Girl in a Blue Dress felt like puzzles or enigmas or mysteries to be solved. Like, why was She wet? Was She sweating? Had She been in water?

Who were the people sitting around the table? I didn't recognize any of them. They all seemed to be in their late teens or early twenties. Nothing about them rang a bell. Nor did I have any clue where the cheap wolf costume came from.

And what was with the gibberish? You'd think that someone motivated enough to come back from the dead, bang around my parents' attic, and worm Her way into my dreams would have figured out how to deliver the message. A million times I've thought about what I remember Her saying, to see if there is even a pattern or anything that sticks out. To be honest, I'm not even sure She repeated the same thing—it could have been different every time.

And the biggest mystery: Why Her? There were no dead girls in my past. I had nothing in my family tree about blond girls who died young.

I have spent countless hours over the years going over those dreams in my head, trying to find any connection, any literal, metaphorical, or figurative symbolism or meaning in *any* detail of that dream, and I always come up with exactly nothing.

Which is when it starts to get scary to me. I mean, there has to be *some* connection. It happened to me—and it happened for some reason. She is my Jacob Marley. Somehow the wetness, the people, the forest, the man in the wolf costume—those were somehow Her version of the chains Marley forged in life and had to drag with him through eternity. If I didn't recognize what they meant, that meant I hadn't figured something out yet and the connections would present themselves only *after* all the bad stuff She was warning me about eventually happened.

Then there was the message itself. Just as Marley came back to warn Ebenezer Scrooge about the coming visits from the ghosts of his past, present, and future, She was warning me about something, too. Or at least I've always accepted it as a warning, but it equally could be a threat, a prophecy, a harbinger of *something*. Something that someone/something else was going to do—or that She planned to do Herself. The only thing I knew for sure was that it almost certainly couldn't have been good news. The Little Girl did not come into my dreams to wish me a good day or compliment the shirt/pants combo I'd worn earlier. She had something to tell me that was very important.

I feared that whatever it was had to be *so bad* that only She could deliver it. I feared what She'd do when She tired of trying to communicate with me in my dreams. I feared I had only come so far in my experience of Her. And it could get worse at any moment, any time.

I also feared that it might be impossible to heed Her warning. When Marley came to visit Scrooge, he said it was too late to save his own soul but that Scrooge had time to be redeemed. But what if Marley and the Christmas ghosts spoke gibberish? Would Scrooge miss his one and only chance to redeem himself? Because I couldn't understand the Little Girl in a Blue Dress, would I miss Her warning? Would I miss *my* chance?

So, it wasn't an apparition I feared. I was scared of what I didn't know, simply because I didn't know it. My life began to feel like that flash of a moment between when you know you're going to be in an auto accident and the impact itself. Like that moment between when the wave crests above your head and when it comes crashing down on you. Even if it is only for an instant, the waiting is the worst part. Worse than the collision. Worse than the injury and damage. Whenever Little Girl came to me in my dreams, my whole life started to feel like that moment. Just waiting, knowing and not knowing, all at the same time.

Two aspects of my life blossomed as I headed into my teens.

I started to become heavily involved in my church. From simply attending Sunday service I felt increasingly drawn into joining the Sunday school, youth group, and confirmation classes, mostly because I wanted to hang around with the other kids. I looked to my fellow teen parishioners to fill the human void in my life. My family had kept attending the same church after we moved to the house on Thirty-fourth Street a few years earlier. Since I now lived in a different neighborhood and school district, I rarely saw most of these kids more than once a week. When I was at church, I was on my best behavior. The lack of regular exposure, plus me being on my best behavior, made it easier for me to make friends at church than at school. Though at the time I wasn't terribly interested in all the Jesus stuff, this group became the one area of my life where I was deeply involved with other people.

I also quickly embraced the self-righteous "stick it to the Man" vibe of the church's social activism and attitude toward the outside world. This led to the other blossoming area of my early teens: my letter writing, which grew into something more purposeful. As I became more involved in the church, the subjects of my letters switched from complaining about budgets, parks, and proper signage at crosswalks into the need for politicians to address poverty and injustice.

Writing letters soon led to social action—doing walkathons for cancer research, volunteering for food pantries, boycotting products, marching against nuclear arms, and just about anything else I could fit into my schedule. I was a full-time bringer of truth and righteousness. I felt I'd found my purpose and calling, a way to realize my potential. My goal was nothing short of changing the world, but underlying it was a strange and uncomfortable anger. I was upset that there were so many things wrong with the world and that adults had allowed things to get so fucked up. I felt that while it was profoundly broken, it was also profoundly fixable. All I had to do was try.

But of course, nothing changed.

I'd write letters. I'd attend rallies. I'd protest. And nothing ever seemed to change.

Because the world allowed all these horrible things to happen, I believed that it was tacitly saying these things were acceptable. Yet I also slowly came to realize that no matter how many marches I attended, no matter how many letters I wrote or bake sales I ran or cans of food I collected or miles I walked, there was nothing I could ever do to stop it. I thought I could make a difference in the world, but often there was no difference to be made. We march and protest and express our opinions, and all we accomplish is making ourselves feel better. I think I was angry because not only did I know that nothing would change, I felt foolish for thinking that I could ever make any substantive difference in the first place.

Despite my growing apathy, I kept writing letters, kept boycotting, and kept attending protests and rallies. I did this mostly because I was so desperate to hold on to the small amount of human connection that surrounded these activities. I thought it was useless work, but I didn't want to stop. Even though I felt less and less connection to and tolerance or trust of other people, at the same time I could not bear to let them go. I figured there had to be some formula—some combination of actions—that would result in the world accepting me, and me feeling wanted. While part of me wanted to keep trying different tactics until I got the equation right, I was also feeling increasingly desperate.

During this time I noticed that both the Little Girl dreams and the terror spells in the attic were accelerating. You might think the connection was simply a matter of circumstance and suggestion. At the time, though, the dreams began to feel like a validation of some impending doom.

I was just a teenager, and I was already haunted. Haunted by my own disappointment. Haunted by a disconnection from the world around me. Haunted by a festering depression. Haunted by loneliness.

I never knew why or how, but I felt the Little Girl in a Blue Dress was the harbinger of my own self-destruction. I had no idea who She was. I had no idea how She was connected to me. All I knew was that the Little Girl in a Blue Dress knew the truth.

I felt trapped. Trapped between the world I didn't understand and a ghost that I didn't understand. That's when I asked my mother if I could move my stuff up into the attic playroom. I wanted to make it my bedroom. It was like I was magnetically drawn to the attic. As much as I was scared to face down whatever I felt was there, I equally couldn't stand the thought of staying away. Given the choice between my fear of the outside world and my fear of Little Girl, I had to choose which I wanted to be closer to and which I wanted to distance myself from. Even though I was terrified of Her and what She might mean, She also felt like my future, my journey, and my path.

My mom was a little shocked that I wanted to be up there. I just shrugged it off, saying I thought it would be cool.

"This room is a little drab," my mother said. "We should paint it. Any color you'd like?"

I thought for a moment.

In confirmation class, we'd just finished learning about the colors of the liturgical seasons in the church year—white and gold for Epiphany and Easter, red for Pentecost, dark blue for Advent, and purple for Lent. I really had had no idea what Lent stood for before we talked about it in class. But afterward I thought about it all the time. Most people think of Lent as being the six weeks before Easter where you give up chocolate or swearing or something. In the church year, Lent is supposed to be a time of prayer and preparation, of introspection and self-examination. Most people also mistake the purpose of giving things up for Lent. It isn't to deny yourself something, it's to let go of distractions. To focus on your true calling.

"Purple," I answered.

She probably wasn't surprised, as I had recently decided to adopt purple as my official color. Anytime I could have anything in purple, it was the color I chose. The color of Lent.

I never admitted this to anyone. I just told them that I really liked purple.

But in truth, I saw myself as preparing for something. Something I didn't know. Something I didn't understand. Little Girl was trying to tell me what it was, but I wasn't ready to hear it yet. So I waited, and reflected, and prepared.

A lot of church literature refers to the season as the "Journey of Lent"—as if it is not a mark of time but a passage with a destination. I knew I was on a journey myself, though I had no idea where or why. I just wanted to be alone, surrounded by purple walls, ready for Her and as far above the rest of my life as possible.

• • •

After that first drive, Laura and I talked on the phone just about every night for a week. Then we went driving again. Then we talked on the phone every night again for another week.

It didn't take long to pick up that Laura had a habit of interrupting conversations with non sequitur questions like "When you think of ravioli, do you think of meat ravioli or cheese ravioli?" Or "Did I ever tell you that both of my grandfathers died in gruesome train accidents?" Or "If you could start today over again, what would you do different?"

Here I was trying to blow her mind with deep thoughts about truth, art, hypocrisy, and whatever—and she couldn't stick to the same topic for more than a minute before uttering something like "Do you think you'd make a good burlesque dancer?"

"I'm not even sure what a burlesque dancer is."

"You know, a striptease dancer."

"Well, it depends who I'm stripping for."

"Well, let's say you were a woman and were stripping in a bar. Do you think you'd be any good?"

"That's like asking, 'If you were a potato, do you think

you'd taste good with sour cream on top of you?' It makes no sense."

"What kind of question is that?" she responded. "Of course you'd be delicious. What kind of potato *wouldn't* taste good covered in sour cream?"

"I think you are missing my point," I said.

"No, I think you asked a question and I answered it."

That was annoying thing number two: She was nearly impossible to peg down about anything. She often answered questions with more questions. Whenever you tried to force her into a yes or no answer on something, she'd just smile and masterfully work her way to talking about something else. For example, for all the time we spent together, she rarely would eat in my presence, even when we went to a restaurant. I'd ask if it was because she wasn't hungry or had just eaten or didn't have money. She'd then tell a story about how she used to try eating paper as a child, because she imagined it would taste delicious, completely ignoring my question.

Yet, for all her evasiveness, she had this otherworldly, enchanting quality that made you never want to stop talking to her. She made you feel that she was keenly interested in what you had to say; that everything was about the moment the two of you were sharing. You could tell she was absorbing everything and was deeply interested in knowing as much about you as she could. She'd often recall, verbatim, things you'd forgotten you had shared months earlier.

We gradually started to see each other more, settling into a few times a week. Something would come up in a phone call that would segue into a suggestion that we hang out. Hanging out usually meant me picking her up (I was always told to wait in the car and not approach the house), then, without much discussion about where to or why, I'd just start driving off down some road. The car was like a rolling clubhouse, a safe place where we could say anything, do anything, and be anything without anyone staring or judging or wondering what we were up to. But the motion was important, too. We both were often desperate to get away, even when we had no idea where to go. Driving, motion, not being still—it all felt as essential as breathing.

But moving required gas. Gas cost money—something neither of us had in any measurable quantity. So we started to seek out places, hidden, secluded places, where we could camp out for a few hours unnoticed. Places where we could just be.

On the night we played Beer Golf with Jimmy, we spent the rest of the evening just driving around back roads, talking endlessly about anything that came to mind. As we drove back toward town, Laura lay down on the bench seat, resting her head on my leg, and fell asleep.

My heart immediately shot up into my throat and started racing. On her part, it was just a simple acknowledgment of closeness, trust, and intimacy. My leg just happened to be a perfect place to rest. However, I was, as should be clear by now, not someone accustomed to large degrees of closeness, trust, and intimacy. I had no idea what to do with myself. I felt like anything I said or any motion I made would screw this up. My arm had been extended behind her headrest and was getting numb. I slowly moved my arm out from behind the seat and just kind of let it hang there in midair. I didn't know what to do with it. Lacking any better idea, I just slowly let my hand come down to rest on her shoulder. She let out a deep sigh and continued to sleep.

We drove that way for about another twenty minutes until we came to a small manmade lake named Lake O'Dea. At least I guessed it was called Lake O'Dea. A large apartment building next to it was called the Lake O'Dea Apartments, so I just assumed. There was a dead end road that ran behind it that was perfect for hanging out. No traffic. No cops. No bother.

As I shut off the engine, Laura awoke, looking up at me.

"I really liked *Music for Airports*," she said, sitting up and back against her seat. "I don't have it with me, but I'll give it back next time."

"Oh no," I replied. "You can keep it."

That was at least my sixth copy of *Music for Airports*. I kept giving them away to people that I felt should have the record. *Music for Airports* was Brian Eno's first album of "ambient music"—sparse, simple music meant to create mood and ambience for spaces (like an airport, for example). *Music for Airports* contained only four songs, if you can call them that. Each featured a series of tape loops of a few simple notes (or sometimes just a single note) from a piano, synthesizer, or human voice. These notes would loop on intervals—one loop would repeat every twenty-three seconds, another every thirty-nine seconds, another once a minute, and so on. The randomness generated unexpected harmonies and moments of beauty, surrounded by periods of reverberance and near silence. It was unlike anything anyone I'd known had ever heard.

"Here," I said to Laura, reaching for my cassette case to give back her dub of Killing Joke's *Fire Dances*. "It was pretty good. I might pick it up sometime."

I didn't want her to know how quickly I'd fallen in love with *Fire Dances*. Most punk rock was like listening to a food processor. You hit the button and it just went, full bore—chopping, spinning, and tearing shit up. Killing Joke was different. The songs sounded like anthems; they had emotion, range, and subtlety. Sure, all their songs were about the end of the world, but hey, at least they brought a little style to their nihilism. I'd been so willing to return Laura's tape because I'd already secretly bought my own, as well as every other Killing Joke record I could find.

"Where did you ever hear about Killing Joke?" I asked.

"I saw them in Germany," she said. "When they played, the club pulled barbed wire across the front of the stage. When everyone was slamming . . . every once in a while . . . someone would get thrown against the wire."

"Oh my God."

"No, it wasn't a bad thing . . . I guess. People would get cut . . . there was blood all over . . . but it was okay. It was like a release."

"A release from what?" I asked.

"Pain," she replied.

"What? That makes no sense. How can thrashing into barbed wire—"

"A different kind of pain."

"When they played 'Frenzy,'" she continued after a brief moment, "people started to really flail around and it was getting a little violent. The singer, Jaz, brought out a bottle of rum, and the guys who got cut were begging him to pour it on them. So he did. And then the guys really started to flip out from the burning in the cuts. But then, when it was over, they pulled the barbed wire back, and they brought out jugs of water, and everyone sat around together. It was a shared moment."

In the years since that night, I've often wondered what she felt was so honorable about this story that she would remember and share it. I think she expected me to be impressed with people who controlled their own pain. Rather than get beaten up by life and a world that doesn't understand you, don't wait to get hurt—throw yourself against some barbed wire. Hurt yourself before someone or something else does.

"If you like Eno, you'll probably like this one, too," I said, pulling another tape from the box. "It's different. It's him with David Byrne from Talking Heads."

As the music started up I pulled out a little tin box from the glove compartment, opened it, and tipped it toward Laura, like I was offering her a breath mint or something. It contained about half a dozen pills of various sizes, shapes, and colors.

"No, thank you," she said, though she did accept one of the leftover beers from the backseat.

Then she said, "You sure like that stuff, don't you."

"Is that a question or a statement?" I asked, washing down a pill with the remainder of my beer.

"What does that do for you?"

"It makes me fucked up."

"No, I mean, why do you take it?"

I wanted to trust her, but trying to explain how I felt was just so damn exhausting. "Let's just say it helps me," I said.

She didn't say anything, which to me meant she was expecting more of an explanation.

Pause.

"Why aren't you going to school in the fall?" she asked.

"I think I might take some commuter classes."

"Didn't you apply anywhere else?"

"Wait-listed—every single one," I said. "Even the state schools that have to take you."

"I figured someone like you would have no trouble getting into college."

"Everyone tells me that the stuff I like will never amount to anything," I said. "So if you aren't interested in anything else, what is the point of trying? So you can end up sitting in an office and wearing a tie and being miserable until you die—is that what I'm supposed to do with my life to make everyone happy? That doesn't sound like much fun. It's easier to deal with other people's disappointments than to deal with your own."

"Yeah, that seems like it's working out well for you," she said.

"What do you mean?"

"You seem so happy," she said sarcastically.

"Oh . . . fuck off."

We sat silent, listening to the tape.

Though she didn't notice, I spent most of the silence looking at her face. As she stared out the window, her face showed all these tiny gestures and expressions as her thoughts moved along with the beat.

"What's this called again?" Laura asked.

"My Life in the Bush of Ghosts," I replied.

I drearily rocked my head and shoulders to the beat. I could start to feel the pill kick in, forming a haze around my thoughts.

"Have you ever seen a ghost?" I asked nonchalantly.

It was a weak segue, admittedly, but I had been looking for a way to bring up Little Girl to Laura. As much as I wanted to share it with her, I cringed at the idea of talking about it. Too late; I'd laid it out there.

"You mean, like a spooky ghost? Like something floating around?" she asked.

"Yeah."

"No," she said.

Pause.

"Have you?" she asked.

Pause.

"Since I was a kid I've felt this . . . ghost, I guess . . . in our attic. It's kind of fucked up."

"There's a ghost in your attic?" she asked, getting very excited at the idea. "Can we go see it? Have you ever talked to it? Does it move stuff around?"

"It's not like that," I interrupted, feeling a slow wave of calm seep through my body. "I think She's kinda mean."

"Mean?" Laura replied. "How is she mean?"

I thought for a moment about how to answer. It would be really easy to make something up and get out of this, but I was also almost compelled to tell her about it.

"She comes to me in my dreams," I said, instantly regretting it.

Silence.

"Oh, come on," she said, hitting my arm. "What a bullshitter you are."

"Actually, no," I said. "I'm not kidding. I think there really is a ghost in the attic that has it in for me."

"What?" she exclaimed. "Who is it?"

"I don't know."

"What does she want?"

"I don't know."

"What makes you sure she wants to harm you?"

"I . . . don't . . . know."

"Well, then, what *do* you know?"

I sighed, lit a cigarette, and took a deep drag.

"I guess I need to figure this out before She does whatever She wants to do to me," I said.

"What does that mean?"

"You know, in order to catch a fox . . ."

"So you are going to try to outghost a ghost?" she said. "How does that work?"

"I don't know . . . What am I supposed to do?"

"Find out what she wants."

"I can't," I said. "She . . . speaks gibberish."

"Gibberish."

"Yes, gibberish. None of it sounds like words. When She looks angry, it seems like it's because I don't understand what She's saying."

We both just stared out the windows silently until we got to her house. She told me, again, not to get out of the car.

There was an awkward few seconds, which to me felt like an awkward few hours, while I looked at her face, trying to get a read on what she'd do if I tried to kiss her.

While the time we spent together was definitely not like any date I'd ever heard of, it still kind of felt like a date. Or at least my heart was beating in my throat the way it did at the end of a date.

I slowly leaned over and kissed her.

She touched my cheek and kissed me back.

She reached into her bag and pulled out a copy of *Slaughterhouse-Five*. When we were on the phone, she often talked about books she'd read that had meant something to her—none of which I'd read. She placed it in my lap and raised her eyebrows. She didn't need to say anything—I knew that this was her attempt to get me to read it, partially because she felt it might have the same effect on me and partially because she wanted someone to talk about it with.

"Sweet dreams," she said with a smile. "Tell your ghost girl I said hello."

Then she climbed out of the car and ran into her house.

NOW

It's pretty obvious right away that I'm in the right place. As I pull in to the hotel parking lot, three women are circling my car while chanting and holding out dowsing rods to lead their way. Once I walk into the hotel lobby, I'm greeted by a sign that reads: NO READINGS, HEALINGS, CIRCLES, OR SÉANCES IN THIS AREA, PLEASE.

Lily Dale, New York, is pretty tiny—two hundred homes—and about an hour south of Buffalo. However, Lily Dale is quite different from the dozens of other towns that dot northwestern New York. The hamlet is entirely owned and run by followers of the Spiritualist religion. Spiritualists believe that they, as mediums, have the ability to communicate with the dead, using the dead spirits as life guides, predictors of the future, companions, and emissaries to God. Starting out as a Spiritualist church summer camp in 1879, Lily Dale grew into a town. Its guesthouses, hotels, museum, and library—not to mention its restaurants, post office, and fire department—are all run by people who believe they can see and talk to the dead.

During the summer, tens of thousands of people descend on Lily Dale for private consultations with its registered mediums, to attend lectures, church services, and workshops, and to receive healings.

The hotel where I'm staying, the Maplewood, is old, as in falling-apart old. It's been hosting summer guests since the 1880s and looks it. There are no televisions, telephones, or air-conditioning. Everything creaks and is lumpy, slanted, or sunken. There are signs everywhere warning guests not to smoke, slam doors, light incense, flush sanitary napkins, burn candles, or shower without the curtain completely closed—all because these activities will push the building over some kind of functional abyss.

And of course, the place is supposedly teeming with ghosts.

In fact, ghost sightings are so common in Lily Dale that some claim they can't tell who is alive and who is dead. Pass a person on the street, and it could be someone staying in the hotel room next to you or it could be someone who stayed there in 1928. Some visitors and residents of Lily Dale have taken to referring to themselves in the plural—as in "We are going shopping today" or "We might stop over later for a visit." They're referring to themselves and their spirit posse.

I have no time to investigate the Maplewood's otherworldly residents, as I am on the verge of being late to the five-thirty Stump Service.

Inspiration Stump is a tree stump in the middle of the Leolyn Woods, a towering old-growth forest on the outskirts of Lily Dale. There are no bells or announcements when it's time for one of Lily Dale's four daily public services. At five-fifteen, almost every person in town simply exits home, hotel, or guesthouse and quietly walks to the far end of town and the trail into the woods.

The Stump itself is huge, probably three feet in diameter.

It's thought by Lily Daleans to be an "energy vortex"; standing near it will amplify a medium's abilities. For some reason that no one has been able to explain, in 1898 the residents of Lily Dale decided to encase the Stump in cement, later adding a short fence around it. Lily Dale mediums are no longer allowed to stand on top of the Stump when giving readings and messages. Some say it's because it is too powerful (according to a long-repeated rumor, a medium had a heart attack while channeling atop the Stump). Others suggest it is too unsafe, as the cement covering has caused the actual wooden Stump to rot away completely, leaving an empty shell.

From the 1880s to the 1920s, Spiritualism was the fastest-growing religion in America. Spiritualism was founded, albeit loosely, in 1848, when Kate and Margaret Fox started to receive spirit messages from a murdered peddler who was buried in the basement of their family home. The Fox sisters began demonstrating their medium abilities to others and quickly grew into a national sensation. Other mediums began to emerge, and Spiritualism slowly grew from a curiosity into a movement, then a religion. By the late nineteenth century there were more than eight million followers. And all this despite there being no centralized anything in Spiritualism—no religious texts, no core sets of beliefs, organization, or dogma—except the belief that adherents speak to the dead.

During Spiritualism's peak, thousands of people would fill this clearing in the woods to hear the Stump-fueled mediums shout out messages from long-lost relatives and friends to those assembled. Today there are about a dozen wooden benches, capable of holding about 150 people, arranged in a fan shape in front of Inspiration Stump.

For my first service, it's a packed house. As we're sitting

around waiting for the service to begin, I notice that at least ten of the people attending are already crying. Outside of a few bored children, most of those assembled are middle-aged and older; all rather pasty, plump, and plain-looking—the type of people you expect to see at a Kiwanis pancake supper or in the cheap seats at a Wayne Newton concert, rather than at a gathering to invoke the dead.

At precisely 5:30 P.M., a man walks up and stands in front of the Stump. "Good afternoon. My name is George Kincaid, and I'd like to welcome you all to the five-thirty Stump Service."

George looks like a standard-issue retiree—unextraordinary in every sense. He stands in the small clearing separating the Stump from the first row of pews.

"How many of you are here for the first time?" he asks.

A few dozen hands shoot up, including mine.

"Good, good," George continues. "First, I'm gonna tell you how this works. Several of Lily Dale's registered and visiting mediums will take turns coming up here and tuning to the spirit world. They bring your loved ones from the other side to prove the continuity of life between the physical world and the spiritual world. If the medium receives a message for you, they will ask to come to you. You need to acknowledge this—out loud. They need to hear your voice vibrations—it helps them make a connection. Different mediums work in different ways, but make sure to respond to everything they ask, verbally. Now, because we treat this as a religious service, let's all stand for the opening prayer."

"Oh Lord, Father-Mother God, as we come once again to the Stump, to prove the continuity of life, we ask that the loved ones from the other side manifest to show their love and guidance. Amen."

"Okay, our first person to serve spirit tonight is Brenda Hawkins, a registered medium here in Lily Dale. Brenda?"

Brenda thanks George for letting her serve spirit that evening, says a brief silent prayer, and surveys the assembled crowd.

Then she points right at me. It feels like winning the lottery the first time I buy a ticket.

"Sir, may I approach you, please?"

"Sure," I say.

"A little louder, please?"

"Sure, yes," I call out. "Absolutely."

"I'm sensing a spirit . . . a maternal spirit, please . . . perhaps a mother or grandmother. Is your grandmother on your mother's side in spirit, please?"

Assuming that "in spirit" is a euphemism for "dead," I guess she is referring to Bobalu. I reply, "Yes."

"Okay, that's it," Brenda says. "Tell me, please, was she a little round in the bottom?"

Now, how am I supposed to answer that? Bobalu wasn't really overweight, but she wasn't rail thin, either. Imagine how pissed off Bobalu would be if she traveled back from Grandma Heaven to deliver a message to her oldest grandchild, just to arrive as he says, "Oh yeah, she had a huge ass!"

I just shrug and say nothing.

"That's okay," Brenda says. "I feel the spirit that is reaching out to you is definitely Grandma."

Brenda pauses.

"She wants to surround you with light and love right now and let you know that she watches over you and is proud of you," she resumes. "She knows that you have a job that is difficult and demanding, and she is proud that you do this work. That . . . that is mostly it . . . she just wants you to know that she misses you and knows how much you loved her. She wants to leave you with blessings . . . oh. There is one more thing, please."

I nod, then catch George's glance and remember to say "Yes" out loud.

"Grandma wasn't much of a car person, was she, please?" Brenda asks.

"No," I reply. Outside of smoking in them and driving them to the grocery store, my grandmother had no particular connection with cars.

"Well," Brenda says with a slight chuckle. "Your grandmother wants you to check your tire pressure over the coming weeks, please."

"My tire pressure?"

"Yes, she says that it is nothing dangerous; just make sure you are watching it carefully to be safe. That's it. And I leave you with God's light and love."

Brenda then receives a message from some woman's uncle and is off in another direction.

Tire pressure?

I drove seven and a half hours to have Bobalu tell me to watch my tire pressure? People come to Lily Dale to connect one more time with the recently departed, find out what will happen to themselves and their loved ones, understand the afterlife and how to prepare for it, and finally figure out where Aunt Myra hid her jewelry. All I got is some car advice from a woman who couldn't tell a tire gauge from a meat thermometer.

Over the rest of the hour-long service, about five other mediums get up to deliver messages, each connecting with three or four spirits. Unlike Brenda, many mediums start off by focusing on the spirit that's reaching out, then identify who in the audience the message is meant for. Regardless of tactic, things often start off vague and general and end up slightly less vague and general.

A normal message will start off like this:

The medium says she has someone in spirit with a *J* name, probably a generation or two back, who would have died of something in the chest area.

Now, think about how many people have a deceased relative who has a first, middle, or last name that starts with *J*. Add that they died of something "in the chest area," and see how likely it is that no one in a crowd of 150 has a connection. Of the two dozen or so mediums I saw deliver messages at public services in Lily Dale, more than half of them started off trying to identify a spirit as being overweight or having died of something in the chest area.

After a large number of people raise their hands at the chest-area description, the medium adds something slightly more specific, like that the *J* relative is wearing a uniform in spirit, meaning that in life that relative was in the military, a delivery person, a policeman, worked in a medical field, et cetera. A few hands go down. Then another level of mild specificity: something like that the spirit loved music, knitted, or clipped items from the newspaper to send to relatives and friends. Sooner or later, the medium has it down to a specific person.

One particularly bold student medium at the service gets up and says he has a spirit with him named Eunice and wants to know if anyone in the audience has an aunt or sister in spirit named Eunice. Nothing.

Then he asks if anyone in the audience is named Eunice or has a living aunt or sister named Eunice.

Crickets.

He looks over at George, shrugs, then attempts to connect

with another spirit. He asks if anyone has a deceased relative, a woman, who was short, round in the bottom, and dyed her hair. Lots of hands go up.

When a medium delivers a message to the living, it is almost always loving, supportive good news. The spirits have come to let the living know that everything is going to be okay, that they love them and are always with them. The spirits want the living to know that while other living people don't understand them fully, or don't appreciate all the work they do, or judge them, the spirit is there to let them know that everything will be fine, and if they believe in themselves everything will work out. That son who hasn't come home in years—the spirit knows he will soon. The uncertainties and difficulties in a career—rest assured that the spirit will help guide them and they will be successful. Every man is acknowledged for his hard work; every woman is counseled to slow down and take care of herself for a change.

Even after all I've been through, at this point in my life I am not, by any standard, a pessimist. Yet even I can acknowledge that sometimes bad things can happen and things *don't* work out very well. Not according to the spirits of Lily Dale. They have traveled back from the great beyond to let us know everything is going to be all right. All we need to do is chill out and follow our heart/head/spirit.

After the service ends and George says another quick prayer and sends everyone on their way, the first thing I notice is more crying.

In my reading about Lily Dale before visiting, there was one curious tidbit that I couldn't get my head around: Most of the summer visitors aren't Spiritualists. If people don't practice this religion or identify with all this dead-people stuff, why do they flock here? After that first service, I figured out why.

People come to Lily Dale because they are grieving.

They've lost loved ones and are desperate for a sense of closure or completion. They need answers and are hard up enough to schlep out to the middle of nowhere to listen to people who claim they can talk with the dead. Many of those crying before the service were anticipating a message. Many of those crying afterward are upset that they didn't get one.

I feel like a bit of an asshole. I came to Lily Dale expecting to encounter a bunch of weirdness—which, frankly, I found. However, I expected the people who came here to be guileless kooks. In truth, their motivations for coming here aren't that different from my own. I want answers and closure; so do they. Instead of being an outsider, I'm one of them.

The next morning I begin my hunt for a Lily Dale medium to consult with one on one. In order to conduct readings or deliver spirit messages in Lily Dale, especially if you plan to charge—I mean, accept "love offerings"—for doing so, you need to be registered and approved by the church. Lily Dale mediums go through an exhaustive vetting and testing process to demonstrate their gifts before being allowed to practice in town. Visiting or student mediums are allowed to give messages at Inspiration Stump (or at Lily Dale's other outdoor venue, the Forest Temple), but they're forbidden to do private readings or accept money—I mean, love offerings.

At the time, there were roughly forty registered mediums hanging shingles in Lily Dale. How do you choose one? Well, if you see a medium you like at a Stump service, you can look her up in town and set up a consultation. Other visitors go by the recommendations of friends or mediums they've visited in the past.

For me, it's all about style. I simply walk the streets of Lily Dale, making harsh choices about the spiritual abilities of Lily

Dale's mediums based solely on their home décor. A few tattered angel flags on the front of the house? No. A full-sized Buddha statue on the front porch? Awesome, but not someone I want guiding *my* life choices. Poorly hung Christmas lights in the front window? Maybe next time. New Age music playing on a boom box on the front porch? No way.

After perusing the options, my first choice is a medium named Lynne Forget. To be honest, while her house is a little rough around the edges, I just decide the last name Forget is kinda fantastic for a medium. However, when I go to Ms. Forget's porch to sign up for a session, every slot is filled.

Okay, no problem. I'll just go with the next passable choice I come across: James Barnum (whose home has a tasteful and well-kept red-and-white exterior with some meticulous and lovely landscaping). A sign is hanging on his porch, ALL FULL TODAY. I move on to choices three, four, and five—all full, no appointments available. On a Monday in late August, Lily Dale is hopping.

I run into two women sitting outside a medium's home (one that I originally passed by due to purple wind catchers and a rain-forest tape playing on the porch). I ask if they have already booked their appointment.

"Oh, yes, we booked our appointment six weeks ago," one says.

"The good ones fill up quickly. I don't think there's much room for walk-ups," says the other.

In other words: I am screwed.

I spend most of the morning going door-to-door looking for any available medium. Knowing there are forty mediums around town, I scour every driveway and sleepy side street. I even revisit all the tacky houses I passed over earlier. Eventually, I find one with a name crossed out for four o'clock that afternoon: a cancellation. The medium's name is Patricia.

I write my name above the scratched-out cancellation. I'm in.

At four, Patricia meets me on her porch and invites me into a back room near her kitchen. After stepping into the kitchen to yell at her grandchildren, she comes out and rubs some essential oils on her hands, holds her newly scented palms to her nose, and takes a deep breath. She never asks me what I'm doing there or what I want; she just dives in.

"I'm sensing someone in spirit who had trouble breathing. A grandfather? Or some other male figure?"

"I'm sorry," I reply. "That really doesn't seem like a connection to me."

"What did your grandfather die of? I assume one or both of them are dead."

I tell Patricia that I didn't know either of my grandfathers well, and I'm not sure what they died of, but trouble breathing isn't ringing a bell.

"I'm still getting a male—and trouble in the chest. Could there be a younger man who passed?"

Sure, there are plenty, I tell her. But she seems to get really hung up on identifying the spirit, for at least another five minutes.

"This male energy says that you are very creative and there are other things you want to do with your life, but that you took a career for stability and money."

This is so vague, kind of applicable and kind of not, that I really don't give much of a response. I just nod.

"Something with your hands," she continues. "Do you do creative things with wood?"

After another few minutes of these misfires, I decide to tell her why I'm here. I lay it all out. Dreams. Little Girl. Laura. Death.

"Of course there was a little girl in the attic!" she exclaims. "She came to you in your dreams to try to communicate with you and couldn't, so she became increasingly frantic and desperate. You need to start thinking about what she would have wanted to tell you. Why it was so important."

I suddenly feel riveted by her words. She should have no credibility with me—everything she's told me so far is so off base. But now I'm hanging on everything she says.

"Sweetheart, you are asking all the wrong questions," she continues. "You need to stop asking *if* this happened and start asking yourself *why* it happened. There is something that drew her to you. Something she wanted you to know—a warning— and she kept trying to tell you and couldn't reach you."

"Okay," I say. "Then why did She want to hurt me?"

"What specifically did she do to try to hurt you?" Patricia replies. "What you experienced was your own fear and misinterpretation. With this Little Girl, you were basically dealing with a lost soul. We see lost souls all the time—drug addicts, people putting themselves in pain. They are just lost souls still attached to bodies. You don't doubt they are real. Why do you doubt her?"

Patricia reaches over and takes my hands.

"From what it sounds like, honey, you were a lost soul, too."

The leader for the 1 P.M. Stump Service on my third day in Lily Dale is Neal Rzepkowski, a family doctor and ordained Spiritualist minister. Neal is famous outside of Lily Dale for being forced to resign in 1991 as an emergency room doctor from the Brooks Memorial Hospital in Dunkirk, New York, because he was HIV-positive. The story made it to the front page of *The New York Times*. Neal was on *Oprah*, too.

Now he is offering a prayer and setting up a message service for dead friends and relatives to reach out to the living. The first medium called forward to share spirit was Jessie Furst, who, in addition to giving private readings, runs a guesthouse in town.

"Okay," Jessie calls out. "I'm sensing a woman . . . forty to forty-five . . . and breast cancer. And I'm getting the name Deborah. Does anyone here have a Deborah?"

A woman sitting about ten people to my right tentatively raises her hand. As she tries to tell Jessie about her connection, she's becoming visibly upset. It takes a couple of tries to get it out through the crying, but the woman says *her* name is Deborah and that she receives grief counseling from a forty-three-year-old woman who'd recently been diagnosed with breast cancer.

"Sometimes spirit sends us messages that get all confused and mixed up," Jessie says.

Then Deborah blurts out that she's receiving the counseling over the recent death of her son. Deborah's husband is sitting next to her, with his arms around her shoulders as she sobs. They're about fifty years old.

"Yes," Jessie says with sudden assurance. "The message is from your son."

"He wants to tell you he loves you and that he misses you," Jessie continues. "He wants you to know he is okay and there is no pain."

Deborah starts to wail, placing her head in her hands while Jessie speaks. Deborah's husband starts to sigh heavily, then tears pour down his cheeks.

"He knows how much you loved him and how much you sacrificed for him," Jessie says. "He just wants to surround you with love and tell you that whenever you think of him, he is right there with you. You know those times when you are sitting alone and you think you can sense him?"

Deborah nods.

"That's him. And he loves you so much and says he will always be with you. And I leave you with that, with light and love."

Jessie moves on to other spirit messages—from someone's dead aunt, someone's dead father, and someone's dead brother. As her time ends and she begins to walk away from the Stump, Neal stops her.

"Jessie, I think you need to stay up here another minute," he says, waving his hand toward the treetops to his right. "There is a very persistent spirit here that wants to reach out through you."

"Yes!" Jessie exclaims, raising her hand high above her head and walking back toward the Stump. "I can sense him, too. His name . . . is Peter."

I hear a cry out from my right; it's Deborah. She's so upset she can't speak. Her husband, openly crying as well, finally speaks out. Peter was the name of their dead son.

A chorus of gasps rises from the crowd assembled at the Stump; many begin crying, too.

"Boy, Peter really loves you," Jessie says, beginning to choke up herself. "He just wants to take another moment to reach out to you. To surround you with all his love and make sure you know that no matter what happens, no matter what is going on, he loves you and will always be *right there*. So much love from this spirit for you. He wants to thank you and say God bless you."

Jessie walks away in tears. For all the emotion I've seen in the audiences at message services, I've never seen a medium show much at all. They're a generally stoic bunch—receiving messages is a pretty routine part of their lives. But Jessie seems sincerely moved by what has happened. Neal calls up another medium, but for all intents and purposes, the service is pretty much over. By the time it officially ends and Deborah and her husband rise to look for her, Jessie is gone.

To this day I'm still torn about what I witnessed that afternoon. On one hand, the way Jessie identified the couple and the spirit was just a shade away from the fishing you'd see from a five-dollar psychic at a state-fair booth. It felt manipulative, overly vague, and a little dirty.

However, if you spoke to Deborah and her husband, what they experienced was nothing short of a miracle. They traveled to Lily Dale for a connection and closure to this tragic event in their lives, and they got what they needed. The whole first encounter identifying Deborah and her counselor was probably a standard Lily Dale fluke. The name Peter popping up was probably just dumb luck.

So if no one was being financially scammed and poor Deborah and her husband walked away feeling like they connected to their dead son, where's the harm? It could easily have been a complete coincidence. So what? What's wrong with it?

This service would become the defining example of the dichotomy of Lily Dale in my eyes. I know that 90 percent of everything I saw in Lily Dale was pure bullshit; I just don't know which 90 percent.

On my way back, I stop at the Lily Dale Museum. It's in the old one-room schoolhouse and pretty much serves as a dumping ground for all of Lily Dale's historical artifacts.

The main table in the center of the room is covered by photos and albums of clippings about Lily Dale's history and its more famous residents. There's even a box of bent spoons, evidence of some medium's cutlery-twisting skills.

One wall is devoted to "spirit precipitated art"—meaning that it was created and/or guided by the dead. A few famous Lily Dale mediums from the late nineteenth and early twentieth centuries used to place a blank canvas and a bowl of paints on a table at the beginning of a séance. Then, two hours later, at the séance's conclusion—*bang*—a painting would be there. The painting was often a portrait of a spirit that was present during the séance. Following Spiritualism's descent into charlatanism in the early twentieth century, this and all other forms of physical mediumship, including levitation, manifestations, and dripping ectoplasm, have been strictly forbidden in Lily Dale, but that doesn't stop them from displaying artifacts all over town. There are also a number of spirit slates (aka "automatic writings")—small chalkboards and pieces of slate that would, during the course of a séance, become filled with drawing and writings from the great beyond.

When Spiritualism was at its peak, it was arguably too big. As it became more and more popular, there was an increasing movement toward showmanship and pressure to produce increasingly astounding acts of spiritual communication. Fraud became rampant, but the popularity of the religion remained high. People come to Spiritualism through grief, and there is never a shortage of people in pain.

By the beginning of the twentieth century, there was a movement within Spiritualism to clean house, get a bit more organized, and weed out the sensationalists and obvious fakers. Probably as a result, Spiritualism began to wane in popularity. After World War II, it slowed to the trickle that it is today.

Today's Spiritualists are almost obsessed with recognition and things that sound official. They are all certified in different areas of mediumship and spiritual work from organizations with vague but quasi legitimate-sounding names. Many have divinity degrees, clergy status, and even Ph.D.'s from organizations controlled by other Spiritualists. They may be nonconformists, but they want to be certified nonconformists.

My next appointment is with a veteran medium named Joe. In addition to being a registered medium in Lily Dale, Joe and his wife are also the proprietors of a Lily Dale coffee shop, which is right across the street from my hotel. Joe, like other Lily Dale mediums, has a full schedule most of the days I'm in town. Hanging out at the coffee shop during my stay got me friendly with Joe's wife, who helped me arrange a session.

Joe takes me into a private office off the main room of the coffee shop for my consultation. It's covered with his own spirit-guided paintings and artwork. I know this because he tells me. Joe tells me a lot of stuff. Even though we have only forty minutes together, he spends the first fifteen minutes talking about himself and his abilities. He recites his entire bio to me, recalling his recognition, even as a child, that he had the gift of visions and the ability to speak with the dead, his stint in Catholic seminary, and his mastery of Usui Reiki. I don't get in a single word.

If you didn't know Joe was a medium and coffee entrepreneur, you'd think he was a longshoreman or some other tough blue-collar worker. He is bald and a little on the short side, yet stocky and sturdy. He has big, thick hands that you just can't imagine holding the delicate, small paintbrush used to make his spirit-aided art. After we say a prayer together and meditate for a bit (now almost half our time is gone), Joe says that he feels tremendous sadness around me.

"I'm sensing that this loss is fairly recent, like within the last several months," he says.

"No," I respond softly. "That really doesn't have a connection to me."

"I'm sensing some spirit guides around you. Yes. One is definitely Eskimo. Does that resonate with you at all?"

"I have nothing against Eskimos, Joe," I say. "That's about it."

Joe continues with a series of fairly random observations, delivered to him by my spirit advisors. None completely off mark, but none particularly on the mark, either. With only ten minutes left in our session, I decide to cut to the chase. I tell him everything, just like I did with Patricia.

When I relate my story, Joe, who until now has been quite jovial, turns very solemn, almost angry.

"When I was a boy, I hated to touch people or be touched," he says. "Why? Because whenever I touch people, I know what's going to happen to them. When I was twelve years old, I was at the beach with my family. Then my mother grabbed me and started tickling me. I started fighting her off, because I knew what would happen. While she was holding me, I got a vision."

He pauses.

"I saw her body being eaten by wild dogs," he says. "Two years later, my mother died of cancer, weighing seventy-two pounds. Here's the thing: When you focus on the literal meaning of messages—what you see—you often miss the point. With my mom, those dogs were her illness. I saw the whole thing coming. But you know what? As a little boy, I was worried about dogs, not cancer."

I ask if he thinks the Little Girl in a Blue Dress is a symbol of something else.

"I'm saying that whatever needed to talk to you chose the form of a little girl. Perhaps it thought it would be less scary for you."

"It would have been incorrect in that assumption, Joe."

Joe continues for a few minutes about remaining open-minded, the importance of meditation to unlocking the mystery of my past, and about the importance of consulting my spirit guides. Then he looks at his watch. He pauses and takes a deep breath.

"What are you doing now?" he asks. "Are you busy?"

"No."

"Wanna go on a walk with me?"

"Sure," I say.

A minute later we're walking across the park, destination unclear. Even though Joe had a tight schedule and bookings throughout the day, he's generous with his time. He seems intensely interested in sharing whatever we are going to see, appointments be damned.

"I think I've seen your Little Girl before," he says. "Several times. Right here in Lily Dale. Before I moved to Lily Dale I used to come out here for a few weeks in the summer for workshops, classes, and training. I always stayed in a guesthouse on Cottage Row," he says. "Sometimes, you know, I'd get up early in the morning and go downstairs. Several times, I walked into the library . . . and I saw a little girl. She had blond hair, a blue dress, just like you say. She'd be there for a moment looking at me, then she'd be gone. Maybe, now, just maybe, it's the same girl. Your Little Girl."

Joe continues to share his theory: Perhaps Little Girl came to me in my dreams knowing that one day I would need some answers, and my quest would lead me to Lily Dale. Perhaps she knew that it would take twenty years before I would be ready to hear what She had to say. Perhaps this was all part of the plan from the beginning—that coming to Lily Dale is my destiny.

Joe says that several years after seeing the girl in the library he was in the National Spiritualist Association of Churches office next door, which has a spirit painting hanging in the mailroom. The painting, almost one hundred years old, is of the same girl he'd seen in the library, blue dress and all.

I can feel a knot forming in my stomach. What if this is true? Fuck, what if *half* of it is true? What if this whole nonsense is all part of a larger puzzle? Little Girl, Laura, my dreams, all these years of wondering and unanswered questions—all leading me here. All pieces to a puzzle that is about to be solved in a church mailroom. As we walk up the steps to the church office, I feel my skepticism ebb and flow again as I wonder whether the mystery of my life is about to take a quick and definitive left turn.

Joe waves at the secretary and says we're just stopping in to look at a painting in the back. We weave through the former home now commandeered as office space.

As we walk into the mailroom, Joe points up to a painting.

"There she is," he says with an empathetic smile on his face.

It is a young girl. Blond hair. Blue dress.

I take a deep, long look at the picture.

"It isn't Her," I say.

"What? Are you sure?" Joe says.

"Yes," I reply. "The hair is wrong; her face is too round. It isn't Her."

We stand there for a moment.

"Now think about this for a minute," he says slowly. "Are you sure?"

I don't question Joe's sincerity or intentions, but there is no doubt he is enabling. All it would take is one small leap over some minor inconvenient truths to make my good story into, literally, a fantastic story—one with an unthinkable conclusion and new direction. I'm sure Joe is just trying to help me find an answer.

"No," I say. "I am absolutely positive. This is not the Little Girl I saw in my dreams."

Joe sticks out his lip and shrugs.

"Just keep that image in your mind," he says. "Don't close yourself off to possibilities. You never know, you may wake up in the middle of the night and think, 'That's her!' Or maybe you'll have another dream and notice more of a similarity."

I can't help but wonder how many times similar things have happened. People come to Lily Dale looking for answers, and if they don't find one, they kind of hammer one into place.

"Now, I'd suggest you just be patient," he says. "I get the feeling that all the pieces of the puzzle are in front of you; you just need to put them together. Try different arrangements, different orders. Just keep an open mind."

The Wednesday-night Lily Dale Ghost Walk is a big deal for tourists. People flock into town to take part in the popular tour, and by the time it starts at nine o'clock, the firehouse is packed. A stretch limousine arrives with about twenty middle-aged women here to take the tour as part of a fiftieth birthday party or something. T-shirts are sold. Everyone gets a com-memorative Lily Dale Ghost Walk flashlight.

The tour is hosted by Neal and Joe. After welcoming every-one, Neal shares a PowerPoint presentation covering some complex and confusing explanations of ghosts and spirits.

"There are several different types of ghosts," explains Neal. "They all have different traits and are here for different reasons. Some are 'Halloween ghosts'—those are simply an evaporation of the ethers—or the spirit from when the body had life. Seeing them is like watching a film loop. They can't interact with you—they are simply an image. There are also spirits that are astral beings; those are the kind that try to communicate with someone who is mediumistic, like the people of Lily Dale."

Neal goes on to explain that many Spiritualists believe that there are different planes of existence and, frankly, offers a bit more detail than the tour attendees seem interested in. They want visceral freaky ghost stuff. They want Lily Dale to be like walking through a haunted house.

"You know, you can actually see your spirit form—we call it the 'prana aura,'" Neal says. "If you look at your hand and defocus a little, you can see it. It's an energy field that is about a sixteenth to an eighth of an inch around your finger. A healthy prana aura looks like fur sticking out—like static electricity. If the 'fur' looks wet or flattened, there is a lack of energy."

All of the tour attendees start looking at their hands, hoping for fuzzy, and comparing notes with their friends or fellow birthday celebrants.

Then Neal shares a bunch of photos taken on previous Ghost Walks—spirit orbs floating overhead, ethereal fog in the distance. The attendees are getting a bit restless, so Neal breaks us up into three groups. I end up in Joe's group.

"I bet you went back to the office to look at that painting again, didn't you?" Joe asks me as the tour heads out into the night.

I did, I admit. Even though I am dead certain that it isn't Her, the whole notion is simply too weird to let go without at least taking a second peek. Under the guise of taking a better photograph, I asked the office secretary if I could go back and look again. With a wave of her hand, I was again standing in front of a spirit-guided painting of a little girl in a blue dress. Just not *the* Little Girl in a Blue Dress.

Joe just smiles, nodding, and winks.

The Ghost Walk itself is a pretty cut-and-dry walking tour, except it takes place in the middle of the night. We walk by the historic places of Lily Dale and learn lots of trivial things about them. We see the homes of famous Lily Dale mediums and hear stories about their wild séances and works of spirit mastery. We learn about what it's like to live in a place like Lily Dale (turns out the church owns all the land underneath the businesses and homes and leases it to property holders, thus making it impossible to get a mortgage for a home in Lily Dale—homes have to be bought with cash). One of the last stops on the tour is the Maplewood Hotel, where I'm staying. During this stop, I learn that all the bad art in the hallways that I'd been cringing at all week is, in fact, spirit art. After explaining the concept of spirit art to the other tour attendees, Joe stops in front of a large red tapestry. He says the Spiritualist woman who created it was a quadriplegic, blind, and mute and that she stitched the tapestry with her mouth.

"Her mouth?" I ask.

"Yes," Joe replies. "She was in a trance state for the nine years she spent working on it, and she embroidered it with her mouth."

I stand there for a moment letting that sink in.

"Her mouth," I repeat.

"Yes," Joe repeats.

"How is that possible?" I ask.

"With the help of Spirit . . . ," he says, trailing off to what he assumes is an obvious conclusion.

"I'm not even sure I can grasp the physics of how that would work," I say.

Joe just smiles.

"I'm sorry," I say. "Talking to dead people . . . I'm willing to accept that. Hearing voices that others can't hear—I'll go there with you. Astral projection—I'm skeptical but willing to listen. But creating a queen-sized tapestry only with your mouth—that's too much. That falls outside what I'm willing to accept."

"Well, being skeptical is good," Joe offers. "Questioning things is good. When it all comes down to it, it is simply a matter of whether or not you choose to believe. And I choose to believe.

"But then again," he continues, "I also believe I can talk to dead people."

True, Joe. Very true.

I notice a small framed paper to the left of the tapestry. It's the official Lily Dale version of the tapestry's history, which, as it turns out, is even *weirder* than Joe's.

While the official version makes no mention of her creating the embroidery with her mouth, it does say that Mollie Francher, the stitcher, "suffered a severe accident which resulted in a development of inflammation of the lungs, paralysis, blindness, periods of deafness, occasional loss of speech, then spasms, followed by a trance condition."

Mollie stayed this way for nine years, supposedly refusing all food and drink, saying, "I receive nourishment from a source of which you are all ignorant." And not only did Mollie manage to embroider the tapestry during that time, but she also wrote more than sixty-five hundred letters of encouragement and support to other Spiritualists. Instead of making a tapestry, Mollie should have written a book on time management.

As we head out of the hotel to the next tour stop, I walk up to Joe again.

"You do realize that when you say, 'I also believe I can talk to dead people,' you are providing someone with the ultimate trump card against any argument you make," I say.

"What do you mean?" he replies.

"Well, let's say we're having an argument over who was the director of *One Flew Over the Cuckoo's Nest*. I could say it was Sidney Pollack. You would say, 'No, it was Milos Forman.' Then I would say, 'Yeah, but you also think you can talk to dead people.' Then I automatically win the argument."

"Why's that?"

"Because there would be a third dude with us," I say. "And when he heard all this, he would say, 'Wow, I'm gonna believe the guy who *doesn't* think he can talk to dead people.' And side with me, two to one."

"But who directed the movie?" Joe asks.

"Milos Forman."

"Then I'd be right after all," Joe says.

I decide it's better to let it go.

After visiting a few more Lily Dale sites, we head out to Inspiration Stump. The capper on the Lily Dale Ghost Walk is a special midnight service at the Stump, completely and totally in the dark. As we work our way through the forest, we almost don't need flashlights. This is due to the paparazzi-like explosion of camera flashes. Earlier, Joe had said that many people capture orbs in photos taken in the woods—or their cameras stop working entirely—and everyone is taking pictures into the darkness, hoping to capture a spook.

I settle in on the front bench at the Stump, surrounded by some women whom I don't recognize and assume are with the birthday party group.

Neal leads us in some silent meditation to align ourselves with the spirits and open ourselves up to communication. As we sit there, the woman on my left starts crying. I'm clueless about what to do. Should I comfort her? I mean, I don't even know her. Should I just leave her alone and ignore it?

"Now that we've become in tune with the Stump and the spirit energy, does anyone have anything to share?"

"I was just touched on the arm by my grandmother!" the woman at my left yells. Even though it's pitch-dark, I look at the people around me, I guess to make sure they understand that it was Grandma touching her, not me.

"I'd know her touch anywhere!" she cries out. "I can feel my grandfather, too. It's like they are standing right here with me."

Then the woman sitting on my right starts to sob. Again unsure as to what I should do, I lean in toward her in a gesture meant to ask "Are you okay?"

"Can't you see him?" she whispers through her tears.

"Um, who?" I say.

"He's sitting right there on the Stump," she replies.

Even at night, I can clearly see the entire Stump in the moonlight, just eight feet in front of us.

"I'm sorry," I say. "I don't see anything on the Stump."

"The boy," she insists. "He is sitting right there in front of you."

I just sit up straight again. Probably best to leave the two of them alone.

Neal and Joe both offer a few messages, then everyone gets up to walk out of the woods and head back to town. On the way, my fellow tour takers are aflutter over what happened and what they experienced. Several of them are pretty freaked out. However, I'm not at all, which surprises me.

It's something I came to understand about myself in Lily Dale, but I'd felt it on Clinton Road as well. While these places are scary at first, the more time I spend around them, the less frightened I am. Even though there is no less of a reason for being afraid, I kind of get used to them. For the first time, I catch myself wondering if perhaps it isn't the ghosts I'm scared of.

Nine days after my return from Lily Dale, a few friends and I are going to a movie. I'm driving and my friend Joe (of Clinton Road fame) is giving me directions. Bad directions. After turning the wrong way, I attempt a three-point turn to head back the other way. In the middle of my second turn, I bump up against a curb and hear a loud *pop*.

A flat tire.

We get it fixed and still make it in time for the movie, but it's close.

The mechanic later told me the tire blew because it was only half full.

I should have checked my tire pressure, he says.

THEN

"You! I would. Die for. You!"

Two women at the end of the bath-towels aisle stood open-mouthed, watching as a young woman sang a Prince song in front of the T.J. Maxx layaway counter.

I, myself, was paying little attention to her. I was too preoccupied trying to figure out if 316 came after 276 or before 276.

The singing was accompanied by a rusty bump and grind while she outlined her lower back and rear end with a freshly licked forefinger. I think this was supposed to look alluring or something.

The lip-syncer was my co-worker Annette. She'd taken to quoting lyrics and occasional pieces of dialogue from the movie *Purple Rain* every time she saw me.

I had a mild crush on Annette almost as soon as I started working at T.J. Maxx. She was the women's fitting-room attendant, and I was the janitor. Had you been there when we were both working, you might have noticed that the floors around the fitting room were always spotless and her trash can was always empty. Soon after I started there, *Purple Rain* came out and I tried unsuccessfully to get her to come with me to see it. In Canton, Ohio, at the time *Purple Rain* was released, Prince was seen as some unknown bizarre alien creature. Annette didn't want to go. In truth, Annette used Prince as a convenient excuse to turn me down, just as she had declined my invitation to go out to dinner, and lunch, and one or two other invitations I'd offered over the previous few weeks.

Even though Laura and I were together a lot of the time, she took every opportunity to subtly reinforce that we were not "together" together. I was actually okay with this—or at least I pretended I was. I didn't want to do anything to upset the balance. It was the one thing in my life that wasn't completely fucked up, and despite my lack of concern about anything else, I would go to great pains to keep it not fucked up. To help demonstrate that I didn't consider Laura to be my girlfriend, and to forward the illusion that I didn't want Laura to be my girlfriend, I went out with other girls (or tried to).

Those girls who did take me up on a date were scared off when they'd learn about all the time I spent with this other girl I supposedly wasn't dating. Well, a lot of them were put off when they realized that my fun demeanor was chemically driven and could swing into unpredictable chaos at pretty much any moment, but my relationship with Laura didn't help.

By that time, Laura and I were spending two or three evenings a week together. One of us would call the other, proclaim our boredom, and then feign a mild interest in getting together. We'd usually just spend the night driving around or finding someplace to just sit, drink, smoke, and talk for hours.

I'd stopped telling Laura about my dreams with the Little Girl in the Blue Dress, and the same with the feelings I'd get in the attic. She treated my Little Girl revelations as if I was relating a metaphor. She would always ask me lots of questions about what I experienced and how it felt, but it ended there. No concern, no advice. It was just something I experienced. To her, it was just a story.

As much time as we spent together, she would rarely, if ever, be open to discussing the rest of her life. Ask about her other friends, family, or what she did when we weren't together, and she'd become wildly evasive. Sometimes I'd imagine that the rest of her life was dull and uninteresting, with our friendship the only breath of fresh air. Other times I thought that *she* was the breath of fresh air, and probably had a lot of similar relationships with others she'd allow relatively close to her. I even wondered if, perhaps, she had many intimate friendships and I was the only one she kept at arm's length.

Though she refused to talk about such things, I'm pretty sure Laura saw a number of other guys during this time. I'm sure some of them had the same reaction to learning about me that girls like Annette did when they learned about Laura. Or maybe they didn't have the opportunity to. Given how cagey Laura was with me when it came to revealing any detail about her life outside of our friendship, I can only imagine she was cagey with others as well.

At some point after I'd lost interest in her, Annette changed her mind about *Purple Rain* and, apparently, about spending time with me as well, and became almost obsessed with impressing me with her love of the movie. *Purple Rain* maintained a run as the Saturday midnight movie at the Mellett Mall Cinema for almost a year, and Annette was going almost every weekend.

When Annette finished her *Purple Rain* recitation, she stood motionless, staring at me as if waiting for me to do or say something.

I stared back, unsure what I was supposed to do or say.

"Yeah, right," I said, trying to sound enthusiastic. "Prince . . . awesome."

I liked working in the Receiving Department. As long as I met the low, predefined expectations of me, I was pretty much left alone. I mopped, wiped, swept, and dusted. I broke down boxes and took out the trash. I had a set list of things I had to hobble through in the course of an evening, and if I played my cards right, besides the occasional cinematic reenactment from Annette, I could go through my entire shift with only minimal interaction with my co-workers and even less with customers.

One day I was notified that I'd received a promotion—one that I hadn't sought and didn't want—at the request of the regional manager. A few weeks earlier one of the store's delivery trucks had overturned on a highway outside of Akron. The regional manager showed up and carted off a handful of the guys working, including me, to help clean up and salvage stock—piles of argyle sweaters, white tube socks, and designer jeans with the wrong color top stitching on the seams were all wet from rain, as well as splattered with mud and diesel fuel.

The next day the regional manager came back into the stockroom to thank me again for my help with the truck and to tell me how impressed he was with my tenacity. Obviously his definition of tenacity revolved around not puking at the overwhelming diesel fumes, as I was the only one of the cleanup crew who didn't have to stop a few times to vomit. I didn't want to tell him that my extensive mastery of drinking and pill taking had taught me tremendous control over my gag reflexes.

"I told Jennifer that we need to find something new for you to do," he said. "Something with a bit more responsibility."

He winked and gave me a light punch on the shoulder, very proud of himself for boosting my career opportunities with T.J. Maxx.

The following week the schedule said I'd start training for the Layaway Department.

Layaway is a concept that seems better in theory than it was in practice. At T.J. Maxx, most items put on layaway were never picked up. I think the only real value of the service for the store was pocketing leftover deposits from those too lazy or embarrassed to come retrieve them.

Plus, at our T.J. Maxx, the customers who *really* wanted something they couldn't afford just stole it. One of the few benefits of working as a janitor is that no one, including those about to swipe something, paid any attention to the untouchable mopping up a spilled soda at the end of the aisle. I saw everything. Most would come back thirty minutes later and return the item for cash. At that time, T.J. Maxx had the most ridiculous exchange policy in the history of retail. They'd take back any merchandise, regardless of when you purchased it, what condition it was in, or whether or not you had a receipt. People would bring back dress clothes after wearing them to a wedding, a pair of trousers that had been worn regularly since they were bought four months earlier, or a dress their girl-friend had just lifted from the Juniors Department earlier that morning, right in front of the dude sweeping the floor.

At first, the shoplifting bothered me. But after a while, I, like almost every other employee in our store, stopped caring. I mean, I was getting paid less than four dollars an hour to do this; there was no call for heroics.

My friend Todd had recently received a promotion as well. Todd and I had become friends shortly after he started at the store, when I started buying drugs from him and his roommate. They sold dry, crumbly pot and whatever pills they could find. In addition to being the drug dealer of choice for half the store's employees, Todd had recently been made assistant lead of the Housewares Department. I think it went to his head, as for the previous several weeks he had decided that it was hilarious that I had to clean the employee restrooms, including whatever he did in there.

One day, a few weeks before I started in Layaway, Todd came into the break room and informed me he'd just left an upper decker in the restroom. I had no idea what an upper decker was, so I stopped by the men's room to try to figure it out. I looked in the toilet—nothing. In the trash can—nothing. I searched the entire men's room, nothing. I figured Todd was just pulling my leg and went back to work.

The next morning I came into work to find a note taped to the supply closet. Apparently there was a very strong odor coming from the men's room. The note asked me to investigate first thing and then clean up whatever was causing the smell.

I stopped by the Housewares Department on my way to the men's room, found Todd, and insisted he tell me what an upper decker was.

"Just look under the lid," he replied.

"I did," I said. "There was nothing there."

"Not that lid," Todd said. "The other lid."

Two minutes later, I discovered what an upper decker was. The next day, Todd stopped by the Layaway counter.

"Sorry about dropping that mysterious turd worm on your watch, man," he said. "That was a really fucked thing to do."

He reached into his pocket and then slid something small across the counter. A little blue pill with a heart shape cut out of the middle.

"This should make us even," he stage-whispered. "Make the day a little shorter."

He raised his hand toward his face and popped two pills into his mouth, swallowed them dry, winked, and walked back to the Housewares Department.

By the time the first customer showed up, I was in a blissful fog. However, I couldn't remember any of the codes for the register and just slowly pounded in different number combinations.

"I think the register is broken," I said as the person scooped up her pile of khaki pants and headed to the front of the store. I stumbled over toward Housewares and found Todd standing in front of a shelf of bud vases, mouth hanging open, staring blankly, motionless feather duster in hand.

"Dude, I need your help," I said. "I can't remember any of the codes I learned today."

I wasn't sure what I expected Todd to do, but I repeated my plea three times before he shook his head a few times, reached in the front of his smock, and pulled out a cheat sheet of register codes from his own failed attempt at the Layaway Department.

I found my khaki customer up by the service desk and lured her back to the layaway counter. With one hand over one eye, I read Todd's notes, typed in all the item codes, took a ten-dollar deposit, and stuffed the pants into cardboard box number 316.

Later, Annette stopped by to perform her choreography routine.

Soon afterward, Todd walked up to the counter.

"Dude, did I piss myself?" he asked, looking at his crotch.

"I don't think so," I replied.

"Man, I feel like I'm pissing my pants . . . right now."

We both stood staring at the crotch of his pants, waiting for a wet spot to surface, for the next minute or two.

Eventually, I reached out to hand him his cheat sheet back, lightly knocking him on the shoulder to get his attention. He stared at it for a moment, briefly returned his attention to the crotch of his pants, wished me a pleasant evening, and walked away.

When the store-closing announcement came over the PA at 8:55, I realized that I hadn't really moved or done anything since staring at Todd's crotch almost two hours earlier. I had a list of things I had to do to close out Layaway. The first was to take all the day's new layaway boxes upstairs to the storage room, a long windowless aisle of identical boxes lit by a single fluorescent bulb. I walked all the way to the end and halfway back before I realized I'd passed box 316 about four hundred boxes earlier.

After expending a considerable amount of mental energy determining that 316 should come directly after 315, I started hearing some soft taps—the sound of someone slowly walking up the stairs to the storage room. It was probably Todd, looking to score an unsellable pair of pants to wear instead of his pee-stained pair. Or perhaps it was Annette, now forward enough to suggest we do it on top of a stack of layaway boxes.

But as I heard the footsteps reach the top of the stairs, I felt a wave of cold hit my back.

At first, I was confused. Did someone open a door? How was cold air making it all the way up here?

Just as I was about to turn around toward the stairs, it dawned on me what was happening.

I could feel my stomach fill with adrenaline. I couldn't move.

It was Her.

I was sure the Little Girl in a Blue Dress was standing directly behind me, no less certain than if I was standing in the hallway of my parents' attic. It was almost as if I could hear Her gibberish—like it had somehow bypassed my ears and was penetrating directly into my head. I felt like I could hear Her mumble out Her nonsense, taking hard breaths between each sentence. I envisioned Her standing there behind me, dripping wet, mouth running in a silent fury of gibberish.

I'm going to close my eyes, I said to myself. *And if there is a ghost here, I will see it when I open them again.*

I couldn't open my eyes.

I fought every impulse I had to turn around and confront her. I was frozen, with every muscle in my body fighting to turn toward and away at the same time. I could feel all the air and energy in the room sucked into a void behind me. My back just kept getting colder and colder. Just as I could imagine Her about to reach out and touch my back, it was all gone.

In an instant, the cold, the feeling of presence, Her—everything just switched back to normal. I didn't want to know what had happened. I also didn't want to hang around to see if it would happen again.

I just turned—nothing was there—and ran.

I jumped down three steps at a time, raced through the store, and bolted out to my car. I took off down the road and drove for hours.

In the morning I got a phone call from the store manager reaming me for the condition of the Layaway Department. The boxes weren't put away properly, the register was an indecipherable mess of transactions. I had really blown it, she told me, really disappointed her after she'd gone out on a limb for me. I apologized, saying that I had no excuse for what happened and didn't know why I had made so many mistakes. But I did have an excuse. I did have a very clear reason.

In the few years since she'd come into my life, I'd never felt Her outside my parents' house. But now the equation had changed. She had followed me into the real world. The boundary was broken. If She could reach me in the layaway storage room, that means she could reach me anywhere.

••

"Okay, this is how we operate," Steve said, speaking slowly, like he was already exhausted six words into our conversation. "WKSC has been blessed with . . . how do I describe it . . . 'working' equipment."

As of a week earlier, I was a student at a local eight-hundred-student Kent State University satellite campus. As I made clear to Laura, I had very little interest in attending college. Funny enough, colleges had very little interest in having me attend them. You'd think the thing to do would be to simply not go to college. But I felt suddenly compelled to find a college that would take me—for two reasons.

First, since I'd stumbled through my final months of high school that spring, every awkward conversation I had with any-one I ran into—former friends from school, people from my church, distant relatives, and so on—always started with the same question: "Where are you going to college?" I really wanted to answer by saying, "I hate college. I hate the idea of college. And now I hate you, probably for several reasons, but mostly because you asked me about college."

Even more compelling was my lack of alternatives to school. Logic would dictate that someone skipping college would go out and join the workforce. However, with my inability to show up anywhere on time, dyed hair, piercings, frequent state of inebriation, and verbal explosions, my employment options were somewhat limited. That left me with a simple choice: either work more hours at T.J. Maxx, the one place that seemed happy to have me, or enroll at least part-time at Kent Stark. As far as I could tell, Kent Stark was mostly for students, like me, with so little college potential that they couldn't handle going to the actual Kent State University thirty miles north. It was a legitimate college, at least on paper, and I now had a response (which only required me to utter two syllables) whenever someone asked about my plans. I figured I could just sign up for a few basic, embarrassingly unchallenging classes to get everyone off my back.

As soon as I had, I sought out the campus radio station. Almost the entirety of my knowledge about new wave and punk had been formed in two ways: from music discovered while listening to WAUP late at night and from music shared by friends who discovered it listening to WAUP late at night. WAUP was a small college station, attached to the University of Akron, bringing fifty thousand watts of Hüsker Dü, Laurie Anderson, the Damned, X, and Television to throngs of rural kids who never thought music could sound or feel that way. My goal at WKSC was simple: to blow people's minds. I knew the effect WAUP had had on me, and I intended to use my slot on WKSC to do the same to others, whether they wanted me to or not. Because I was a freshman, and because I had no experience, and because I was late to sign up, I got the one shift not yet claimed: Thursday mornings from eight to ten.

WKSC seemed to be classified as a "radio station" solely because those involved wished it to be. I don't think there was ever any broadcasting involved, as it had no transmitters. It was "broadcast" through the PA systems in the hallways and lobbies of the three campus buildings, was featured as the "on hold" music in the Theater and Art Departments and as background music in the school's grim early-seventies-era cafeteria. In this regard, it was caught somewhere between being Muzak and a bad club deejay system.

The entirety of its studio equipment looked as if it was about to explode—and in a glorious manner. The broadcast console was probably World War II vintage, featuring large fist-sized knobs for mixing that let out bursts of crunchy noise and distortion every time you moved them. The two turntables worked, though Steve pointed out that I should never touch the metal platter of the left one, or I could expect a pretty severe shock.

"Yeah, you could empty your bladder on that one," he said, slapping me on the shoulder.

There was also a monstrous open-reel tape player, which Steve said hadn't worked in the three years he'd been there, a microphone for announcing, and a cassette player the size of a suitcase.

"You know, if you get the tape in there just right, it'll play without eating the tape," he said. "But it probably isn't worth it. Even by 'KSC standards the thing sounds like caca."

The most troublesome feature of the WKSC studio was that the entire station was located in one corner of the cafeteria, blocked off by two glass walls. That meant that at least 90 percent of your listening audience was in clear view, no more than forty feet from you. This would lead to a lot of unwelcome audience interaction, especially considering my musical choices.

"Oh, and one more thing," Steve said, leaning down to draw my attention underneath the broadcast console. "If you ever get complaints about the volume being too low or too high or too whatever, here is where the Secret Volume Knob is."

Steve pointed to a numbered dial bolted to one of the console table's legs. Above it was an embossed plastic label that read SECRET VOLUME KNOB.

I have no idea what became of Steve after WKSC. He could have become a dope dealer, a congressman who fucks young pages, a life insurance salesman who steals money from old people—it doesn't matter. That moment, showing me the location of the Secret Volume Knob, was the single stupidest thing Steve would ever do in his life.

"Whatever you do," he added with a giggle, "don't turn the Secret Volume Knob completely up. The compressors can't handle it, and the results are thunderous, man. Shit will blow up."

Steve looked at me with a large grin. My training was complete.

Buying drugs from my co-worker Todd and his roommate Andre was a novelty to me. Before I met them, all my drugs were acquired from friends or friends of friends. It was mostly appallingly low-grade pot and random speed. We were teenagers; often having drugs was more important than actually using them. Sometimes we'd hold on to the stems and seeds that had cost us our entire allowance, just so we could say we had it.

I developed a mental image of what a real drug dealer's life must be like. I imagined a big house, a Cadillac, and chicks running around in bikinis while everyone played extremely loud music on their massive stereo system. Even considering Todd's employment in Housewares at T.J. Maxx, I was still willing to fantasize he had a bitchin' existence.

In truth, Todd, his girlfriend, Andre, and Andre's girlfriend all shared one room at the Traveler's Inn Motor Lodge on West Tuscarawas Street. There were two chairs, a small table, two beds, a barely functional television on a small dresser, and a bathroom. There were also piles of clothes, empty food containers, and a bicycle in the room. It smelled like a hot, dirty sock.

The only one walking around in anything close to a bikini was Andre, whom I rarely saw wearing anything other than his underwear. Andre didn't seem to have a job or anything to do. He sold crap drugs to high school kids at football games and the roller rink. That seemed to be enough to pay his share of the weekly rent at the Traveler's Inn. Andre loved to complain about white people and make jokes about how stupid white people were, but I never recall seeing him with anyone other than white people.

I imagine that I was different from a lot of Andre and Todd's meager assortment of customers. Most people got high to feel good. Not me. I wasn't there to feel good. I was there to feel nothing. It seemed that my life was full of reminders of how fucked up I'd let it become. It wasn't that I wanted to feel everything was okay, or that I wanted to forget or feel absolution or oblivion. I wanted to be a blank slate. The pills were a way to achieve that for a few brief hours. Good or bad, it didn't make a difference. I just didn't want to feel.

The deal was pretty simple. I would buy a twelve-pack of beer (not Wiedemann) and take it over to Todd and Andre's. I would make small talk, have one beer, buy some mildly overpriced drugs, and then leave the rest of the twelve-pack with them. I usually just wanted pot, but if they had something more, I would try some pill roulette. In truth, a lot of the cheap pills that I bought from them just made me breathe heavily and fall asleep, which, arguably, could be considered the same thing as feeling nothing, especially when I didn't dream.

"How about those blue ones, with the hearts cut out of them?" I said. "You know, like the one you gave me at work."

"Those ain't hearts, fool," yelled Andre from the bathroom. "Those are little *V*'s cut out of them, for the name, Vali—"

"La la la la la la la," I interrupted, putting my fingers in my ears.

Andre had forgotten my rule—not that he cared enough to remember: I didn't want to know the names of the drugs I was buying. I just wanted to know what they'd do to me. I had these bad visions that one day I'd learn that because I took Drug X, I could only have kids with two heads, would eventually stop getting erections, or would develop some terrible disease. In my mind, if I didn't know what I was taking, I wouldn't have to worry about what it might do to me long term. Problem solved.

"How much?" I asked.

"Three a pop," Todd replied.

"If I buy this crap pot you have, I'll only have enough cash for five," I said.

"Take six," Todd said. "Last one's on the house."

"Like hell it is," Andre called out from the bathroom. "You buy five, you take five."

"Deal," I said, throwing the cash onto the bed, putting four pills in the bag with the weed and holding the last one up to my eye. It did look like a tiny heart. I popped it onto my tongue and reached for my beer.

"Oh, no, like fuck you won't," Andre said, running toward me from the bathroom and grabbing the beer from my hand.

"What the fuck, Andre?" I said, pulling the bitter tablet off my tongue.

"Man, you are not doing that here. You take that with beer, and you'll be seeing shit that isn't there, man. That will seriously fuck you up."

"Really? I'll see things that other people can't see?"

"Bitch, you will be drooling in that chair for six hours. I ain't gonna have you hanging around here all night."

"No, seriously, this stuff can make me see things that I can't see straight?"

I pulled my wallet out of my pocket. I still had about seventy dollars from my paycheck that was supposed to go for car insurance.

"I'll buy all of them." I said.

"What?"

"All of them," I repeated.

"Three apiece," Andre said. "And no freebies," he added, hitting Todd on the back of the head as he walked over to change the channel on the TV.

I planned out my first WKSC playlist for the next week. While I was supposed to be studying polynomials and reading *The Good Earth,* I was worried about my second set of songs and whether the Smiths' "How Soon Is Now?" should go before or after the Butthole Surfers' "Concubine." I think I had the entire first month mapped out before my first shift.

Asking me to wake up and be somewhere at 8 A.M. was pretty much the same thing as asking me to get up and be somewhere at 3 A.M., so I knew from day one that the only way I'd pull it off was to take a bunch of different pills and stay up all night. Which, like every time you try to keep yourself awake all night, backfired completely, resulting in me passing out at around 5 A.M. and waking up just a few minutes before I was supposed to be "on air" (if you could call it that).

All my dramatic running around to get the shift started, interrupted by mad, sickness-fueled dashes to the bathroom, seemed to distract the meager listening audience from what I was actually playing, which was probably a good thing. The complaints were few that first show but really started to pick up as fall got rolling.

"I don't think people want to hear 'Holiday in Cambodia' before their second cup of coffee," Steve offered in my first (and only) feedback session. The criticisms slid right off me. Someday, I thought, these people would hum "Holiday in Cambodia" while rocking their kids to sleep at night, and they'd have me to thank for it.

As I came in one morning a few weeks into my deejay career, I noticed three black women sitting at a table chatting and drinking coffee. They'd been there every Thursday morning. The woman who seemed to do most of the talking was wearing knee-high red leather boots. I recognized her because she had winced and looked up at the overhead speaker several times during my previous shows.

While I was getting settled in, I dropped my first record, "Institutionalized" by Suicidal Tendencies, and, as was my norm, gave a good twist to the Secret Volume Knob.

They stuck me in an institution.
Said it was the only solution.

I looked up and noticed Red Boots.

"I'm sorry," Red Boots said, smiling wide, as I opened the door and stuck my head outside. "I was wondering if you could do me two little favors."

"Okay," I said.

"Well, first, it is hard for us to talk when the music is so loud," she continued. "I was wondering if, perhaps, maybe, you could, you know, turn it down."

"Sure."

"I mean, like, way down."

"Well, like all the volume settings are automatic and can't be changed, but I'll see what I can do," I said. "What's the second thing?"

She grinned.

"Well, we were wondering if you could, perhaps, take requests, or try, like, playing some different music."

"Hey, I know it may not be to *your* taste," I said. "But I have to keep the entire audience in mind."

She crunched up her brow.

"Entire audience," she said loudly. "Look around."

Besides Red Boots and her friends, my "entire audience" consisted of a handful of half-awake fellow students and two cafeteria workers.

Her tone suddenly shifted.

"Our table is the simple majority here, and if we don't want to hear this screaming 'I hate you' junk, you will play what we want."

"Hey, if you don't like it, you can come sign up for your own shift and play what *you* want."

"Or I can just tell your tragic mopey ass that *I* pay for this school, too. And I pay just as much as *you do*," she said, tapping her finger against my chest.

"Write a letter," I said, stepping back to close the door. "Because then you'll learn how little other people care about what you think." I shut the door and reached for the Secret Volume Knob, turning it up even higher.

Red Boots started to shake her head as she rejoined her

friends, shouting, "Oh, hell no!" so loud I could hear it through the glass wall.

I dropped my Flipper record on the other turntable and played "Living for the Depression"—a minute and a half of mostly lo-fi shouting over a simple (and sloppily played) three-chord progression. The speakers barked out:

> *I'm not livin' life to be*
> *A real cheap fucker like you,*
> *Cop-out.*

Red Boots was now standing up, addressing the few occupied tables around her, and pointing at me through the glass. Eventually she just turned toward me and shouted. Inside the 'KSC booth, I couldn't make out a single word, but I think I still pretty much got what she was trying to say.

I grabbed David Bowie's *Lodger* album from my bin, pulled the needle off the Flipper record, dropped the needle in the middle of the first track, and walked out of the deejay booth toward Red Boots and her friends.

I jumped up onto the table and began stomping up and down and dancing along with Bowie. A flurry of books and beverage cups flew off the table. I kicked the remaining items off the table and across the room.

There's no doubt that Red Boots brought a little drama to the situation, but none of it justified what I was doing. It wasn't like I used her behavior as an excuse, but as license to let go. Rather than take the upper road, I felt compelled to take a lower road. I knew this situation would not end well, so I decided to let my rage flow. Why work so hard to contain myself when it felt so good to just let go?

"I am a DJ," I sang along with the record. *"I am what I play."*

"Get off my table, you crazy motherfucker!" Red Boots screamed. I could tell she wanted to reach up and smack me or swat me away. For some reason, she restrained herself. It was more self-control than I think I could ever muster about anything. No one would have blamed her for hitting me over the head with a ketchup bottle, but Red Boots just stood there shaking her head.

I picked up some discarded Styrofoam coffee cups off the next table and started heaving them at the wall in time with the song, splattering small amounts of backwash against the brick wall. Then I turned back to Red Boots and her friends and started to dance around in front of them, suggestively wrapping my fingers around my belt as if I was about to strip.

They, and the rest of the cafeteria's occupants, just stood or sat there, staring at me. I remember one of the food servers stood with her mouth open holding a full spoon of oatmeal.

I knew that what I was doing was an overreaction. I really didn't care that it was an overreaction. I knew that in a few minutes I'd regret everything I was doing and feel horrible for scaring them. But the feeling became like trying to hold back an orgasm. The tidal wave of hate-fed euphoria was just too tempting, too overwhelming. I just had to let myself go, even though I knew the chaos that it would create.

"I am a DJ, I am what I play," I sang. *"I got believers, believing me!"*

I jumped down and returned to the 'KSC booth, locked the door, threw the Bowie disc back into my bin, grabbed my *Music for Airports* tape, slammed it into the ancient player, hit Play, and slumped down into the chair. The loud, distorted etherealness of *Music for Airports* seemed to confuse people more. Most just got up and filed out of the cafeteria.

I played the tape because I wanted the situation to melt away. *Music for Airports* always made me feel calm. It reminded me of feeling peaceful. It reminded me of sitting in the car late at night with Laura. I wanted to let *Music for Airports* pour over everyone there and have the same effect on them. Just let this situation I'd created wash away.

I felt like a fool. Not for behaving so badly, but for taking it out on Red Boots and her friends. They were probably scared— and how could you blame them? They just asked that I turn down the music. The next thing they knew, some idiot was kicking coffee around the room while dancing like a lunatic on top of their table. I was an asshole for sucking them into my bullshit.

A few minutes later a campus policeman showed up and told me to turn off the tape and leave the station.

When I came out of the booth, Red Boots launched into how much of an asshole I was.

I started to scream nonsense, partially because I wanted to freak her out, but mostly because I was overwhelmed by the torrent of rage and anger that I felt. If you had sat me down at the time and asked what was making me so upset, I probably would have spouted off about how much work I'd put into my playlists and how I was doing this for free and how if she didn't "get it" then that was her fault and how dare she complain and ruin something that was so important to me.

In truth, that would have just been a cover—something to shroud my confusion at how quickly I'd given over control to my darkness. Whenever something, anything, happened in my life that could possibly justify being pissed off, I ran with it.

Every time it happened, my fuse just got shorter and shorter. It shocks and embarrasses me to think back to how quickly I could be overwhelmed by life, leaving me feeling like I had little control over myself—almost as if I went into a trance and became only a witness to my own emotions and actions.

I stood there and screamed. I wanted to smash things up. I wanted everyone else to feel as horrible as I did. Red Boots, the cop, the cafeteria worker—I wanted them all to know how angry I felt and how simple shit like this was just too much. I couldn't take any more. When my rant ran out of steam, my face was red and had snot and tears running down it. No one seemed to know what to do or say, including me.

I picked up my crate of records and walked out the door.

When I next picked up Laura for a trip out to Lake O'Dea, at first I didn't mention anything to her about getting kicked out of the radio station. I would have done whatever I could to keep the conversation away from anything in my real life. Instead, I baited her into an argument.

We'd argue about anything—just for fun. We'd argue about Bruce Springsteen or telekinesis or architecture or some other subject that, often, we knew little about. Most times we ended up passionately defending ideas that we really didn't believe. It felt good to let out the rip cord and be overtly animated and passionate about *something*.

If Laura was mildly impressed or entertained by my zealous argument for, say, everyone in the Western world abandoning their own language and speaking Latin, the evening might end with a short kiss.

It became the big moment of truth between us after the nights we spent together: the kiss attempt. I tried to kiss her at the end of every evening we spent together, sometimes in the middle of an evening we were spending together. Sometimes she kissed me back, sometimes she didn't. Sometimes it was a deep kiss. Sometimes it was just a peck. Sometimes she'd stop me from even trying to get close. I always tried to guess what was coming, tried to find some rhythm or pattern. There was a formula for everything, I always reminded myself. From the combustion inside my car engine to a guitar amplifier to how the bricks and mortar were held together in a building foundation to an egg frying in a skillet to a kiss from a girl—everything happened based on an equation. I believed nothing happened by chance—it was all just simple math. Variables and constants were combined to achieve a predestined outcome.

This time, while I was in the middle of making some point about something, Laura turned in her seat and slowly climbed into my lap. She reached for my cheek and started to kiss me.

In that moment, everything—Little Girl, work, school, my family, Red Boots, everything that pissed me off or upset me—just vanished into the warm softness of her mouth. It seemed like a frozen moment, like everything around us simply stopped.

I didn't want it to end, but soon enough she stopped, turned herself back around into her seat, smiled without looking at me, opened the door, and left without saying a word.

The next morning, I just kept thinking about that kiss. I kept thinking about the smile on her face as she got out of the car.

The problem was, everything horrible in my life came rushing back as soon as she closed the car door, trying to drown out the memory of that kiss. I didn't want to let it go, but felt I had to.

Every time I thought of that kiss, I thought that I didn't deserve to feel good. Rather than comfort me, the kiss just reminded me how far from normal and good my life really was.

I even tried to take some of Todd and Andre's little blue pills. All I did was fall asleep, waking a few hours later to a world just as fucked up as it was before. The kiss stung. The kiss made it worse.

I needed to remove the memory of that kiss.

As soon as Northeast Electronics opened that morning, I walked in and asked to see stereo receivers. I picked out the most beautiful Sony model they had and paid with a check. Five inputs; 120 watts per channel.

It cost almost three hundred dollars. That was more than I brought home in a month of cleaning toilets and taking out trash at T.J. Maxx. I had less than twenty dollars in my checking account. I wrote a check anyway.

After walking out the door with the receiver, I drove back to Lake O'Dea, where Laura and I had hung out the night before. I opened up the carton, unpacked the receiver, and set it up on top of its cardboard box in the middle of the road. Then I went into my trunk and got a crowbar.

I took a long look at the receiver. This thing wasn't built for what was about to happen to it. It was built to look beautiful in some rich guy's house and fill his parties with loud shitty music that made him feel cool. The guy's friends were supposed to look at this stereo with envy, hoping that if they put up with idiots like him long enough, they might be able to squeak their way up high enough to be able to afford something like this someday, too. To be honest, I wanted it too. It was a symbol of success and wealth that I would never have.

I took the crowbar and dragged it across the metal top, leaving a deep, long scratch. There was no turning back at this point. It took three strikes before the front broke off. Then I started swinging at the insides, bits of plastic and circuit board flying everywhere.

I'd needed to balance out warm feelings before, of course. In the past, I'd just throw some bottles across an empty parking lot. I'd slam my fist into stacks of cardboard boxes in the backroom of T.J. Maxx. I'd dig my fingers into the side of my chest until I drew blood. This was different. That kiss needed a greater response. For a brief moment, that simple passionate gesture had made me feel wanted, like I'd actually succeeded in bringing some joy to someone. In the moment, it made me happy. A new kind of momentary happiness called for a new kind of sabotage. There was only one thing to do with that stereo: Make it into an offering.

Within four minutes, the receiver was reduced to a pile of broken plastic and metal. There were pieces of it stuck in my hair. I felt an almost orgasmic wave of relief. For just a moment, I felt calm.

In three days the check I'd used to buy the stereo would bounce, then bounce again, then Northeast Electronics would start calling me, and eventually threaten to send the check over to the authorities. They'd tell me writing a bad check for that amount could be a felony. I would create all kinds of chaos and drama and scrape together just enough cash and make just enough excuses and get just enough leeway to pay them their money and fees hours before they turned the check in to the police department. Everyone involved would treat me like a fuck-up.

When I think back to that time in my life, I remember saying that I never wanted to have any regrets. I wanted to follow my instincts regardless of the consequences or outcome—to ignore convention and expectation and pressure. To be free. But I was actually doing the opposite. Eliminating options, creating chaos, and reinforcing the idea that my life was irreconcilable.

Standing in the sun on the road behind Lake O'Dea, I looked at the pile. Black plastic shards, scratched and twisted metal, cracked circuit boards, and stray letters from a chrome logo. Scattered. It matched me, a broken machine. No purpose. No future. Nothing more than fodder for chaos yet to come.

Eighteen-year-olds were supposed to have bright futures. They weren't supposed to be broken. They weren't supposed to be haunted by dead girls. They weren't supposed to feel so much anger and pain with no reason why.

I knew I needed to leave. If I looked at those pieces for another moment, I knew I would pick them up and start digging them into my arms, neck, and eyes. As I started walking toward the car, I didn't feel regret or fear or sadness. I felt nothing.

Exactly as I'd hoped.

• • •

One of my classes was Introduction to Philosophy, taught by a little man who looked like he'd just walked out of an R. Crumb cartoon, whom we called "the Instructor." A generic "IN-STRUCTOR" had appeared on the class schedule where his name should have been. It never got corrected, and he never once told us his name. On the first day of class, he simply walked in and asked if we had read any of the assigned texts. Since we had never received a syllabus or a list of required books, several people shook their heads no, while the rest of us just stared blankly. He pulled a pile of barely legible mimeographed course outlines out of his bag, plopped them by the door, and began talking about Socrates. That's how we started.

The Instructor would rant for an hour about truth, the Federal Reserve System, cinema verité, and Ronald Reagan—and I was transfixed. For the first time in my brief college career, I actually read the assigned texts. Not only did they prime me for whatever mind blowing the Instructor was about to lay down, but they offered the benefit of giving me something brainy to talk about with Laura.

Shortly after I started the class, Laura and I drove up to the Flats in Cleveland to see a band she'd heard on a mix tape, the

March Violets. Laura was driving home afterward because (a) she loved to drive but didn't have a car, and (b) I had shown up at her house so fucked up that I passed out in the three minutes between arriving and her opening the passenger door to jump in. The only thing I remember about the show was that the March Violets were fronted by a woman with huge hair who was not wearing a bra (and really should have been). When I mentioned the bra thing to Laura after the show, she refused to unlock the car door until I took it back.

We continued to argue about the piggishness of my boob observation as we drove out of the Flats and through a neighborhood of empty warehouses overlooking the Cuyahoga River.

"Stop the car!" I yelled, leaning toward the window and fixing my attention on one passing building.

"What? No," she replied.

"I need you to stop the car right now," I said.

"Are you sick or something? I'm not going to . . ."

I reached in between us and pulled up the emergency brake. Luckily, we weren't going that fast, and we quickly skidded to a dead stop in the middle of West Ninth Street. A car honked and swerved around us.

"What the fuck was that?" she asked.

"We have to go in there!" I shouted back, annoyed that I had to explain my instant obsession.

"Where? There is nothing here."

"Right there," I said, grabbing a small flashlight from the glove box, opening the car door, and walking toward a dilapidated warehouse. Laura parked the car and followed. By the time she caught up with me, I had already broken off the padlock from the front door. It was barely held in place by rusty screws embedded in the weather-beaten frame. It came out with about as much effort as it takes to pry a pit out of a ripe peach.

"How are you sure that we aren't going to get caught?" Laura said.

"I'm not sure we won't get caught," I answered, turning on the flashlight, handing it to her, and walking into the cavernous space. I saw a metal staircase off to the side and started to climb four stories to the top. The floor was one large room with a small, cheaply built office against the far wall. The space was flooded with moonlight through six-foot-square windows of small glass panes. It was almost bright enough that we didn't need the flashlight.

"Why are we here again?" she asked.

"Because I think we should live here," I said.

"Live here?"

"Yeah," I answered. "We could move in here and clean it up. It would be amazing."

"Live here," she repeated flatly.

"Yeah, together," I answered.

"We'd live here together? Why would we live together?" she said.

"Don't you think it would be cool?" I asked.

She paused and looked me in the eye.

"I don't know," she said, turning the light away to find the stairway back down.

Once outside again, I grabbed a bottle of cheap wine from the back of the car and we sat on the loading deck of the warehouse. I decided to drop some philosophy on her.

"Well, as you know, Socrates was like Jesus, he didn't really write anything—it's all told to us through others," I said, making it sound like the most obvious thing in the world, even though I had only learned it myself twelve hours earlier. "Plato was just one of them."

"Really," Laura said.

"You have to break things down into a series of questions. Then you will find the ultimate truth you seek."

"Is that so?" she said.

"Socrates felt he'd be better off dead than have to conform to society's expectations," I said. "He'd rather die than live on his knees."

"You try to make that sound so noble," she said.

"Are you mocking me?"

"Yes."

As we lazily walked around the warehouse's loading area, I started quoting the Socrates passages I'd copied into my notebook, reading them to Laura by the light of my Zippo. Passages about the evils of piety, the virtue of sacrifice, and quotes about the gods, beauty, and wrongdoers. I still have that notebook, though for some reason just a few random pages remain in it. It was cheap—more than likely the binding got loose and disintegrated over time.

"No one knows whether death may not be the greatest of all blessings for a man yet men fear it as if they knew that it is the greatest of evils. And surely it is," I read.

After that, I stopped reading, mainly because I simply couldn't read what I'd written. My letters and words started to morph into scribbles and random shapes, less and less legible as they stumbled down the page.

I looked a few pages further into my notebook. All scribbles. Not a single legible word. It went on for at least a dozen pages.

The final few pages contained just wild loops, scratches, and thrashing lines. I had pushed so hard that I'd dug the pen into the page, putting small random tears into the paper. I must have broken the pen, or it had run out of ink, because it just suddenly stopped. Then the writing switched from black ink to blue for one final quotation, one that I'd copied repeatedly over several pages, written neatly and precisely:

"But it is clear to me that it was better for me to die now and to escape from trouble. That is why my divine sign did not oppose me at any point."

As I stood silently staring at the pages of my journal by the light from the Zippo that was about to burn my fingertips, I realized that I had no recollection at all of writing any of this. Seeing the progressively manic scribbles was just as shocking to me as it would have been to a stranger.

We got into the car to head home. By this time, I was sober enough to drive. As we got onto I-77 and headed out of Cleveland, Laura thumbed through my notebook. She eventually laid her head down in my lap, took my hand, and placed it across her collarbone. We sat there in silence for a few minutes.

"Am I pretty?" Laura asked.

"What do you mean?" I asked.

"You know," she said. "Do you think I'm pretty?"

"I thought you didn't believe in conventional beauty," I said. "You are probably the last person I'd ever expect to hear that question from."

"Just answer it," she said. "Is that so hard?"

"Yes," I said, pausing. "I think you are pretty."

She wrapped her fingers around mine and closed her eyes for a few minutes.

"Tell me what you're thinking," she said.

I hesitated.

"Why don't you want to live in the warehouse?" I asked. "With me."

Laura slowly sat upright.

"It isn't that . . . ," she said.

"What?" I interjected.

"Eric, I have no interest in living in Cleveland," she said.

I just stayed quiet.

"I mean, is that what you want?" she asked. "Downtown Cleveland? Some rat-filled warehouse?"

"We could clean it up," I said.

"That isn't the point. Don't you want something more?"

"Like what?" I asked.

"Eric, there is a whole world out there," she said. "Don't you want to be a part of it? Don't you want to see what's outside Ohio?"

"In a world full of ignorant fucks who hate you, what difference does it make if they're in Canton or Amsterdam?"

"You wouldn't know, would you," she said.

Laura started paging through my Socrates quotes until she found what she was looking for. " 'The most blameworthy ignorance is to believe that one knows what one doesn't know,' " she read.

"What's that supposed to mean?" I asked.

"You tell me," she said. "You wrote it in your amazing notebook of truth.

"And what is the deal with this one?" she continued. "You highlighted and underlined it four times: 'Now the hour to part has come. I go to die, you go to live. Which of us goes to the better lot is known to no one, except the god.' Huh?"

"I guess I thought it was important," I said.

"Plainly," she said, leaning her body against the passenger window.

Recently I dug through that weathered journal filled with Socrates quotes, which I've managed to hold on to all those years, and my heart almost stopped beating when I came to that quote. I remember reading it for the first time. I remember how clearly it seemed to express my feelings about wanting to end my life. I remember copying it from my textbook and underlining it again and again. I remembered Laura's reaction to reading it. But none of that is why it affected me so much to look at it again today. I underlined it because I had felt it applied so clearly to my life, when clearly it had applied to hers.

Neither of us said a word for a while. I drove and kept turning up the music. Laura thumbed through the notebook.

I pulled over a few blocks from her house. I turned the lights off on the car and reached for my book bag in the backseat, fishing around for something to write with. I wrote on a blank notebook page, "Don't you want anything normal out of life?"

She looked at me for a moment, slightly puzzled by why I would write this instead of saying it aloud. She took the pen and notebook from me.

"What do you mean?" she wrote, handing them back.

"You always talk about exploring places and roaming around the world looking for something," I wrote. "But don't you want a normal life at some point? Like having a family and stuff?"

She visibly shuddered when she read it.

"I can't think of anything more repulsive than the thought of having a baby," she wrote. "The idea of something growing inside me, it's just . . . SICK."

Everything was quiet for a moment, then she grabbed the notebook back from me and continued to write.

the most blameworthy ignorance to believe that one knows what one does not know."

—J.

"...but it is clear to me that it was better for me to die now and to escape from trouble. That is why my divine sign did not oppose me at any point."

—S.

Now the hour depart has come. I go to die, you go to live. Which of us goes to the better lot is known to no one, except the god."

—S.

"The most important thing in life is not life, but the good life."

—S.

"One should never do wrong... retur...

"So if you are asking if I want to be happy, and happy means being somebody's wife and somebody's mother and somebody's neighbor or somebody PINNED DOWN to some warehouse because it would be cool . . . then NO. I guess I don't want to be happy like that."

Everything stayed silent for a moment.

"And you are wrong," she said aloud. "That isn't happy."

"I never said that," I answered. "I just asked if you wanted that."

"You asked if I wanted normal," she snapped. "And I don't have any idea what normal is, though I'm pretty sure I wouldn't care for it. And I wouldn't be hanging around with you if I thought you had a clue about normal, either."

I didn't know whether to take that as a compliment or not.

As much as I found myself battling against convention and rules regarding everything else, having a relationship with her was one area where I decidedly longed for "normal." Perhaps it was because everything else in my life was such chaos, but I wanted to make sure my feelings weren't in vain. I wanted to know that this one thing in my life was real and had meaning. I wanted to know it was true.

When we reached her house, I slowly leaned over to try to kiss her good night. Laura softly shook her head and reached for the door.

I was spending an increasing amount of time in my car, basically because I had nowhere else to go. I could go home, but that would mean dealing with my parents. I could go to class, but that would mean explaining why I hadn't attended most of them in weeks. The only place I didn't feel any pressure to explain myself was work, where few people seemed to notice me at all. But I only worked twenty hours a week, which left me with about a hundred and fifty-odd hours to fill.

So I just drove. Drove around Canton. Drove to my favorite hidden places. Drove nowhere in particular—just around.

One of the best parts of driving was being able to listen to music. I'd added an amplifier to the tape deck in my car, which turned the volume inside the vehicle from loud to obscenely loud. I liked it loud enough in the car that I could feel the music rattle against my body, throb inside my sinuses, and pulse in waves along the hair of my arms.

It isn't that I loved what I was listening to as much as I loved the way it made me feel. Listening to music that loud has a way of blocking out your other senses. You start to taste music and smell music. It makes you numb to your emotions and the world around you.

A few nights after the March Violets show I was driving around after work, trying to burn off enough time so that I could go home after my parents had gone to bed. I'd just bought some Burger King and was driving up and down Cleveland Avenue, eating fries and listening to Gang of Four.

As I drove, out of the corner of my eye I noticed a dark flash across my rearview mirror. By the time I focused my gaze, it was gone.

Odd, I thought. Probably a bird flying behind the car or a piece of newspaper in the wind or something. Still, I could feel my heartbeat quicken.

I reached under the dash and clicked off the amplifier. Perhaps it was better to be less numb, I thought, and continued down the road munching on my fries.

About ten minutes later I saw it again. The headlights from the car behind me were suddenly blocked by something.

Before I could even turn my glance toward the mirror, I knew what it was.

It was something in the backseat of the car.

It was Her.

I could feel Her there, leaned forward in the seat, sitting perfectly still. Mouth moving silently, blankly gazing at the back of my head. No sound, just presence.

There was no brief flash this time. I didn't dare look directly into the rearview mirror, but I could see that She was still blocking the headlights. I could feel my chest tighten as confusion turned into panic.

Without stopping the car, I whipped my body around to look.

"What are you waiting for?" I screamed out before I even noticed that the backseat was empty.

No sign of Little Girl. No sign of anything.

"No, no, no!" I yelled, beating my fists against the car seats with every syllable.

I'm shocked at how mercurial my emotions could be back then. Twenty seconds earlier I was complacently eating a French fry. Then I was in a full-blown rage.

I heard a car horn coming toward me, getting louder. I turned back in my seat to face forward and saw two headlights, about forty yards directly in front of me. I'd drifted into the oncoming-traffic lane.

Time seemed to slow. My rage evaporated as quickly as it had risen, leaving me wanting to just shut my eyes to make everything go away. I didn't lift my foot from the accelerator; I just steadied the steering wheel straight ahead.

No one knows whether death may not be the greatest of all blessings for a man.

For a moment I thought I could see the words in front of me, scribbled in my frantic handwriting in the illumination of the headlights. I just wanted everything to stop. I was tired of being alone and confused and overwhelmed and uncertain and out of touch and wishing for things to be better.

But it is clear to me that it was better for me to die now and to escape from trouble.

I shook my head from side to side, making the headlights dance and swirl like the writing in my notebook.

I thought to myself: Let it happen.

I pushed the accelerator down further. I exhaled deeply, letting all my emotions go. For a moment, I felt peaceful.

The horn grew louder. The lights got closer and brighter and then swerved off the side of the road.

I could see the bright brake lights in the rearview mirror as the other car came to a stop.

"You are quite the Humean."

"Pardon me?" I replied.

"Hume. Your essay. Very interesting," said the Instructor, pointing a finger toward the essay blue book he'd just slapped down on my desk.

"Cortez," he called out.

A girl meekly raised her hand.

"Read the book next time," he stage-whispered, slapping a blue book down in front of her.

While he called out to other classmates, I flipped through my blue book. After the first few pages, my legibly written answer seemed to fade in and out, with drawings, arrows, and scribbles in between. After manically writing, then scribbling out the last page and a half, I ended my essay with a quote from the reading, which I had memorized: "I believe that no man ever threw away life while it was worth keeping." The quote was followed by a drawing of a hangman with a happy face.

Below it was written in red, "Provocative. Strong case. B+."

It was the highest grade of my college career.

The Instructor's class was the only one on my schedule that I attended regularly—or pretty much at all—anymore. Even though I knew I was looking at a grade card filled with Incompletes and F's, I still diligently attended the Instructor's course, read all the material, and did all the assignments and tests.

Our midterm was devoted to the second book in class, David Hume's *Dialogues Concerning Natural Religion*. In hindsight, I'm sure the Instructor had assigned us Plato and Hume to help us learn the basics of critical thinking. Socratic method. Scientific method. The world seen through empirical skepticism. Come up with a question or idea, then let your experience be your guide to the truth. However, to me, they started to mean something else entirely.

They were Suicide 101.

I knew I'd stumbled onto something big one night when I was struggling my way through the Hume book. I was really excited that the Instructor planned to cover one 125-page book over a month's time. Then I realized that the work of the Instructor's favorite eighteenth-century Scottish philosopher wasn't exactly a page-turner. I spent three weeks attempting to force myself through the main text, though I eventually skipped ahead to a collection of posthumous essays. Late one night when Laura was busy and there was nothing to do, I drove out to Lake O'Dea on my own and started reading the second essay, "Of Suicide," by the dome light of my car, Public Image's *First Issue* in the cassette deck.

"The superstitious man is miserable in every scene, in every incident of life. Even sleep itself, which banishes all other cares of unhappy mortals, affords to him matter of new terror; while he examines his dreams, and finds in those visions of the night prognostications of future calamities."

I jumped out of the car and started walking toward a streetlight, reading and rereading the passage over and over again, while I felt my stomach sink.

He wrote this about me, I thought.

The dreams. Little Girl. Visions. Everything. Hume was speaking directly to me.

I put the book down just long enough to run back to my car to find a pen and my highlighter, almost as if I had to capture the text immediately or I'd somehow lose it forever. I started to highlight and underline almost everything, turning every page of the essay into a sea of yellow color and bold black strikes.

In the essay, Hume makes the case for providence: that everything happens according to the rules and laws established by God; that these rules govern everything, from the temperature at which water boils to the amount of force you must assert to move a large rock.

Hume then argues that suicide is only a crime if it is a transgression against God, our community, or ourselves, then strips down the case against suicide from each perspective.

I kept reading, highlighting, and scribbling notes as the argument unfolded in front of me.

"Whenever pain or sorrow so far overcome my patience, as to make me tired of life, I may conclude that I am recalled from my station in the clearest and most express terms. Both prudence and courage should engage us to rid ourselves at once of existence, when it becomes a burden."

Basically, Hume was arguing that if your life sucked or you were contemplating suicide, go for it. If you found yourself questioning whether or not you should die, you were, in his eyes, already checked out—or so far gone that there was no point in turning around. Your fate was already cast, game over.

Many years later I learned that Hume did not believe in God, providence, fate, divine intervention, or divine anything. He just liked to mess with the feeble minds of religious folks. To him, the whole essay was a carefully constructed mind fuck. But back then I accepted it as truth. Genius written down more than two hundred years before I was born. Genius meant to guide me.

Shortly after finishing the essay, I drove to a nearby pay phone and called Andre and Todd's room at the Traveler's Inn.

"What the fuck do you want?" Andre bellowed.

"You know those little pills I get from you," I asked.

"Motherfucker, it is two-thirty in the morning!" he yelled. "Can't it wait?"

"No, it can't," I replied. "Do you have any?"

"Sure, I got a couple."

"How many?"

"How the fuck am I supposed to know? Ten, maybe."

"Can you get more?"

"How many more?" Andre asked.

"More," I replied.

"I don't know, probably about thirty. They ain't cheap, though."

"I want more."

"More than thirty? What the fuck do you want that many for?"

"What do you care, Andre. I want more."

"How many more?"

"Fifty."

"Fifty sleeping pills? You know how much that is gonna cost?"

He told me. I immediately consented. Andre told me to stop over tomorrow evening and pick them up.

"And I want cash, motherfucker. Not excuses. Not promises. Cash."

The next day I cashed my paycheck, drew whatever embarrassingly small amount of money I had in my bank accounts, and cashed two bad checks at grocery stores. On the way, I stopped by a thrift store and picked up a beautiful glass vial, just big enough to hold fifty tablets. After stopping by Andre's and enduring his questioning and threats about not trying to sell these at any of his regular hangouts, I drove up to Lake O'Dea. I put all the pills in the vial, screwed on the lid, and placed it on the dashboard. I felt an amazing sense of relief, as complete as the day I smashed the stereo.

This vial was my emergency escape plan.

Part of me was resigned to the idea that the only way I could gain control over my life was to end it. The only way to take back the power of the Little Girl and the darkness surrounding me was to end my existence. Part of me finally felt peace, knowing that when things got really bad, I had a way out.

Of all the emotions I felt, despair wasn't one of them. I had torn apart everything in my life. I knew it. My friends and family knew it. I had turned out to be nothing but a disappointment and a failure. A doped-up, undependable, unpredictable mess who thought he was being followed around by a dead girl he didn't know. Little Girl wasn't my problem; Little Girl was a symptom of my problem.

The real problem was me. The only way to fix it was to get rid of me.

It's obvious to me now that there was a small part of me, a very small part, that didn't want to give up. I could have very easily opened the vial and swallowed all the pills, right then and there. But I didn't. Instead, from then on, every moment became a choice.

For example, Laura and I might have had plans or I would have internal discussions with myself along the lines of, "Yeah, I could kill myself on Tuesday night, but then I'll never know for sure if Greg [one of my fellow WKSC deejays] was right when he argued that Guadalcanal Diary sounded better live than on their record. So maybe I'll wait until the weekend to overdose on pills. But, wait, there will be a new Iron Man comic out the following Tuesday, so maybe I'll wait until after that."

Every time I'd get scared or angry or impatient or someone would start yelling at me for some dipshit thing I'd done, I'd just reach into my coat pocket and brush my fingers against the vial. It was cold. It was real. It was comfort.

It was a choice. My choice: Do it now, or wait awhile longer. A choice I made every time I touched it.

Of course, David Hume would probably have laughed at my little vial of pills and sense of power and control. He'd argue that my fate was already sealed one way or another. All I was doing was acting out the formula. It was only a matter of time. Just as certainly as those pills would cause a chemical reaction in my stomach, I was simply working my way through the stages of a predictable and predestined outline, step by step.

The only thing I could hope for, Hume would say, was an error in the equation. To find something broken and, thus, working against the rules. An exception. A way out.

. . .

I had made a feeble effort to make some new replacement friends by seeking out some of the punk kids that took classes at Kent Stark. I'd long ago given up on making friends with normal people, which was good, because they had about the same level of interest in me. Seeking out the company of people who appeared as odd as—or odder than—me felt more like working at my pay grade. Phil and Ben fit perfectly. Between their total lack of initiative, underwhelming delivery on their potential, and love of beer and punk rock, they were complete fuck-ups. Just my kind of guys.

Most of the time we just sat around the cafeteria talking about bands and bitching about classes. On Thursday nights we'd grab a couple of others and go to the Galaxy Niteclub because they served twenty-five-cent drafts and twenty-five-cent hot dogs. We'd gorge on hot dogs and swill, then roam the dance floor, concealing our contempt for our fellow patrons just enough to keep from getting beaten up. Usually the night would end with us slam dancing out in the parking lot at closing time as the frightened drunks stumbled wide around us to avoid a stray arm or bead of sweat.

One night I was at Ben's for a party when he noticed me staring off into some void in his kitchen. After catching the attention of a few others, he waved his hand in front of my eyes, asking me what I was looking at.

"I hate that motherfucker."

Pause.

"Who are you talking about?"

"Him," I said, pointing at the shelf next to the refrigerator. "Cap'n Crunch.

"I hate that mouth-breathing dumb motherfucker," I said as I walked across the room toward the shelf, picking up the box. "He is basically Mr. Magoo in a sea cap. I always rooted for the Soggies."

"Umm . . . what are the Soggies?" Phil asked.

"From the commercial," I said. "The Soggies. The blobby things on springs?"

Ben and Phil looked at me blankly.

"The fucking Soggies try to ruin the cereal, making it soggy. Then dipshit Cap'n Crunch shows up and scares them away," I said. "I used to root for the Soggies. I'd just look at this ballsucker and wanted to punch him in that big fucking nose."

We all have cringe-inducing moments in our lives, moments that when we think back on them make us shudder. It doesn't matter if it's a week, a year, or a decade later, we can't ever get used to the thought of what we've done. Of all the stupid things I did during this time in my life, this is the one that still makes me cringe. The more I spoke, the more I felt people staring at me, wondering what I was talking about, wondering if I was ever going to make any sense. The more I struggled to connect, the further I reached. Acting this way was my "Hail Mary" play—either I'd finally be able to make a meaningful connection to people, or my behavior would expand the chasm even further.

"Okay," Ben said while looking over at some of the other people gathered in the kitchen.

"You want to know what the problem is?!" I yelled, digging my hand through the top of the unopened box. "This shit . . . this shit that you eat? It looks like fucking macaroni and cheese." I threw a handful of cereal on the kitchen table.

A few people stepped back, somebody groaned, and others

started whispering. They knew what was about to happen. I knew what was about to happen. Nobody could do anything to stop it. It was like some sad, terrible play.

"This shit . . . it isn't food!" I screamed, banging the box against the table. "It is Yellow Number Five!"

I smacked the box against the table again, returning it to my face to read again from the label.

"It is thiamin mononitrate."

With the next smack, cereal started to fly around the kitchen.

"Pyridoxine hydrochloride . . . mmm, sounds delicious!"

Cereal was spraying around the room.

"And reduced iron! What the fuck is reduced iron? And why are you eating this shit?!" I was now flailing the empty box against the tabletop.

"I fucking hate this motherfucker!"

"Man, you need to calm down," Phil said.

I threw the box at his head. He started toward me; two guys put their hands on his shoulder to hold him back.

"I will cut out your fucking heart and eat it in front of you," I said calmly, not moving an inch.

Everyone just stood staring. No one understood the point I was trying to make. I'm not even sure *I* understood the point I was trying to make. I just remember someone gently grabbing my arm and steering me toward the door.

"You should go," I heard someone utter.

The next time Laura and I went to Lake O'Dea I told her about the Cap'n Crunch incident.

"What were you thinking?" Laura yelled at me.

"It didn't mean anything," I replied.

"What do you mean? You threatened him. Not cool."

"I didn't mean it."

"Then why did you do it?"

"What do you care?" I added. "What difference does it make to you what I do?"

"It makes a difference."

"How?" I asked. "You know, I just don't get you."

"What is there to get?"

"I mean, what is going on here?" I asked. "What are we?"

"What do you mean?" she said.

"I mean you and I. This, between us. What is this?"

"I don't follow," she said.

"Our relationship," I answered. "Are we friends . . . or are we more than friends?"

"What difference does that make?"

"Because it does make a difference," I answered.

"It is what it is."

"That isn't good enough," I said. "We hang out together all the time. We talk all the time. Where is this going?"

"I don't understand why it has to *go* anywhere," she said. "Why do you have this sudden need for things to be defined?"

"How come whenever something is important to you, it is important. But when it's important to me, I'm just boxing you in?"

"I didn't say that," she replied. "If you feel the need to define things, you'll ruin them. I mean, aren't you happy? What we have, doesn't that make you happy?"

"Of course I'm happy," I said immediately.

I don't know why I said that. Even then I knew it wasn't true. Or at least it wasn't entirely true. Yes, being with her did make me happy, but my joy being with her was quickly overwhelmed by the emptiness I felt about everything else. My answer at the time was that I just needed more of her.

"You don't need a permission slip to do something or be something," she said. "Stop waiting for it; it isn't coming. Just let it be what it is."

"And what is that?"

"You and me," she said. "Just this moment. Not the moment before, not the moment after."

While we talked I was nervously rolling a lit cigarette around between my fingers, occasionally holding it close to the underside of my forearm.

"What are you doing?" she asked while I was brushing the burning end of the cigarette so close to my arm that you could see its reflection on my skin. "The cigarette," she added.

"Nothing, I'm just—"

She thrust her forearm in front of me. "If you need to burn someone," she said, "burn me."

She reached out and grabbed my hand.

"What?"

"Burn me," she said.

I broke away from her grasp, took the cigarette, and held it about an inch from her skin. I looked up and we stared at each other.

"Do it," she said.

"This is so stupid," I said.

"Burn me. I want you to do it."

We kept matching each other's stare; I could feel her arm tense up and brace for the pain.

"Put it on my arm," she said softly and calmly.

I slowly dipped the cigarette down and ever so briefly and lightly grazed it against her skin.

She grimaced, then exhaled, turning her breath into a quick sigh of disappointment. Then she scrunched up her face.

"No!" she yelled, reaching her hand toward the cigarette. "If you are going to do it, do it like this."

She was pulling at my fingers trying to get the cigarette away from me. I fought back. She pried it from my hand and jabbed it into her arm, twisting as she pushed down. Most of the ember had fallen off when she grabbed the cigarette from me.

"What the fuck are you doing?" I said, brushing bits of broken ember and ash away from her and the car seat. She was fine. A tiny little burn, but nothing like what she was trying for.

"Are you attempting to have some kind of fucking crazy contest with me?" I asked. "Because if you are, you will definitely lose."

"You want answers," she said. "There is your answer."

She was staring out the window.

At the time, I just thought she was in a bad mood or something. But in the years since, I often revisit that night. She was in a lot of pain about . . . something. There was anger in her about . . . something. I didn't—and still don't—have any concrete idea what upset her so much. Perhaps she didn't either. Maybe that was one reason why she was so evasive all the time. Perhaps she just wasn't ready to—or couldn't—face her own darkness. Both of us were obsessed with being different, yet it was obvious that being different caused her a bit of pain as well.

We rode in silence until we got to her house.

No good-night kiss.

I was sitting on the floor against the wall in my parents' dining room.

"I will handle it!" I yelled. "Just let me take care of it."

My parents were sitting in their chairs at the dining table. I drew my legs up to my chest and wrapped my arms around my knees, rocking back and forth. They told me they were concerned. They'd noticed that I'd lost a lot of weight and my appearance and hygiene were getting worse.

I was constantly in motion—looking around, scratching, bobbing my head, moving my tongue—anything to keep from being still. They had no idea how bad things were, nor would they have had any idea what to do if they did.

"And your checking account is overdrawn by two hundred ten dollars," my mother said.

"And a hundred sixty is one check," my dad added. "Why were you writing checks for a hundred sixty dollars if you didn't have the money to cover it?"

In truth, I had cashed checks to buy all those sleeping pills I was carrying around, which then had started a daisy chain of bad checks written to cover old bad checks, and they just piled up.

The week before I'd received a postcard from the R.E.M. fan club informing me of a string of tour dates through the Midwest. A few days after that I woke up and impulsively decided that I was going to attend as many as I could. I'd told no one, including Laura, that I was leaving. I hadn't made any arrangements to be gone from work. By then I really didn't attend classes anymore. When I took off for the shows and no one knew where I was for days, everyone feared the worst.

I didn't care. I tried convincing myself that I was having the time of my life. In truth, I knew what I was doing, but that just caused my sense of failure and doom to feed upon itself. I was a fuck-up who was in the midst of fucking up, plain and simple. It felt as natural as breathing.

When I got home, I was honestly surprised that my parents were so upset with me or, frankly, had even noticed that I was gone. It wasn't like we were really seeking out one another's company much those days.

"On days when I get the mail, there's always a returned check notice in there," my father added. "And I know most days you are getting to the mail before we are."

"There aren't any more bad checks; those were the only ones," I quickly offered, hoping the lie would stick.

"Eric, I can't believe you," said my dad, waving his hand across the bank statement he'd opened in that morning's mail. "We don't know where you are. You disappear or come in at all hours."

"I work. I have school."

"I don't think Kent has classes at one A.M.," he said.

"You didn't answer the question," my mother said. "Where is this money going?"

"I wrote bad checks to get money to buy pills."

It spilled out of my mouth before I realized what I'd said. Everyone in my life knew that some bad things were going on, but no one, especially my parents, was allowed to see enough to know how fucked up things had become. I told them lies about my great progress in school. I told them about studying and working on class projects with classmates. I told them about working extra at T.J. Maxx. None of it was true. But this time I had told the truth.

My jacket was thrown over the chair in the corner. The vial was in the pocket. I wanted to run over there and shove the whole vial, still capped, down my throat.

"There was this guy I know," I added quickly, not ready for any more truth just then. "He had a bag of pills. He told me he was going to sell them at high school basketball games." I began to tear up. The tears were convenient but real.

"I just couldn't let him do it," I cried out. "I had to stop him. So I got out my own money and bought them all."

"What did you do with them?" my mother asked.

"I flushed them!" I exclaimed.

"Bullshit," my father said. "You bought them for yourself. This needs to be made right, and fast. If you plan to stay in this house, you need to get straightened out. What are you going to do about all this?"

"I don't know!" I yelled, standing up to face him across the table.

"I asked a question!" he yelled back. "What are you going to do?"

"I have no fucking clue! Maybe I'll just die and stop embarrassing you!" I screamed.

"Are you on drugs right now?" my dad asked.

I looked over at the jacket again. My dad seemed to notice my gaze. I jumped across the table and swooped it off the chair. I started to put it on and headed for the back door.

"Eric, come back here!" my mother called out. "Eric, we need to finish talking about this. Eric!" I heard her yell as I headed down the driveway to my car.

Picnic table. Path. Little Girl in a Blue Dress. Wet. Mumbling. Shaking her head. Screaming gibberish.

I wake up. I hear a bump through the wall.

It's Her.

Earlier that evening I'd quietly snuck into the house after my family were all asleep. Following the dream, I spent the rest of the night trying to calm down after feeling Little Girl. I just sat in my bed and listened for more noises.

I heard the other members of my family get up and start their day. NPR on the radio downstairs. Showers running. One by one they all headed out to their normal lives. The house seemed silent.

Just as I was about to get up, I could sense something standing between my bed and the window.

I opened my eyes and saw my brother, Michael, standing over me. He was holding my old typewriter over his head. As soon as he saw my eyes were open, he threw the typewriter toward my head.

I raised my hands just in time to push the typewriter out of the way and jumped up out of the bed as it crashed to the bedroom floor.

"What the fuck was that about, you fucking troll?" I screamed.

Michael ran out of the room into the hallway and turned back, half hiding behind the door frame.

"You are destroying our family," he said before dashing down the stairs. "Why don't you just go away!"

A few years ago I was visiting my parents and decided to pull out some of our dozens of photo albums from growing up. If nothing else, my family was excellent at documenting everything in photographs: every birthday party, Halloween costume, family trip, home-renovation project, and special occasion. But after I got to the few photos I'd allowed to be taken at my high school graduation, I saw there was not another family photo until Christmas a year and a half later. Given my resistance to being photographed, it would make sense that there were none of me. But there were none, period. Of anyone. Of any event. Nothing, for eighteen months. It's clear now that my problems weren't just hard on me.

I hurried downstairs and got into my car as my brother ran past me on his way to school. I needed to get to Kent Stark that morning to try to beg my way into taking an exam I'd missed two days earlier, for a class that I hadn't attended in three weeks.

I pulled down the driveway and stopped at the bottom to switch gears, but then I just sat there in the car and stared at the pavement in front of me.

I didn't want to go. It wasn't worth the effort to maintain the façade anymore. I was getting close to done.

Without really putting much more thought into it, I put the car in drive, straightened the wheel toward the house, gunned the gas pedal, and tensed my arms as I felt the car lurch forward.

NOW

"You get anything?" a sweaty, lanky guy asks us while momentarily looking up from the display of his camera.

He is so excited he's almost out of breath. He doesn't even wait for our answer before running behind another boulder and taking another picture. In the dimness of our flashlight, I can see him look at his display, shake his head, then start to head off in a different direction.

The hillside is pitch-black, yet we can hear voices coming from almost every direction, accompanied by random flashes of light.

The Gettysburg National Military Park closes at 10 P.M. In mid-July the sun sets at 8:19 P.M. That leaves a little less than two hours of darkness for hundreds of terrified tourists to roam around the park's six thousand acres looking for ghosts.

The ghost-hunting weapon of choice: digital cameras. Tourists climb rocks, slink through woods, and slowly creep down paths clicking picture after picture, hoping to capture some of the ectoplasm, mist, and strange apparitions thought to be as common as Civil War–era bullet fragments. Stand on any high point between dusk and closing time, and the battle-field glows with microbursts of light.

"I got an orb! I got an orb!" someone screams.

You didn't get an orb, I want to tell him. You got a dust ball.

Devil's Den, the boulder-covered hillside near the southern end of the battlefield, is thought to be among the most haunted spots in the entire park. My friend Meghan and I show up at a little past dark to search for ghosts. It seems that well over a hundred other Gettysburg visitors have the exact same idea, though they treat their ghost hunting like it's a ride at the county fair. Everyone seems to be running about screaming, giggling, and snapping pictures, while still being scared of what lies around the next corner. Chances are, it's a sunburned and bloated vacationer from Iowa looking for a ghost, too.

Shortly after arriving, Meghan wondered out loud how long we'd be walking around Devil's Den before we came across someone with a bald eagle or American flag tattooed on some exposed area of the body.

Answer: four minutes.

And both tattoos were on the same dude.

I'm not entirely sure why Meghan joined me on my trip to what many people believe is the most haunted place in the entire country, but I have two theories. First, she's married to Joe, who accompanied me on my trip to Clinton Road. So if Joe got to go on a ghost-hunting trip, she should too, she probably thought. Second, Meghan lived in nearby Hanover for several years. As a result, she knows her way around Gettysburg fairly well and has hung around the battlefield, at night, on numerous occasions.

It's here at Devil's Den where Meghan herself had an experience that she couldn't explain.

"My friend Brian was coming through town on a road trip from New York to Texas," she says. "He's a huge history buff, so we came out here on our way to get beers and pizza in Gettysburg. We were walking up through Devil's Den, and this huge fireball flew right in front of me."

It was a ten-inch ball of light, a few feet away. It just whipped by, then, just as suddenly, disappeared. By the time she realized it was happening, it was over. She's come back many times since but has never seen anything else like it, nor does she have any idea what she saw that night.

Meghan isn't the only one. Hundreds of people report seeing weird stuff such as strangers standing among the rocks, then suddenly disappearing. There are stories of whispering voices, gunshots, and the reported sense of being watched.

In fact, there are literally thousands of ghost stories connected to Gettysburg. Most of these, of course, stem from the 51,000 men who were killed or wounded over the three-day battle in and around Gettysburg in July 1863. At the end of the campaign, more than 8,000 bodies littered the battlefield; many were so hastily buried in shallow graves that rain left exposed arms, legs, and heads popping up out of the ground. This ghoulishness bred ghost lore like mosquitoes in an old tire.

There is one person at Devil's Den who isn't freaking out at the idea of finding a ghost here: me. Before visiting Clinton Road and Lily Dale, I was unable to sleep for days. During the visits themselves, I was constantly on pins and needles. However, this time, it just feels like something to do. It isn't like I had some epiphany or breakthrough, or that I'm not still scared of ghosts in general. But when I see all the tourists jumping around Devil's Den, I just suddenly realize that I'm not experiencing any of the excitement and nervousness and adrenaline that I see in them.

There's precious little in Gettysburg that doesn't center on the tourism industry. At most summer tourist destinations, evenings are spent playing mini-golf, eating ice cream, and watching movies. Not so in Gettysburg. At night, the streets of downtown Gettysburg swarm with ghost tours. The ghost business is big business in Gettysburg.

Walking down Baltimore Street, you quickly realize that ghost tours are to Gettysburg what casinos are to Las Vegas. There are fourteen companies offering ghost tours in and around the city itself and the battlefield. Since most companies offer multiple variations, on any given night you can take your pick of several dozen tours. There are walking tours, home tours, battlefield tours, bus tours, hospital tours, theater presentations, and even ghost tours on horseback and Segway scooters. It seems like just about any building that was standing in the mid-nineteenth century has an accompanying ghost story and can be toured at night for ten dollars.

In addition, more than twenty local hotels and B-and-Bs claim to have spirits-in-residence. One major modern hotel chain claims to be haunted, saying that guests hear ethereal cannon fire from their beds. However, given the target demographic for said hotel chain, the spooky booms are more than likely from an errant Molotov cocktail or a traveling meth lab set up in room 218.

But it wasn't always this way. In fact, not that many people really associated Gettysburg and ghosts until the early 1990s. The man largely responsible for all this is Mark Nesbitt. Mark was a Ranger Historian for the National Park Service at Gettysburg in the 1970s before embarking on a career as an author, with most of his work related to Gettysburg. In 1991 he published a book of ghost stories he'd collected called *Ghosts of Gettysburg*. It was a smash hit. Mark went on to author nine more books of ghost stories and ghost-hunting exploits (including five more *Ghosts of Gettysburg* volumes), as well as several other novels and nonfiction books—almost all related to Gettysburg.

After the initial success of *Ghosts of Gettysburg*, the borough of Gettysburg was soon brainstorming ways to attract tourists downtown once they came to visit the battlefield. They asked Mark if he'd be interested in creating a tour of downtown locations mentioned in his collected ghost stories. Mark hosted his first Gettysburg ghost walk in June of 1994. By that fall, he was running tours seven nights a week. In 1997 he bought a building downtown to serve as his home, office, and retail store for his books and tours. Later that year, another guy in Gettysburg decided to offer a competing tour. And, as Mark says, things just exploded from there.

The competition hasn't hurt Mark's business. On most nights, he runs six different tours. He has expanded his tours to Fredericksburg and Charlottesville as well. He offers ghost-hunting weekends at haunted bed-and-breakfasts, as well as private tours and investigations. He even sponsors a ghost-themed cruise.

"Everyone who comes to Gettysburg will tell you, it has a special . . . feeling," he says as we sit talking in the back room of his house, which he claims—wait for it—is haunted. "I liken it to walking into a church. A church is just a building, but yet you get a special feeling when you go in there. You know, you go out to Pickett's Charge, and you just get this . . . a friend of mine said, 'It's like the great crush of souls' that you feel here. I don't know what another explanation could be, except that they're still here, all those people. The ones who survived, we know they came back to visit. Why wouldn't the dead?"

"So let's just say that a person is visiting Gettysburg," I say. "And let's say this person found all this a little overwhelming.

And let's say he doesn't have a big issue with trespassing or being places you aren't supposed to be—theoretically, of course. And let's say that this person is very scared of ghosts, and if he is going to go through the self-torture of looking for ghosts, this person doesn't want to waste his time. If this person were to go to one place in Gettysburg to have an experience, where would you tell this person to go?"

"To experience a ghost?" Mark asks. "The place that most consistently produces experiences is the Devil's Den and Triangular Field area," he says. "I've had more weird things happen there than just about anyplace."

A few hours later, Meghan and I are dodging tattooed tourists with digital cameras trudging through Devil's Den on our way to Triangular Field—and the clock is ticking.

"We need to be really careful about not getting caught in the battlefield after hours," Meghan says, referring to the National Park Service's unambiguous prohibition of after-hours lurking. "They patrol it pretty thoroughly."

"Who patrols it?" I ask. "Park rangers?"

"No, self-righteous reenactors and Civil War nerds."

Gettysburg is, of course, the Mecca of Civil War battlefields. I guess it shouldn't be surprising that the die-hard reenactors are pretty protective of it.

"Wait a minute," I say. "If the battlefield is supposed to be haunted by the spirits of thousands of Civil War soldiers . . . and the battlefield is filled with thousands of reenactors dressed like Civil War soldiers, how can we tell who's a ghost and who's a reenactor?"

Meghan pauses to consider this.

"The smell," she answers.

The large open field adjacent to Devil's Den, Triangular Field, is the mother lode of Gettysburg ghost sightings. There are entire websites that just collect pictures taken on the field. Strange things are routinely encountered here: "rebel yells" heard when no one is around, peculiar depressions seen in the grass as you walk by, the moans of dying soldiers, and the smell of gunpowder.

As we shortcut down some deer paths, looking for the main trail, we do what everybody does: take photos. Despite the number of ghost photos taken there, an often-told piece of Triangular Field lore is that cameras and video equipment often jam or stop working. If by "not working" you mean "not capturing any ghost images," I'd have to agree it's true. Our photos contain rocks, grass, and darkness. The same rocks, grass, and darkness seen on the Triangular Field websites, minus the ethereal fog, forms, and apparitions. Though before I leave his house, Mark does warn me against expecting too much from my eyes. He says we need to pay attention to our other senses.

"Of all the ghost experiences we document out there, you know, only about ten percent of them are visual. Auditory, now that's about sixty percent. You hear a lot out in that field. In fact, you can experience ghosts with just about all your senses," he says, then pauses. "Except taste. I've never had anyone tell me they could taste a ghost."

As we slog through the valley, the Ghost Meter in my left hand periodically jumps to life, beeping and lighting up. The Ghost Meter was a Christmas gift from Meghan and Joe. It's basically an EMF meter, a simple electrician's tool used by thousands of other ghost enthusiasts, who claim that dead spirits emit a low amount of electromagnetic radiation, which registers on the meter. The Ghost Meter adds a certain flair to the process; it's housed in a casing made of clear and orange plastic that looks like it was designed by Apple Computer in 1997. I tested it around the house before bringing it "out in the field," as those in the field might say. According to the Ghost Meter, the radio in my dining room and my KitchenAid mixer either are haunted or produce a significant amount of electromagnetic output. Whenever it gets a signal that moves the meter at least halfway, orange lights start blinking on top and it starts to beep. My excitement over the intermittent beeping and lights ceases when I realize that it's registering a signal every time it comes within a few inches of my cell phone. It doesn't occur to me until later that I'm not terribly concerned at the time that my cell is emitting enough radiation—four inches from my testicles—to set off the Ghost Meter. Every time it happens, Meghan jumps, looks around, and then yells at me to hold the Ghost Meter in my other hand.

As I snap pictures in the moonless dark of Triangular Field, I periodically catch Meghan in my pictures and notice the look on her face. It isn't quite fear, but there is a growing amount of concern on her face as we walk deeper into the fields and woods, farther away from the picture-taking tourists who seem content keeping close to the road and trailhead.

As we go deeper into the field, our photos still contain nothing significant at all, except dust balls. Oh, excuse me, I mean orbs. Orbs are little balls of opaque light that show up in photographs. According to paranormal investigators, orbs are spirit forms floating around unseen by the naked eye but capturable by a camera.

Ghost hunters will always say there is "quite a bit of controversy" surrounding orbs, but the "orbs controversy" is about the least controversial controversy I've ever encountered. I could not find anyone who actually takes the "pro-orb" folks seriously, except the pro-orb contingency themselves. It's pretty cut-and-dry bullshit.

Because of the cheap and fairly low resolution of most digital cameras, orbs are common in digital pictures. That is, until the photographer cleans the lens. If you are in a location with a lot of dust in the air (like most supposedly haunted locations), you spot a lot of orbs. Also, when you leave your camera on and the lens exposed for long periods (like, for example, when you're on a ghost hunt), you get a lot of orbs.

Some orb catchers will show blown-up pictures of orbs, pointing out facial features in the pixelation. I could take a close-up of a freckle on my arm, blow it up, and put up at least a half-convincing case that you could see in it the features of Chairman Mao. You see what you want to see.

Walking through the field, I start to think about the people who take all these ghost pictures, passing them along to the Triangular Field websites. Are they fooled by what they see? Are they looking for something, and do they keep looking until they find something that fits what they're seeking? Are they looking for acceptance and attention by faking it? I mean, half those ethereal-fog photos could be early-morning mist or stray cigarette smoke.

We pass through downtown Gettysburg once more on our way out to another hot spot Mark Nesbitt suggested, Pickett's Charge. He said it's easy to find—just follow the road until we get to a restaurant called General Pickett's Buffets (that's not a typo, FYI—supposedly having a salad bar *and* a hot-food bar qualifies it for the plural status); the battlefield is just south of the restaurant. As we drive through town, Meghan offers her own narration of Gettysburg history.

"Yeah, I went to a wedding reception over here and got terribly drunk," she says, pointing to some old-looking building near the town square.

"Oh, Jesus, I used to go out there all the time!" she exclaims as we pass another building.

It's very clear to me that Meghan sees Gettysburg very differently than I do. She sees ghosts everywhere, just ones that have nothing to do with the Civil War.

We drop the car and walk to the fence surrounding Pickett's Charge. We stand there for a long time, take a few pictures of the tall grass and blackness, watch the Ghost Meter register nothing, and just stare out into the void.

People claim to witness entire ghost infantry units marching across Pickett's Charge, see ethereal campfires, and hear orders shouted. I'd settle for one spectral rifleman, lost and asking us for directions, but I get nothing. We see nothing, hear nothing, smell nothing, feel nothing. We definitely don't taste anything, either. I don't feel the "great crush of souls"— all I feel is the great crush of boredom and the great suck of mosquitoes.

It's really late when Meghan and I come in and make our way to our rooms at the bed-and-breakfast. No one else in the entire building is up, and the restaurant is long closed. All of a sudden we hear a chirping beep.

I look down and see an orange light glowing through my shorts. It's the Ghost Meter in my front pocket, and it's going ape shit.

It stops almost as soon as I pull it out, so I slowly wave it around the room. Whenever it comes in proximity of a particular armchair in the hallway, it beeps and lights up, and the needle slams to the far right. I pull it away from the chair and it goes silent. I put it back down and move it around the area where someone might be sitting, and it goes full tilt again, staying there until I pull it away. I look behind the chair, thinking there might be a poorly grounded outlet in the wall or something electrical behind it. Nothing. In fact when I run the Ghost Meter right up against the wall, it is totally still. It's the chair that's setting it off, or more specifically, something sitting in the chair.

"Oh, shit," Meghan says. "I don't like this one bit."

I try in front of the spa entrance—no signal. In front of my room door—no signal. But whenever it's pointed at the seat and back of the chair, the meter is slammed to the right and beeping and flashing like crazy.

"Look at it this way," I say. "That chair is out in the hall. It's, like, all the way out here, and, well, you know, you're safe."

I offer my best attempt at a reassuring smile.

As soon as I get near the doorway to Meghan's room, the Ghost Meter starts going nuts again. With her standing just inside her room and me standing just outside the threshold, I wave the Ghost Meter around her entire doorway. It goes totally nuts. I have to admit that even though I've gotten a little used to being in "haunted" places lately, I'm starting to feel some adrenaline take up residence in the pit of my stomach. I quickly stuff the Ghost Meter back into my pocket, hoping that might make us feel better or perhaps forget that it even went off at all. No such luck. Meghan and I just stand there for a minute, unsure what to do.

I turn to look at Meghan, who is staring at me with her nostrils flared.

"Thanks, jerk," she says.

"Have a nice night," I say, reaching into my pocket to shut off the still-beeping Ghost Meter, and head next door to my room.

"Fuck off," she says, closing the door.

THEN

"Would you like a stool softener?" the orderly asked me.

"What is that?" I asked.

"It's a stool softener," he replied. "It softens your stool. Would you like one?"

"Will it fuck me up?" I asked.

"More than likely not," he replied.

After giving me my paper cup of pills, the orderly looked up at the wall and sighed.

On a piece of paper taped above my bed: ERIC NUZUM IS A VICTIM OF MATHEMATICAL ERROR.

"I'm going to turn this in to the head nurse," he said, pulling it down. "You know, when they ask you to stop doing this, you really should listen. They'll put this in your Progress Plan, you know."

I did know.

The ward staff seemed very tired of me and my signs. I'd write them on the back of some form or report, steal tape from the nurses' station, and hang them above my bed.

After putting up signs reading QUESTION EVERYTHING, GO AWAY, and ANARCHY IN THE 5B, I was warned that putting up signs above my bed was not acceptable. When I asked why, I was given the same excuse I heard for everything, from walking around with my bathrobe over my regular clothes to playing the piano during breakfast: It will cause a disturbance among the patients.

There was already *plenty* of disturbance among the patients, I'd argue. My signs weren't going to make any difference.

After the nurses and therapists started to frown on me posting these signs in my room, I started branching out into the ward itself. Signs started to appear above the TV (DON'T LOOK UP!!!), on the back of the couches (THE PUDDING IN THIS PLACE TASTES LIKE DOG SHIT. HMMMM. WONDER WHY?), and elsewhere. After putting up EAT ME in glued macaroni (my first occupational-therapy project), I was warned that one more sign would result in having the issue of sign making added to my Progress Plan: the list of "goals" (read: requirements) that needed to be achieved in order to get out of here.

ERIC NUZUM IS A VICTIM OF MATHEMATICAL ERROR wasn't the first sign I'd made since receiving my final warning. It was the fifth.

I was begging them, taunting them in fact, to whip out the Progress Plan and add the sign making to my list of goals.

The Progress Plan was one of the many euphemism-laden forms, charts, and outlines that the staff dutifully filled out to document my daily routine, goals, and activities. My Progress Plan contained four items:

• Patient will not harm self on unit.

• Patient will report hope for the future.

• Patient will identify three alternate coping mechanisms.

• Patient will problem-solve re: stressors.

On my second day in ward 5B at Timken Mercy Medical Center, a nurse presented me with my Progress Plan and asked that I sign it. I just couldn't bring myself to do it. I kept thinking, if I sign this, what am I admitting about myself? That what they were saying was right? That I believed that being here would make any difference in my life?

Every doctor, nurse, and social worker repeated the same explanation: I wasn't going anywhere until we agreed on a Progress Plan and fulfilled every single item. I explained that while it was very kind of them to put together a Progress Plan, this was all a mistake and that I wanted to leave. They explained that when I was admitted, I'd signed away my ability to make that decision until my doctor had determined that I was no longer a threat to myself and others. I explained that I was fucked out of my gourd when I was admitted here. They produced a statement signed by two witnesses (both hospital staff) attesting to my lucidity and recognition that I understood all the paperwork and was made aware of my rights. I'd explain that they could fuck off.

It didn't go well from there.

At that point, I'd been in 5B, the "high observation" ward (another euphemistic title for a level of care and oversight that was just a small step up from a straitjacket and padded room) for five days. I still had only a sketchy idea of the circumstances involved in how I got here. The morning I was admitted, I had driven my car up my parents' driveway, scraping against the house a few times before coming to a stop. Damage to the house was incredibly minor, a small scratch mark, one chipped chimney brick, and a corner taken out of a limestone stair in the back. However, the process had torn the front driver's-side wheel from my car and chewed up the surrounding body panels. Supposedly, I then tried to drive the car back down the driveway. I got about ten yards in two or three tries, dragging along on the broken axle, before I passed out in the car. Somebody called my mother at work, who came home and announced that we were going to the emergency room. I told the admitting nurse that I'd been carrying around a vial of sleeping pills with the idea that I'd use them to kill myself. I talked with a couple other staff people and was presented with papers to voluntarily commit myself.

The information was sketchy because no one seemed to want to tell me what had happened. Outside of hitting the gas pedal in my parents' driveway, I remembered exactly none of this and very little of the preceding days. I just knew I was in a mental ward of a hospital, which, for the most part (minus the chocolate pudding and gelatinous fried chicken), had exceptionally tasty food.

The doctors and staff were pretty flummoxed about my complete lack of withdrawal and DTs after being in the hospital for five days, consuming nothing stronger than unsweetened iced tea. Shortly after I was admitted, they sent a social worker to inventory the alcohol and substances I had taken in the seven days prior to my admittance. At first, the social worker looked a little perturbed.

"Look, I've heard about you," he said. "You need to cut it out and give me the actual list."

The numbers were so high he thought I was making it all up. Just to be difficult. To be fair to him, I did do that kind of stuff, but this time I wasn't.

Looking at it now, I believe there are two very clear, rational reasons why I was having no withdrawal or cravings.

First, I was not an addict. By now, it's kind of an addict cliché for said addict to declare, "I can stop whenever I want."

However, I actually could stop whenever I wanted, and I did. I never felt the physical need to drink or take drugs. It was an emotional need. There were times when drugs felt like an answer. They felt like a way out or a method to dull my senses into a blissful void of nothing. My world would somehow darken or Little Girl would show up, and I'd scramble to find a way to cope. Coping usually involved a mixture of substances—a cocktail of inebriation—that would make it all better, if only for a little while, until it didn't anymore. Then I'd stop again. I'd kind of lose my taste for it. I'm not saying that I wasn't abusive—with drugs, alcohol, or other things— just that I wasn't addicted. Drugs were never the problem in my life; they were a symptom.

All this considered, take it from me, if you are ever in a circumstance where you are being evaluated for possible substance abuse, *the last thing* you want to tell them is that you aren't an addict. As soon as you try to explain all this and those words—"I am not an addict"—come out of your mouth, opinions are sealed and there is absolutely nothing you can do or say that will convince anyone that you are actually, in fact, not addicted to any substance. I would tell them, over and over again, that I was not an alcohol and/or drug addict and could, really, honestly, stop using whenever I felt like it. They would slowly nod, pat my hand, and tell me they would be ready to talk when I was ready to confront my problems. I'd exclaim that I wasn't being difficult, but that I really, double-swear, was not an addict. They'd offer me some blandly affirming gesture and tell me they were there for me. I'd tell them to eat my ass. They'd decline.

Second reason I didn't suffer for lack of drugs once I was admitted to the hospital: I was high all the time. Three times a day an orderly would show up with a tray of paper cups. At every one of these pill feedings, I would be given, at minimum, four to six pills to take.

"The doctor just wants to determine the right combination of medications to help you."

A lot of the time I felt like a zombie, stumbling around the ward trying not to slip and fall in my own drool trail. I'd have the spins so bad that sometimes I couldn't even contemplate going to sleep at night. I needed to sit upright in a chair, or I'd be throwing up for hours. The staff would tell me to lie down in my bed. I'd tell them I couldn't, that I'd get sick. They'd shake their heads. They'd heard about me: uncooperative. Three times a day an orderly showed up, each time pumping me full of new drugs or new combinations of drugs. Each day I just seemed to get more fucked up than before.

I spent a lot of time asleep or watching television. There were no Little Girl dreams.

The fact that I had no Little Girl dreams once I entered Timken Mercy was odd to me but not nearly as odd as the reason I was given as to why I had nothing to fear while staying there. Shortly after I was admitted, I had told a nurse that the reason I couldn't sleep was because there was a dead girl who would find me there. The nurse reassured me it would be okay.

"These walls and windows?" she said, standing up to run her hand along the plaster. "Ghostproof. No ghost can enter. You are safe."

"Ghostproof?" I asked.

"Sweetie, I've worked here for twelve years; no one comes in or out of here without me saying so." She gave me a reassuring smile.

The one good thing that I saw Timken Mercy providing me

at that point was a break—a break from school and people . . .
and even from Her. I was so desperate to believe that She could
not bother me there that I was willing to accept the nurse's
claim of ghostproofing as reasonable. I really didn't want to
apply too much scrutiny. She wasn't there; that's all I cared
about.

When I wasn't being grilled by doctors, therapists, and social workers, or trying (and failing) to sleep, or swallowing
dozens of pills, I basically spent most of my time roaming
around the ward.

If you weren't suicidal when you arrived in ward 5B at Timken Mercy, a few hours there would definitely get you in the
right mood.

Besides the fact that it was geared toward containment,
there were two terms that described everything in 5B: flame-
proof and stain-resistant. Since it was a psych ward, patients
would do just about every imaginable thing (and then some
unimaginable) with just about every imaginable bodily fluid
and discharge. Therefore, there was a lot of mopping and wip-
ing going on. This required furniture, drapes, floor coverings,
and upholstery that were up to the task. Everything that wasn't
was contained in a Plexiglas box, and that included the television.

For many of the same reasons, the staff of 5B were under-
standably concerned with fire. Every surface was coated in
some kind of flame-retardant goo that left it feeling like slick
plastic. Even the curtains in the dayroom felt like they were
made out of shredded garbage bags. Considering this, it was
odd that they let us smoke. In fact, it was almost like they *en-
couraged* us to smoke. I think several patients who had never
smoked before entering the hospital became chain-smokers

while there. Smoking seemed such a core component of patient care that if residents of 5B wanted to smoke six cigarettes at a time from breakfast until lights-out, the staff seemed happy to let them do it.

Smoking also highlighted the most unusual feature of ward 5B: the wall lighter. If you had a bunch of disjointed folks with questionable compulsions, you certainly weren't going to let them carry around matches or lighters. But the staff had plenty of other things to do than light cigarettes all day. So they came up with what was, frankly, a genius solution: Install an electric coil, like a car lighter, in the wall. You'd walk up to this thing, about an inch around, and press a small button underneath. In five seconds or so, it would start to glow red. There was a small wire mesh cage surrounding it, so it would be impossible to wedge anything other than a cigarette in there. Well, one time I did see a dude stick a pencil in and try to light it on fire, but pencils were contraband to begin with, so, oddly, the staff seemed much more concerned with how he had gotten a pencil than with the fact that he had intended to light it (and perhaps the entire ward) on fire.

Many everyday items were strictly forbidden: For example, we couldn't keep plastic or Styrofoam in our room (the staff feared we'd try to burn it in order to inhale the toxic fumes). Food came precut, and patients were only allowed to eat with spoons. If you wished to shower or shave (and, frankly, few 5B residents seemed particularly concerned about either), you had to have an orderly in the bathroom with you. The staff viewed just about anything not permanently attached to our bodies as potentially dangerous and a candidate for contraband status. This seemed so odd to me. Here was a collection of people who couldn't cope with anything or function in the everyday world. Yet at any moment, the staff believed, we could turn into MacGyver-like evil geniuses able to do immeasurable harm to ourselves and others when left alone with some dental floss, a can of Coke, or a transistor radio.

Thankfully we were allowed to use the toilet unsupervised. If they were so concerned with what I might do with a fork, it was astonishing that they would leave me and my creative 5B brethren alone to drown ourselves in a toilet tank or do God knows what with some fresh feces.

My 5B brothers and sisters were an assortment. of life's walking wounded: failed suicides, alcoholics and chronic substance abusers, crying depressives, head-trauma cases, people caught in the tail end of a massive meltdown, burnouts, and a few who seemed on the verge of being completely and forever checked out. This was before rehab, stigma-free therapy, and Prozac. At that time, they'd simply sedate you into submission and cross their fingers in the hope that you'd work your shit out with endless therapy sessions.

I was one of the youngest patients. There was another kid my age, a really thin boy named Harold. He seemed to be very upset and didn't leave his room much for the first few days. The only time I'd seen him out of his room, he was yelling that he was the son of God and begging for everyone to look at his stigmata.

Besides Harold/Jesus (actually, he was one of two Jesuses on 5B), there were about two dozen other patients. I befriended a few, like Stan, who had purple skin when he first arrived (which turned yellow within a day or so). Also Richie, who seemed normal until he got nervous, and then he'd start to tic with increasing frequency until he stood rubbing his hands together and singing Bob Seger songs. I'd heard that before he came here, Richie was found living in a home with six dogs and no heat or electricity. For the first few days I was there, whenever I tried to talk to him, he'd suddenly pretend to be asleep. I had better luck with my roommate, Silas. Silas was a large middle-aged black man who always seemed happy and was always complimenting the patients and staff, always had a kind word for someone who seemed upset. Silas seemed so normal that you could easily mistake him for one of the staff. In fact, for the entire time we were there together, I never garnered a single clue as to what Silas was doing in a mental ward.

The one thing all us folks had in common: This was where we had crash-landed. This was where our friends and relatives brought us when they couldn't deal with us anymore. This was a place for the broken, those who had completely worn out their welcome, tested patience, and seen wit's end. This is where we ended up when there were no other options. All the residents of 5B wore their pasts on their sleeves, as if they were caught up or frozen in some part of their own history. But once we were here, our pasts, which we held on to so closely, were done with us. As we stewed in 5B, our lives were moving on. We were put here, left behind, as part of cleaning up the mess we'd created.

I remember being escorted into Dr. Blumfield's office. I was told he was my psychotherapist, not to be confused with Dr. Chang, my admitting psychiatrist; Kay, my social worker and substance abuse counselor; or Jo, who coordinated my "multidisciplinary treatment plan," whatever the hell that meant.

"Hi, Eric," he said. "Good to see you again."

"Have we met?" I replied.

"Ah, yes," Blumfield said, flipping through my chart. "We talked for an hour the day after you were admitted."

I plopped down in the chair across from his desk.

"I may have been talking, but I wasn't there."

Blumfield smiled and nodded.

He had a rumpled, pasty, aristocratic look to him—a little weak, a little professorial, and a little like you'd expect him to be wearing an ascot and announce he was late for the opera. He had a thin beard and frameless glasses, kind of hip for a therapist, but not that hip. While we spoke he often ran his fingers over the seams of a beautiful silver cigarette case, which, I'd later learn, contained generic menthol cigarettes.

"Are you telling me that you don't recall our conversation?"

"I'm telling you that you may have very well had a conversation, but I have no idea who you were talking to or what was said."

"Hmmm," Blumfield said, starting to take notes. "We seemed to have a pretty lucid conversation, Eric," he said. "You revealed quite a bit in the assessment."

"Assessment?" I replied. "If you were making judgments based off what you heard the other day, then you definitely need to throw those out."

"How about we start fresh, then?" Blumfield pulled out a copy of my Progress Plan and placed it on the table.

"Jo says that you are refusing to sign this," he said.

In truth, I'd wadded up the Progress Plan and told Jo to go fuck herself.

My problem with the Progress Plan was that it didn't feel like progress at all. Reading it felt like admitting defeat. It wasn't about getting any better; it was about doing what I was told. Not causing problems. Being manageable.

"What are stressors?" I asked.

"Well, your Little Girl is one," Blumfield replied.

"I told you about Her?"

Not only had I discussed Little Girl, I'd also told him that I had just moved back from New York City, where I'd tried unsuccessfully to start a band. (Not true.) I'd said that I had a vial of little blue sleeping pills that I had been carrying around in my pocket for two months. (True.) I'd told him that I planned to slip some of the pills into a stranger's drink before I killed myself. (Not true.)

After hearing all this, I reminded him that I was so fucked up when I arrived that I would have consented to blow a donkey.

Blumfield was unmoved by this. He told me that I had discussed and consented to the goals when I'd first arrived.

"Eric, I'm afraid you've constructed a world where there are no rules you want to play by, where there is no accountability," he said. "Part of moving beyond that is to stick to your word. You agreed to these goals; now I need you to sign the form and let's get started."

"If I was so agreeable before," I said, "why didn't you just have me sign it then?"

"Well," Blumfield stumbled. "You were . . . um . . . you nodded off before you could sign it." He smiled softly. "Do you remember me discussing the basic deal here with you?"

"Just to remind you, I don't even remember meeting you," I replied.

"Basically, we have fourteen days," he said. "We can keep you here that long based on the consent form you signed when you were admitted. We can usually eke out a few more days without much of a problem. You can't walk off this ward without our permission. In fact, you can't even leave your bed without our permission if that becomes necessary. If you have not seen improvement by the end of the fourteen days, we can petition a judge to commit you to a longer-term care facility. Is that what you want?"

"Is that what you all think should happen?" I asked.

"Eric, that doesn't matter," he said. "What I want—what we all want here—is for you to get the help you need. I feel very confident that with your help, we can have you home in less than your fourteen days. But if you can't manage that, then perhaps something more ongoing and stable is the best thing. I don't think you need that, but in all candor, that's up to you."

"Like I said, your plan is shit. And if you think it's a good plan, then I can't do anything except assume the same of you."

Blumfield pursed his lips and looked straight at me. "That language won't get the reaction you're seeking," he said.

The next thing I knew, I was on top of Blumfield's desk, kicking books and stacks of paper to the floor, screaming at him about seeking reactions. Blumfield said nothing to me, just picked up the phone to call the orderlies.

I was confined to my room that night, pacing, crying, and screaming.

"This is Jesus H. Christ," I said, motioning toward the couch in front of us.

"You call him Jesus Christ?" Laura asked.

"No," I replied. "That lady over there, we call *her* Jesus Christ. *This* is Jesus *H.* Christ. Before he became Jesus, his name was Harold, so we call him Jesus H. Christ. Having more than one Jesus makes it confusing."

"Pleased to meet you," said Jesus H. Christ, rolling his eyes toward me in a jovial mocking huff as he extended his hand to Laura. "I don't call myself that, but you can call me whatever you like."

"Nice to meet you," she said, shaking his hand.

"But I am God incarnate," he added. "And I will pray to my father for you, if you like."

"That would be nice, thank you," she said.

I guided her elbow away from the couch.

"Jesus H. Christ knocked up his girlfriend," I whispered. "Then he kinda . . . ," I added, opening my hands next to my head. *"Poof."*

I motioned to the chair in the corner. "This is my roommate, Silas."

Silas jumped up to greet Laura, shaking her hand firmly. "My, my," he said, looking her up and down before turning to me. "You didn't tell me she was so pretty."

"That's a lovely blouse you have on today, sweetie," he said to her, remarking on the black-and-white striped top that looked like an old-fashioned prisoner's shirt.

"Why, thank you," Laura said, smiling. "I figured it was appropriate for the occasion."

On the few occasions that Laura and I had spent time around people she didn't know, she was often quite shy. But that day she was gracious and warm to everyone she met.

Even though I had been on the ward for five days, she was my first visitor besides my mother. For the first forty-eight hours I wasn't allowed to see anyone. Once that was over, I kept scanning the dayroom during visitor hours. My mother started visiting almost every day; my brother and father would not come. And friends? Besides Laura, I didn't seem to have any left.

Eventually I had gotten it together enough to call her. I did so partly to let her know where I was and partly to almost brag about where I was. Whenever I'd get morose, sulky, or stuck somewhere between crabby and suicidal, she was quick to say something disarming or indirectly tell me things weren't that bad. Laura wasn't exactly dismissive of my feelings, but I often left our conversations feeling like she didn't quite get how harsh things felt for me—or at least that she wasn't willing to acknowledge it. This frustrated and upset me. I spent so much time trying to hide the depths of my feelings and the cluster-fuckedness of my life from everyone, except her. The one person I was honest with was often telling me that I was being too dramatic, or overthinking things, or would I just please change the subject. It wasn't like she didn't believe me—it was more like she questioned why I let things bother me so much. In a small way, ending up in the mental ward was a strange kind of validation for me. Being in Timken Mercy proved that when I was insisting that things were terrible, and she kept insisting that they weren't, they were, in fact, kind of terrible.

When I first called her from 5B, she thought I was joking. It wasn't until she hung up and called me back via the hospital's switchboard that she fully believed me. She was full of questions. How did this happen? Whose decision was it to keep me here? Was I in danger from the other crazy people? What were they making me do? Was I getting shock treatments?

Laura went from never wanting to discuss my feelings to wanting to discuss nothing but my feelings.

As we were wrapping up our call that first evening, I remember her asking, "Well, are you any better?"

"What do you mean?" I asked.

"Being there, does it make you feel any better?"

I had no idea how to answer her.

I called Laura almost every night after that to talk about

what had happened that day. Of all the group sessions and analysis and testing and therapy, the only time anything seemed to make any sense to me was when I tried to explain it to Laura on the phone at night.

It was a few days until she could get a ride to the hospital. It was my first chance to show her everything I'd been talking about. Eventually we settled into the corner of the TV room to talk. While she initially seemed very happy to meet everyone and was intrigued by the quirkiness of life on 5B, the reality of the place started to seep in. She slowly wore her revelation on her face. It was starting to dawn on her that this wasn't a joke. These people weren't eccentrics goofing around. I was in real trouble. I had landed in this terrible place, which was potentially just a pit stop before an even more terrible place. I was wearing a thin veneer of jokiness, but she could tell how scared I really was.

"Take those old records off the shelf. I'll sit and listen to them by myself," rang out from the hallway.

"Richie," I said, looking over at Laura. "It must be cookie time. He always sings 'Old Time Rock and Roll' when they hand out cookies in the afternoon."

Richie sang as he walked into the dayroom, rubbing his hands in a blur of motion.

One of the nurses started walking over toward us with a barely polite "It's four o'clock and visiting hours are over now get the hell out" look on her face. Laura picked up her bag and took a last look around the ward.

She looked at me and touched the back of my hand. "We need to get you out of here," she said.

For the first time, I felt like she was getting it. She understood why I had fallen to this point, why I felt the way I felt. I noticed her eyes darting around the room as if she was seeing everything anew. A single tear ran down the side of her face. She got up and walked toward the door.

For the first time in years, I didn't feel alone.

"Hello," said a small Asian man standing at the foot of my bed.

"Hello," I replied.

"You care for milk of magnesssah?"

"I'm sorry."

"Milk of magnesssah . . . I prescribe for you?"

I looked at the embroidered name on his jacket. It was Dr. Chang. The infamous Doctor Chang. I'd apparently met him several times in my first few days here—meetings, like that with Blumfield, of which I had no recall whatsoever.

Dr. Chang was the kingpin of my stay at Timken Mercy. He was the psychiatrist who admitted me in the emergency room. He was the doctor who oversaw all the other various therapies I was assigned. He was also my Dr. Feelgood, coming up with all the pills and combinations I'd been force-fed since I'd arrived. In short, Dr. Chang was "the Man" in my life. Yet, despite his role as a despicable authority figure, I found him fascinating. I kept wondering how someone with such a limited grasp of the English language could become a psychiatrist in the United States. I've never had a complete feel for how the Sharks versus Jets–like relationship between psychiatrists and psychologists works, but I definitely got the vibe that to Dr. Chang, a solid command of the local tongue wasn't necessary for him to know I was a collection of misfiring synapses and nerves in need of chemical balance.

Now, apparently, he was trying to pimp me some milk of magnesia as well.

"Why are you people always trying to get me to take laxatives?"

Dr. Chang started to write notes on his chart.

"You have suicide thoughts today?" he asked.

"Well, I had been so constipated that I thought of ending it all," I said. "But now that I have milk of magnesia, I should be good."

He continued writing, then started to scribble. His pen had stopped working. He put his clipboard down on my bed and looked at me.

"There are two directions here," he said. "Everyone wants to go 4B. With hard work and cooperation, you go, too."

Ah, 4B. The way the staff and residents of 5B talked about 4B, you'd think that everyone walked around down there in satin pajamas and ate Ben & Jerry's all day while getting back rubs and blow jobs from hot nurses in skin-tight uniforms. 5B was kind of like the intensive care unit of the mental ward. Most people started out here with a great amount of supervision and restriction. However, once you got your shit partially together, you'd get transferred to the "open ward"—4B. 4B had board games. 4B had a small library. 4B had visiting hours twice as long as ours. 4B had three TVs, none of which were surrounded by cloudy Plexiglas.

"However, there other alternatives if you cannot try here," he said.

He didn't need to say another word. In one direction lay 4B. In the other: Massillon State Hospital.

I'd heard of Massillon State Hospital before coming here. People would tell jokes about it or you heard about it on the news. One thing was clear: It was chock-full of seriously fucked-up people. It was a padded-cell-and-restraint kind of facility. From what you heard about the place, it was a lot like the Hotel California. People went there but rarely left.

The staff and residents of 5B really didn't color in any details on Massillon; they didn't need to. The reality of a hospital mental ward made it pretty easy to imagine what a worse version might be like. All the 5B staff had to do was remind me that if I couldn't or wouldn't function at Timken Mercy, they would place me in a facility that "better matched my care needs."

"Choice is yours."

But was it?

Choice was often an odd word for me then. There were times, like that moment, when I felt that implying choice gave a glow of false hope. Most times, I reasoned, there aren't choices at all; everything is just following an obvious and unavoidable outcome. In those moments, choice was theoretical. Technically, it existed, but I felt that only a fool would think that events are that easy or able to change.

There were other times when choice indicated that there were unlimited options available at the whim of the chooser. It could imply freedom and range that rarely existed in reality. In truth, having a choice often meant picking your pain. Choice really meant that there was more than one non-great option. It could also imply that you were the one who got to make a decision that pleased you. Especially in this case, I did not feel in charge of the decision or the options at all.

Dr. Chang reached out to shake my hand. Immediately after doing so, he walked directly to the sink to scrub his hands. Then he left my room without another word.

"Would you like another stool softener?" the orderly asked.

"Sure, what the hell," I replied. "Bring it on."

He handed me a stool softener, along with eight other pills.

"What the fuck is this? I just took another handful of pills four hours ago," I said. "How come every day I'm in here, you give me more and more pills?"

"These are what your doctor wants you to have," he replied. "Sometimes they change medications, or combinations of medications, to see what works best for you."

"I mean, I almost fell down this morning from being so damn dizzy," I said. "How am I supposed to get better if you people have me fucked up constantly?"

"You can discuss this with your doctor," he said. "For now, I need you to take these pills."

I pulled each pill individually out of the tiny paper cup, looked it over, sniffed it, put it into my mouth, and swallowed it with some water. Toward the end of my medication-taking regime, I picked up a tiny blue pill.

"Why am I getting this?" I asked.

"It's a sleeping pill," he replied. "Did you mention anything to your doctor about not being able to sleep?"

"Yeah, but you don't understand," I said. "I used to buy these. I mean, I took a lot of these."

"But the doctor wants you to have this," he said. "You need to take it."

I declared I wouldn't take it and threw it down on the tray. The orderly gave me an "Are we really going to start this again?" look. I said that I thought the point of being here was so that I wouldn't take this stuff anymore. If Dr. Chang wanted me to take that pill, he could come down here and hear me say no to his face.

"Fine," the orderly said, taking a moment to rearrange the cups and pills on his tray. "You know, you would move along faster on your Progress Plan if you just did what you were asked to do."

"I'm sure I would," I replied.

Later that day I was due to be in Blumfield's office. It was the second visit since my last blowup. In the previous visit, we'd actually had a good conversation about my life over the previous few years. I was honest with him. I answered every question truthfully. We talked about everything. Toward the end, he asked me to complete an MMPI mental health test.

"Look at this thing," I protested. "There are, like, four hundred and fifty thousand questions."

"Actually, it's more like six hundred. Six hundred questions," he said.

"Six hundred?" I proclaimed. "How about one question, 'Are you fucking nuts?' Check: yes or no."

"It doesn't take as long as you might think," he said. "You can take it back to your room and work on it in your free time."

It didn't take as long as I thought it would—it took longer. Hours longer. I sat there checking boxes following statements like "I am easily awakened by noise," "I wish I could be as happy as others seem to be," "I am very seldom troubled by constipation," and "At times I feel like swearing."

Then I started to think about what I was really saying about myself.

When asked if "I am scared of what others think of me," I had to answer yes. When asked if "at times I have fits of crying that I cannot control," I had to answer yes. When asked if "I see people around me that others do not see," I paused but eventually answered yes for this as well. The more I read, the sadder I became. For every odd statement such as "I like mechanics magazines," there were hundreds of tiny confessionals about my life—things that I didn't like having to put a black or white answer to.

About halfway through, I just started filling in random dots. I stopped bothering to even look at the remaining questions. "Yes." "Yes." "No." "Yes." "No." "No." "Yes." No one was going to learn anything from this test that couldn't be learned from talking to me for a fraction of this time. The next morning I took it to the nurses' station, complete, and asked them to give it to Dr. Blumfield.

"Let's talk about this ghost business," Blumfield said at the start of our next session.

I'd kind of expected Blumfield to bring up the test. But he made no reference to it.

"What about it?" I replied.

"When did you start seeing her?" he asked.

"I've told you before," I said. "I never saw Her."

"Yes, you did," he replied quickly. "You told me you saw her in your dreams, repeatedly."

"Dreams aren't real, Blumfield," I said. "You of anyone should know that."

We talked more about Little Girl. Going over the dreams again. Going over the feelings of Her presence again. My answers became increasingly short. We'd been over and over this. Why did I have to tell him about it again?

"Have you ever contemplated that the Little Girl wasn't what you thought?" Blumfield asked. "Have you ever entertained that it all may not be real?"

"What do you mean?"

"I mean, have you ever entertained the idea that it could all be an illusion . . . or a hallucination—not real?"

"Of course it's real. What are you saying?"

Blumfield stopped and looked at me, then he grabbed a

book on the corner of the desk and turned it to a page marked with a slip of paper.

"That blue sleeping pill? The one you handed back to the orderly and wouldn't take?"

"Yeah, what about it?"

Blumfield turned the book toward me and dropped it onto the desk.

"Triazolam," he said. "A favorite of uptight housewives and pill poppers across America."

I scanned through the gobbledygook on the page without really reading it.

"Yeah, so?"

"So . . . ," Blumfield said, taking the book back. "Twelve percent of patients report experiencing severe hallucinations from triazolam. The effects could be even more pronounced when mixed with alcohol."

"What are you saying?"

Pause.

"Have you ever thought that, perhaps, this is all the result of chemicals you put in your body?"

"But that doesn't make any sense," I said. "I've been having those dreams and hearing Her since I was, like, a kid . . . years. I wasn't taking those pills when I was thirteen, for Christ's sake."

"And you think that it isn't possible to hallucinate a history? Sometimes hallucinations relating to past events are just as powerful as the ones our minds place in the present."

I think I knew, even at that moment, that what Blumfield was suggesting was at least possible. The idea that it all could be a product of my imagination really didn't have to be true. To me, Little Girl was the most horrifying thing I could imagine. It was even more horrifying to consider that I may have invented Her myself.

"Are you suggesting I made all this up?" I yelled. "Well, fuck you. I didn't lie about this."

"I'm not suggesting you lied. A powerful hallucination could feel as real to you as us sitting here right now. I'm just asking that you consider the possibility that—"

"Enough!" I yelled, standing up. Blumfield reached out and picked up his cigarette case and notes—the things he didn't want to see end up on the floor. "I know who I am. I know what happened to me."

Blumfield made a short attempt at calming me down but soon gave up. I stormed out of the room, yelling back at him as I stomped down the hallway in a fury. I ended up in my room, curtains drawn. I skipped dinner, mostly out of fear that I would be confined to my room anyhow. I ended up just sitting there sobbing until my eyes were almost swollen shut and I couldn't breathe through my nose anymore.

If the Little Girl in a Blue Dress was an illusion, I thought, then anything could be an illusion. If I was wrong about Her, I could be wrong about anything. The reasons I ended up in the hospital in the first place could all be a farce, built off delusions and hallucinations.

I knew what I experienced, I told myself over and over again. I knew what was real.

"So Blumfield thinks I imagined the whole Little Girl thing," I told Laura as we sat on the edge of my bed the next day. "All of it."

"What do you think?" Laura asked.

"I think Blumfield is an asshole."

"Well, does it really matter? If you imagined it or not?"

"That's what I said," I replied. "Well, that's what I meant to say. Well, I guess I kinda said it. But I was kinda screaming at the time. And I didn't quite phrase it that way."

Laura just looked at me for a moment and slowly shook her head.

She reached into her bag and pulled out a notebook and pen.

"Why are you here?" she wrote at the top of an empty page.

"I don't know," I wrote after she passed me the pen. "To find something I'm looking for. To chill out. To get my head straight. WHATEVER."

"Do you have any idea what you are doing here?" she wrote.

It was my turn to write something, but I wanted her to write the answer too. I so much wanted her to tell me what to do.

"Outside of not getting myself committed to a mental institution?" I wrote.

"Well, that seems to be working out very well for you," she wrote.

"Very funny."

"What do you want, Eric?"

Pause.

"Honestly?" I wrote.

She looked at me and nodded.

"I guess I want peace," I wrote.

She circled the word *peace* several times, putting a large question mark next to it.

"I just want to be left alone to do my thing," I wrote. "Freedom not to have to explain things. Not have to struggle all the time. Space . . . peace."

"That's not peace, that's complacency," she wrote. "It's false. There's nothing worth having that doesn't require something of you."

"Ridiculous," I wrote after snatching the pen. "Effort is exhausting. What's wrong with wanting peace?"

"No," she wrote. "What you are asking for is to not have to try. You just need to be happy."

"To me, having peace is being happy."

"What good is peace if you aren't willing to set things on fire?" she wrote.

I looked at her and scrunched my face. What did that mean?

"All I know is that I don't want to live this way," I eventually wrote.

She scratched out what I'd written. "Then fight," she scribbled over it

I took back the pen without looking at her.

"I'm sick of—"

She grabbed the pen from my hand midsentence and scrawled "FIGHT" over what I had just written.

"If I can't find some—" I wrote.

She pushed the pen in my hand toward the paper to stop me from writing any more, then reached up and turned my face toward her own.

"Fight," she said out loud.

She placed her hands on my cheeks. She gently drew me to her and kissed me.

"What you need is a reason to want to leave here," she said after pulling back. "You need a reason to want to be happy."

She grabbed her bag and seemed to get ready to leave.

She offered no further explanation. What was happy? Her? Something else? I didn't understand. She didn't seem to think it was important to explain it to me.

"Oh, I thought you might want this," she said, pulling a cassette from her bag and throwing it onto my bed. It was the copy of *Music for Airports* that I'd given her the year before. "Sure beats Bob Seger," she added, nodding and turning to walk out the door.

Later that evening, after the 5B residents had all settled in for that week's episode of *Highway to Heaven*, I snuck off into the Relaxation Room, remembering that there was an ancient cassette player on the corner table. It was placed there for the convenient playing of the Relaxation Room's collection of self-help tapes, such as *Lessons in Hygiene*, *A Better You Through Sharing*, and other similar nonsense.

I pressed the thumb-sized Play button and rested my head next to the speaker, turning the volume up just loud enough that I could start to make out the notes.

I wanted to feel it vibrate against my cheek.

I wanted to soak it in through my pores.

I wanted to breathe it in.

As I heard the first few notes crackle out of the player, I could feel tears roll down my face and collect where the grille of the speaker touched my cheek.

I knew that in a few minutes the staff would notice that I wasn't accounted for. Then they'd come looking for me. Then they'd probably take the tape away, coming up with some improvised reason about how I could harm myself or others with shards of plastic and forty-five minutes' worth of magnetic tape.

I knew I only had a moment, so I wanted to drink it in and savor it.

How did I ever get to this point? I wondered. How did I ever come to the point that I'd have to sneak away from a room full of drug addicts and schizoids in order to listen to some music? A point where my freedom was completely gone? A point where someone had to watch me shave and clip my fingernails?

The sound of *Music for Airports* didn't seem random at all; it seemed very purposeful. Outside of many renditions of "Heart and Soul" on the ward's piano, it was the first real piece of music I'd heard since being admitted, and probably the most powerful medication I'd received. It was beautiful.

It was at that moment that I thought to myself: I've had enough.

Right there in that room, listening to that tape Laura gave me, I decided that I wanted something more than what I'd allowed myself to become. Listening to the voices and piano notes fade in and out, I decided that I wanted to be happy. If I had to fight for things in life, I wanted to fight for something bigger than the right to eat with a fork. I wanted to love and be loved and feel alive. I had no idea how to find my way, but listening to that music wash over me, I felt, for the first time, that the struggle I faced would be worth it.

Evangelicals always talk about being born and then being born again. They speak of the moment they devoted their life to Christ almost as if it were a reboot, starting over, being born anew. I had no idea of this at the time, but when I look back at that evening, with my head resting on that speaker, I know exactly what they mean, and why. It was a simple stolen moment to listen to some music. However, it was also a mark in time. The end of one life and the beginning of another. I don't think anyone, except for Laura, thought I had even the remotest chance of pulling it off. That just made me want it even more.

The next morning I walked into Blumfield's office and apologized for trashing his desk. And for almost doing it again.

And for calling him a needledick motherfucker. And told him I didn't want to live this way anymore. And if he was willing to help me, I was willing to work hard.

Perhaps I'd been wrong about choice. For me, it felt like that moment was a true choice. At that point, I chose to live.

· ·

The first thing Blumfield said after my apology was that he wanted me to take the MMPI test again and actually answer the questions. All of them.

I told him that I'd be happy to do so after they reduced the medication I was on.

No, Blumfield insisted. Test first, then he'd talk with Dr. Chang.

Once again, the test felt like a daylong trip to the dentist. It was awful, and I let everyone know how miserable I was while taking it. I really wanted to tear it to shreds and stuff it down the toilet. But I didn't. I made myself keep going.

The next afternoon Blumfield and I were in the midst of our regular afternoon session when he got a page to the nurses' station. He put my file down on his desk and excused himself.

Lying on top of the open file was a neatly typed "Report of Consultation," dated after my second blowup in his office.

I turned it around and began reading.

Two decades later I'd walk back into Timken Mercy, take the elevator to the records room in the basement, and open up the file containing all my paperwork, nurses' logs, and reports from my stay at Timken Mercy. I was surprised that they still existed, having been retrieved from a warehouse a few weeks after I'd requested to see them. The file jacket said that I had also requested to see these records three years after being released from the hospital, but I have no memory of doing so, or why.

Once the file was open, the first thing I noticed was the "Report of Consultation." Seeing its slightly yellow pages took me back to a vivid memory of sneaking a peek at it that afternoon in Blumfield's office, absorbing every word as quickly as I could.

INTERVIEW AND BEHAVIOR: This patient presented a bespectacled and tall male, of average build, with clear skin and an odd haircut that is similar to that worn by some subcultural "punk" musicians and their followers. . . . Anger was not expressed in a healthy, direct way. The patient is very combative. . . . Much conflict between family and acquaintances over his odd behavior and atypical life style.

Dynamically, this patient has a veneer of socialization that is constructed upon a morass of confused emotions and instinctual drives. He subconsciously realizes this; that his emotional underpinnings are tumultuous and very tenuously balanced within himself. He also feels that he has been irreparably damaged and the pain from this, when at a conscious level, becomes unbearably painful. Although his thinking is yet essentially intact, it too is starting to show signs of deterioration. For example, there is a clear paranoid tendency beginning to develop.

When Blumfield walked back into his office and noticed that I was reading the report, he made no effort to stop me.

At the bottom was his diagnosis: schizotypal personality disorder. I pointed to it and looked at him, as if asking what it meant. Blumfield opened a book on his desk, spun it around, and moved it toward me.

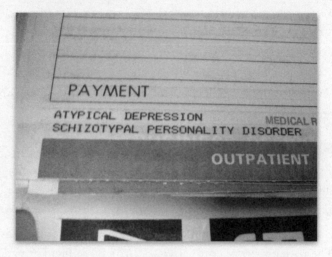

Schizotypal personality disorder: "a pervasive pattern of social and interpersonal deficits marked by acute discomfort with, and reduced capacity for, close relationships as well as by cognitive or perceptual distortions and eccentricities of behavior, beginning by early adulthood and present in a variety of contexts."

It went on to describe a bunch of symptoms and indicators: odd behavior or appearance, poor rapport with others, a tendency to social withdrawal, odd beliefs or magical thinking, suspiciousness or paranoid ideas, and about a dozen others. Some didn't fit, most did. As I read through the entry, I couldn't decide what idea was worse: that someone thought of me this way or that it might be true.

"Do you have any questions?" Blumfield asked.

"So, this is based on your opinion?"

"My assessment, yes," he said. "Plus the tests you've taken."

I remember wondering to myself why he would let me read it. Was it to humble me? Test me? Teach me something? Whatever he was trying to accomplish, it probably worked. After what felt like an hour of processing this in my head, I finally spoke up.

"So where does that leave me?"

"What do you mean?" Blumfield said.

"Where do I end up?"

"There are a few different directions," he said. "Some continue into schizophrenia; others find that they can manage quite well with medication and therapy."

"How do I know where I'm heading?" I said.

"Well, I think a lot of that depends on your treatment—and you have some hand in how that evolves," he said. "Many people who aggressively deal with this live very normal, happy lives."

"I was watching TV once and there was a report on about a guy who had his nuts blown off in Vietnam," I said. "I mean, they didn't say 'nuts' on TV or anything, but it was pretty obvious what they were implying."

"Okay," Blumfield said. "I'm not sure I'm following you."

"Well, he lived in a wheelchair and had no balls," I said. "I mean, he adopted a kid and was married to this woman with big tits and huge hair, but there was a pall over everything: that he couldn't walk and had no balls."

"What is your point?" he asked.

"I guess that all depends on what you define as a 'normal' and 'happy' life, huh? I mean, this guy had all this stuff that was supposed to make him happy, but you could tell that all he really wanted was his balls back."

Blumfield just smiled, then lowered his head to write some

notes, probably something like "Has trouble expressing abstract concepts and ideas." In truth, I had no idea what "happy" and "normal" were, and I doubted I'd recognize either if I found it, let alone be able to express it. And I was positive that whatever would constitute "happy" and "normal" in my life would make no sense to anyone else.

I could hear some guitar chords reverberate from down the hall in the dayroom.

It was Jesus H. Christ singing David Bowie's "Young Americans."

For thirty minutes every day Jesus H. Christ was allowed to play his guitar. He wasn't allowed to keep it in his room or play unsupervised. But for a half hour a day, the nurses would let him set up in front of their station and play. Jesus H. Christ knew a lot of songs.

"Would you mind terribly if we picked this up later?" I asked Blumfield.

"Tell me where you're at. What are you feeling right now?" he asked me.

Over the several days he'd been allowed to do it, Jesus H. Christ's thirty-minute strumming had slowly evolved into unsanctioned sing-alongs. I loved the sing-alongs. There is something about singing in a group that brings you a kind of peace and release that little else can equal.

Stan was also surprisingly well versed in song lyrics. Silas would stand in front of everyone, pretending to conduct the 5B chorus. The sing-alongs were probably the most joyful parts of every day. Patients who hadn't responded to or acknowledged anything since they arrived would suddenly perk up and sing along with "Folsom Prison Blues" or "Let It Be." Nothing brings people together like the shared love of a song.

Our sing-alongs were made even sweeter because we knew that anything we enjoyed doing this much would eventually, and irrepealably, become forbidden. Some doctor or nurse would come up with a reason that singing together would cause a disturbance and suggest some other activity, like checkers or watching TV, and that would be the end of it.

"I guess right now I'm feeling a lot of things," I said. "But I guess more than anything I feel like I want to go sing with Jesus H. Christ."

Blumfield put down his pen and extended his arm toward the hallway.

I was already singing as I ran toward the dayroom.

My therapy sessions continued almost every day, as well as my occupational therapy, moderated study group, and group therapy. In each, I basically learned to tell the counselors and therapists what they wanted to hear. It wasn't like I was lying to them, but I simply learned to convey things in the way they could understand, almost like speaking in another language.

The only time I really expressed myself was during Laura's visits. She came every day or two, and we just sat in a corner by ourselves. By this time, our conversations were less about gossip from the ward and more about untwisting the mess of knots I'd tied through my life. Laura rarely gave advice. Instead, she'd just ask questions about the way I felt and constantly probe by asking me to explain what I meant in deeper detail. She really, never once, pushed or suggested I do anything, but she would quietly nod with approval when she heard things she liked. I learned to live for those nods.

After ten days in 5B, I was moved to 4B. For the most part, I behaved myself, with the notable exception of secretly forcing myself to throw up all my medications. One morning I had woken up to an orderly who wanted me to swallow nine pills—plus a stool softener. Fuck it, I said. No way.

This led to a mini-conference with the nursing staff, then a hallway consult with Dr. Chang, then everyone marching into my room to tell me that I needed to take these pills. If I did not, there would be serious ramifications for my Progress Plan.

Fine.

I took the pills just as I was told.

Then, a few minutes later, I walked into the bathroom, stuck my finger down my throat, and threw them all up again. I repeated this for three days.

Of course, eventually I was discovered; Dr. Chang ordered that I had to take all my medications in the presence of a staff member, then sit by the nurses' station for thirty minutes. Basically, now even my digestion was a supervised activity.

Sitting by the nurses' station kind of felt like wearing a dunce cap in the corner of the classroom. All the 4B residents wanted to know what I'd done and why I was sitting there. After a while, I started to notice how that chair was kind of a perfect vantage point. Jesus H. Christ's new medication had made him calm and no longer interested in screaming and running around naked at night. Therefore, he, too, had made his way downstairs and was now happy escorting his very pregnant girlfriend and his parents around 4B, showing off all the wonderful new features like doors on the bathrooms and leather stamping tools in the occupational therapy room (excellent for customizing the wallets and belts we were instructed to make). There was a blond guy who looked like a roadie for Lynyrd Skynyrd, who'd sit in front of a window rubbing his lower lip for at least three hours. A woman in the corner of the dayroom would start to look very upset, get up and sit in a different chair, and seem fine for another few minutes until she got distressed and moved again. Some dude was playing with himself while watching *The Price Is Right*. Stan was flirting with a woman who'd been brought in a few days earlier. To be honest, the residents of 4B weren't that much better off than the residents of 5B—in fact many of them had been on 5B when I arrived—but 4B had a more relaxed vibe, a feeling that things were a bit more under control, less frantic, panicked, and harsh, as well as mildly less depressing.

I kept wondering to myself what these people's lives would hold. They, like me, were just a few days from getting tossed back into the world. What would happen to them? How would they cope? How long would it be before one of them was back here? Or somewhere worse?

One day, as I digested my meds, I saw a girl named Sarah smiling at me from across the dayroom. She was sitting at a table with a tray in front of her. The natives of 4B had gone into quite a flutter when she arrived. The waves of people, specifically men, who paraded over to wherever she was dwindled a tiny bit when word spread that she was seventeen. Simply because she was the subject of so much ward gossip, I'd pretty much avoided her. It seemed that the only people more gossiped about than Sarah were the men who went over to talk to her.

I looked away for a moment, then looked back. She was still looking at me and smiling.

What the hell, I thought.

As I approached I could see that food on the tray in front of her was barely touched. Her arms were spread out away from her and lying on the table, making the mounds of gauze and pads wrapping her wrists even harder to ignore. She seemed like she was in pain whenever she tried to move them.

"What's the matter?" I asked. "Is the chicken casserole so delicious it's blowing your mind?"

She laughed. "No, it's still just kinda slow going with this," she said, rolling her palms up. I could see some seepage coming through the bandages. "I asked the orderly to help me, but I guess he got busy. They keep fucking with my meds."

"Amen to that," I said, sitting down next to her and picking up her spoon.

I scooped up a small bite on the spoon, brought it up to her mouth, then slowly swung it over to mine. Just before it reached my mouth, I gave her a look of faux shock.

"Oh, did you want this?" I asked.

She laughed again.

I brought the spoon up to her mouth. She backed away slightly and looked into my eyes, then slowly opened her mouth and took in the bite. We just sat there silently for a few minutes. Me scooping up spoonfuls and feeding them to her. Her smiling between bites.

"Hey! Hey!" we heard some staff person yell from the nurses' station. "What are you doing? You aren't permitted to feed another patient!! Stop that right now! Stop!"

"In about thirty seconds they are going to force this spoon out of my hands," I said softly, continuing to serve her while I spoke. "And if they forget to feed you at breakfast, I'll be back."

"Put that down!"

As I expected, an orderly grabbed my hand and took the spoon, while a nurse quickly looked over Sarah.

There was some yelling back and forth, and the scene ended with me walking back to my room before they had a chance to order me there. I didn't act out or throw a fit. It was the first time in years I'd made an effort toward anything that wasn't

meant to fuck things up. It was the first time in years that I'd
stood up for someone other than myself.

"Well . . . you ready to go?" Laura asked.

I thought for a moment.

"No," I said. "I doubt it."

Both of us sat there, looking toward the door, neither of us
sure what we were supposed to do next.

If there is one thing I'd learned about hospitals, it's that
they aren't interested in healing you. They are interested in
stabilizing you, and then everyone is supposed to move on.
They go to stabilize some more people, and you go off to do
whatever you do. Healing, if it happens at all, is done on your
own, long after the hospital has submitted your final insurance
paperwork.

While I was in Timken Mercy, I often expected that when I
was discharged I would walk out to a bright sunny day and
simply skip off into my newly retooled and absolutely perfect
life. The reality was far different. After twenty-two days of almost constant confinement in the mental ward, I was what
could loosely be defined as "stable," but that's about it.

I'd been allowed outside the ward on two occasions. Once,
I was given a one-hour pass to walk around in the hospital's
garden with my mother. The second trip was a six-hour "day
visit" back to my parents' house. My brother was away from
the house all day, and my father barely spoke to me. Basically I
spent the entire visit listening to my records and walking
around the backyard alone.

Dr. Chang had decided to try out a new drug mixture for
the day of my visit home, which had left me barely able to
stand. He'd finally cut back on the number of pills he was pre-
scribing. I was now down to three pills, three times a day. But

they must have been horse tranquilizers or something, as within an hour of taking them, I could barely spell my name.

In hindsight, I can see that numbing me up before sending me back into my real world might not have been all that bad an idea. Before going into the hospital, I'd managed to turn my life into a huge shell game. It wasn't until I went into the hospital that my family really figured out the extent of what was going on. For example, no one was aware that in the few weeks before I was admitted to the hospital, I'd written all over all the posters and artwork I had hanging on my bedroom walls. After covering them with ramblings, I'd slashed them to shreds yet left them hanging. I'd also scorched a ventriloquist doll and then hung the charred remains from the ceiling light fixture with an improvised noose. Those surprised by these discoveries initially included me, as I had, at first, no recollection of doing any of these things. Though once I was reminded of them, I knew I had done them. It is one of the strangest memory experiences I've ever had, then or since, almost as if my mind has erased any detail of these acts yet somehow managed to hang on to the utter certainty that they were my own.

My parents had decided to move me out of the attic into a room across the hall from their bedroom. I was pretty livid when my mother told me, but even I realized I was lucky to have a place to go to after leaving the hospital. T.J. Maxx was going to let me have my job back, which I equally didn't deserve but was grateful for. It wasn't really an act of compassion on their part—they were probably just happy to have someone to do the cleanup work.

At the ward there really was no big goodbye. With the exception of Jesus H. Christ, most of my original 5B brethren had already gone, tossed back into the chaos of the lives they'd

left. No exchanged addresses or phone numbers. Our time together was simply over. The only person I ever saw again was
Silas, when I went down to the courthouse to pay a parking
ticket a few weeks later. Despite our having been roommates
for most of our time at Timken Mercy, Silas pretended he
didn't remember who I was.

I was set up to see both Blumfield and Dr. Chang again
within a week, so they didn't feel the need for a goodbye either. The nurse simply told me that I was free to go home
whenever I chose. Since both my parents were at work, I asked
Laura to borrow a car and come pick me up.

We were sitting on my bed talking when she suddenly
looked at me.

"Wait, do we even need to be here?"

"I don't know, I guess not," I said.

When we stepped outside, the sun was bright, blindingly
bright. It would disguise what lay in front of me. Broken relationships that would take years to heal. Questions I wasn't
ready to answer. The previous twenty-two days hadn't really
solved anything. All my problems and issues were still out
there, waiting patiently for me. The only real question was
whether I was now any better prepared to deal with them.

As we got up and started toward the door, one of the nurses
ran up to me.

"I almost missed you," she said. "You got a package this
morning. We didn't want you to leave without it."

The package had been opened and checked for contraband,
like all incoming packages were. I reached inside the open envelope and fished out a piece of paper.

"Hear you are getting out," it said. "Thought we'd send
you a little something to celebrate." It was signed by Phil and

Ben. I reached inside the envelope to pull out the present they'd sent me.

It was a single-serving box of Cap'n Crunch.

She came back on my first night home from the hospital. I saw a flash of Her in a dream. As soon as I saw Her, I was awake, and stayed that way for the rest of the night, upright in my bed in my new bedroom, shivering, staring into the dark stillness, waiting to hear another noise or for the door from the attic to open.

I don't think I ever really expected that She'd stay away forever, but the Little Girl dreams I began to have seemed different. Sometimes I was blind, my head was covered, or my eyes could not open, and the scenes of the Little Girl dream would play out around me, though I couldn't see them. The new abbreviated ones terrified me just as much as every other Little Girl dream I'd had. As long as She remained upstairs, I figured I could deal with it—just hold on and bear it. If She started showing up in other places again, I had no idea what I'd do. That would definitely be a big problem.

The deal my parents offered was pretty simple. I could stay at their house until we determined what was best long-term. During that time, I could borrow my mom's car to go to work and a limited number of activities. I had to sign my paycheck over to my parents, who would, in turn, give me an allowance. Even if I wasn't using the car, I had to let my parents know where I was going when I left the house and when I'd be back. I also needed to keep myself out of any flavor of trouble.

For some reason, which I was thankful for yet didn't understand, my parents were open to planning a move up to Kent State's main campus in the fall so I could take another stab at classes. I'd start out on academic probation, but by some miracle or legal requirement, Kent agreed to give me another chance. Given what I'd been through, it was a risky move, but I think everyone, including my parents, realized that if I stayed in Canton, I'd just end up in the same cycle. I needed a change of scenery, a chance to be around different people. Plus, when I moved up to Kent, I'd be out of their house. Though they would never have said this out loud, I imagine that they were happy to see me be somewhere else for a while. Most of all, the idea of moving to Kent was a goal, something to aspire to and work for. In a life still filled with smoldering embers from my efforts to torch it, I was happy to have anything to look forward to.

"Dude, they told us you had bronchitis, but I knew it was bullshit," Todd said, trying to make conversation as I swept up in the Housewares Department Saturday night. "Nobody goes into the hospital with bronchitis for weeks and comes out alive, man. I figured you got busted and went to jail."

I told Todd there really wasn't a whole lot of difference between the hospital and jail.

"So, did you nail some crazy bitches while you were in there?" he asked.

I just shook my head.

Todd kept following me as I brushed the dust balls toward the stockroom doors.

"Oh, and by the way, if you need anything to help you reac-climate to society, just let me know, I can set you up," he said.

I told him no thank you, I had plenty of drugs at home that I was trying hard to avoid taking as it was.

"If you ever want to unload any of that stuff, that works, too," he said.

After Todd went back to the Housewares Department, I saw Annette standing by the women's fitting room. She leaned to her left and said, "Okay. What's the password?"

She leaned to the right. "You got it."

To the left. "Got what?"

To the right. "The password."

I think this new *Purple Rain* dialogue was her attempt to cheer me up. Though I'd been back at work for a week or so, it was the first time we'd been scheduled together. While I was given a job, I was back in Receiving—sweeping, mopping, and taking out trash. Despite assurances from the managers that my "medical situation" had been kept in confidence, it was quite clear that word of where I'd been and why had spread throughout the store. I'm pretty sure it was the managers themselves who did the gossiping, as no one else would have had any idea where I was. Now even some of the regular shoplifters seemed to have gotten word.

I really wasn't concerned with who knew what, but watching everyone try to cheer me up all the time quickly got old. I mean, what else would you do for a depressed and suicidal drug-abusing co-worker but bring a smile to his face by reenacting a scene from *Purple Rain* that wasn't all that funny to begin with?

Annette leaned to the right. "The password is what?"

"Exactly," she answered herself, forgetting to lean in the other direction.

"The password is exactly?" she said, realizing her mistake, and then leaning to the left briefly, before leaning to the right.

She burst out in laughter when she finished. I applauded for her.

"That was great," I said. "What did you do, write down all the parts during the movie?"

"Yeah, I took shorthand," she said sheepishly, instantly realizing that it sounded a bit weird.

"Well, good for you," I said. "That was very nice."

Nice. I was trying to be nice. In a strange moment of synergy, both Laura and Blumfield had given me the exact same advice, on the same day, about dealing with people.

"Okay, so you say that when you talk with people, you assume that they judge you or don't like you or have other negative impressions of you," Blumfield summarized.

"That's correct," I said.

His real-world office was filled with even more crap—piles of books, files, stuffed bookshelves, and yellowing photographs. Why would one person need all this, I wondered, let alone be able to find it or use it when he needed it?

"When someone comes up to talk to you, they not only want to express an idea or feeling, they want to express it to you," Blumfield said. "That means that you have value to them. They are interested in having you hear their thoughts, and they value your opinion. I think that's implicit in the gesture."

"The other day when I was sweeping up in the Men's Department a woman kept staring at me," I said. "I asked her if I could help her with anything, and she told me that she prayed for my soul."

"Did you ask her why she wanted to pray for you?"

"No, I didn't have to," I said. "She told me I was going to hell."

"Why did she feel you were going to hell?"

"Because I was wearing earrings."

"Earrings?" Blumfield repeated.

"Yeah, so I asked her about this," I said. "She just looked me up and down and said, 'Yes, those faggot earrings.'"

"I'm not sure what that story means to our conversation," he said.

"I don't think she was very interested in my opinions," I said. "I don't think she felt I had value, implicit or otherwise."

"Eric, you probably interacted with a hundred different people that day," he said. "And you are allowing your experiences with one to determine how you react to everyone. Doesn't that strike you as unfair to the dozens of other people who *do* think you have value and find pleasure in sharing their thoughts and experiences with you? I think you'll find that when you stop assuming a defensive position that you'll be pleasantly surprised by what you find.

"You are such a compassionate and curious person by nature, Eric. You spend a lot of time and energy fighting against it, trying not to be compassionate. Just be with them, acknowledge their interest in you, and let your natural curiosities go."

Laura's fourteen-word version of the same speech, delivered while sharing a Frosty in a Wendy's parking lot later that night: "Just don't be a dick. Listen to people and realize they are trying, too."

Despite thousands of dollars spent on counseling and medication and hospitals and tests, the best therapy I received happened late at night, in parking lots, cheap restaurants, and driving around town with Laura.

Just don't be a dick.

I don't think there was ever a time that the staff of Timken Mercy was convinced that I could live without doing drugs. They really didn't know what advice to give me. One counselor suggested that I attend NA meetings after I left, if for no other reason than to learn from other people's experiences. (I never went.) Another stressed that I needed to avoid any narcotic, powerful stimulant, or mind-altering substance for life, or I'd just end up back in the hospital again. But it was actually Blumfield who, kind of off the cuff, came up with the solution that I've tried to live by ever since. He suggested that if I could enjoy something without it making me high, fine. If it was impossible to enjoy something without becoming inebriated, then avoid it. In other words, it is pretty difficult to "enjoy" pot or pills without feeling something. But a beer or two beers? Shouldn't be a problem, he suggested; don't think of it as a problem. But I was still scared to test myself. My challenge was just keeping it to those two beers. No one other than myself had any faith that I could actually pull it off. Except Laura.

She decided that we should put Blumfield's theory to the test on one of the first nights I was allowed out. We went to the College Bowl, just a few blocks away from my parents' house, and ordered a draft.

The bartender sat it down in front of me. It was golden and cold and looked perfect. We stared at it for a few moments. It was the first alcohol I'd seen in over a month.

"Should I drink it?" I asked Laura.

"Sure, why not. What's the worst that can happen, right?"

I picked up the draft and downed the whole thing in about six seconds.

Pause.

"How do you feel?"

"I feel good," I said.

"Do you feel any different?"

"No."

"Are you angry?"

"No."

"Are you sad and upset?"

"No."

"Do you see any dead children?"

"That isn't funny," I said.

"Great," she said, grabbing my arm and pulling me toward the door. "Let's go."

We had a new hangout spot: a gravel pad surrounding a natural-gas well hidden across the street from the Sportsmen's Shooting Center, way out of town on State Street. It was one of those large pumps that looked like a giant bobbing bird toy. One of the pieces of advice I'd been given when I left the hospital was to find new routines and avoid places and people that always led to trouble. Lake O'Dea was a great place, but it was time to move on. Laura seemed to like the gas well. We never actually saw it move or pump anything. It seemed to have been randomly plopped down in the middle of an open field. The gravel path leading from the road curved off behind a ditch and small mound, making it easy to pull in and be completely hidden from the view of passersby. We'd often lay a blanket on the gravel and stare up at the sky, sit around and talk and smoke cigarettes, or just sit in the car and listen to music. There was no one around, or any reason for anyone to be around, for a long while in either direction.

Increasingly, it wasn't just my future we might talk about.

Laura had always been a stellar student and had great grades. There was no doubt she could go just about anywhere she wanted for college, yet she wouldn't commit herself to anything. She would wonder aloud whether she should go to school or stay home for a bit and save money. Maybe she'd go somewhere far away to school, or maybe she'd go to one of the Kent campuses. Who knew?

As time went on, I found her lack of clear decisions increasingly hard to believe, and I'm sure it was evident in my tone.

By now, in June, every time I'd bring up the subject, she seemed visibly uncomfortable.

"Who knows, I guess I'm going to have to figure something out soon, huh?" she'd say. "Hey, what are you doing on Saturday? Wanna go see *Rocky Horror*?"

The Rocky Horror Picture Show is something that people rooted in the modern world of YouTube and Twitter can never appreciate. It isn't that things like *The Rocky Horror Picture Show* couldn't happen today, it's that they can happen too easily. Viral videos, photos, and websites become sensations, get millions of hits, and are forgotten in the course of a week. We have no patience for organic phenomena today. There was no email or Internet when *Rocky Horror* became what it was, no cell phones, no VCRs or downloads, either. It took years to formulate and spread, one person at a time, until it had morphed into a Saturday-night ritual for freaks and weirdos across the entire country. Instead of building organically over years, today something like *Rocky Horror* could spread in hours, if not minutes, and burn out almost as quickly.

I'm always surprised by the number of people who think the audience participation and gags in *Rocky Horror* were always meant to be there. They weren't. It is a horrocious film. All the talking back to the screen and throwing stuff and squirt guns were always a way to make fun of this terrible movie.

The closest place that showed *The Rocky Horror Picture Show* was a dive movie theater in downtown Cuyahoga Falls, which was an absolute ghost town late on a Saturday night.

I had never seen *Rocky Horror* before but knew a group of older kids who had all gone a bunch of times when I was still too young to get in. I'd picked up on all the routines and audience antics vicariously through them. I also had a copy of the soundtrack album, so I knew all the songs already.

All of this led to me hitting the ground running. I did a lot of ritualized screaming, singing, and dancing on my very first viewing. Laura seemed to have a lot of fun, though she wasn't nearly as enthusiastic about it as I was. Participation, especially group participation, really wasn't normally her thing. For me, it was probably the most I'd ever smiled in any ninety-minute period in my life. It was being in a place with a bunch of people, being ridiculous and loud and having fun. The sense of joy and freedom was infectious. The people there didn't give a fuck if anyone understood them or not—they got one another. They were a group of people sharing some unbridled joy over something that they all had in common but the rest of the world didn't get at all. There was a clear sense of purpose—to have fun and let go.

A guy in full makeup and wearing a corset, fishnet hose, and insane pumps had been sitting next to us all evening, jumping up and down with us every time. After Riff Raff sent Dr. Frank-N-Furter to say hello to oblivion and the movie ended, he turned to us and extended his hand.

"Hi, I'm Jamie," he said. "You're new, right? Well, a bunch of us get together every week afterward at the shit-stain diner down the street for breakfast. You two bitches are welcome to come if you like."

"This is my Vikki," Jamie said later as we joined the group for our first diner visit.

"I'm his fag hag," she chimed in.

"Vikki works at the dirty-book store," Jamie said hurriedly. "If you're ever in the mood to spend a quiet intimate evening with a large black rubber penis, Vikki is your connection."

Vikki waved her hands whenever she burst out in laughter,

which seemed to happen several times a minute. Having an awful job myself, I tried to bond with Vikki over her work.

"It really isn't that bad," she said. "I keep the tissues stocked and make change. Then I just read the rest of the night."

I asked if the patrons ever tried to hit on her.

She laughed and waved. "Yeah, I really don't think I'm what they're looking for, if you know what I mean."

When Vikki wasn't laughing at everything Jamie said, she spent most of her time talking with a rather stern androgynous woman named Val who she sat with during the movie showings. Val seemed to take her *Rocky Horror* very seriously, acting out routines, doing dances, and singing with almost military precision. She would almost crack a smile every time Vikki burst out in laughter but otherwise sat there looking rather drill-sergeant-ish.

Throughout the diner, people would periodically switch places around the big table to converse with different others. Since we were new, many people came to sit with us and learn who we were. Even though we'd only just met these people, they immediately welcomed us as family. They were a collection of eccentrics, outcasts, homosexuals, degenerates, drama-club officers, attention whores, and oddballs. All were square pegs wrapped in some flamboyant combination of leather, fishnet, sequins, odd hats, and tons of makeup. Laura and I never dressed up for any of our *Rocky Horror* excursions but still fit in pretty well, mostly because our everyday attire wasn't that far off of what they wore on Saturday nights. Compared with the normal clientele in a late-night diner, our group seemed as if it had been beamed down from some futuristic other planet (one with a considerable investment in hairspray and eyeliner). They had nasty mouths and were funny and alive. They all seemed to have a chip on their shoulder or some baggage from years of trying to find a home in the real world. Here were the only people in Ohio who were weirder than I was.

So started a kind of ritual. Almost every Saturday night Laura and I would figure out who could get a car, then we'd drive up to Cuyahoga Falls and get to the theater for the midnight show. Afterward, we'd all head down the street to the all-night diner for breakfast.

We'd sit and drink coffee and order just enough bad food to keep from getting kicked out. The diner staff seemed to genuinely dislike us, always giving us reminders that we were the reason they hated their jobs. We talked about deep stuff and silly stuff. It was a venue to entertain one another and a forum to discuss things the rest of the world wouldn't understand. None of us seemed particularly concerned about what went on in the others' lives the rest of the week, but on early Sunday mornings, we would become best friends, chatting until near dawn. At some point the whole culture around the movie became almost trivial. Eventually I'd find myself kinda bored and antsy during the movie. The real attraction was hanging out at the diner afterward.

I'd been up late listening to music and reading when I heard a *click* come from the hallway. I looked up to see the attic door slowly open halfway and stop. After a few seconds, my stomach started to heave.

This is it, I thought to myself. At any moment, She is going to walk out beyond that doorway and corner me in this room. You'd think by now, years after this started and after my hospital stay, that I could feel fairly certain that She wasn't coming. That, of course, is how rational people would think. But every time I'd get it in my head that She was coming—perhaps I'd just woken from a dream or heard a strange noise—it seemed imminent and unstoppable.

I tried calling out. "I'm going to close my eyes," I said. "And if there is a ghost here, I will see it when I open them again."

Nothing.

It happened again the next day while I was getting ready to go to work. Just a subtle *click* from the door latch. The door opened about a foot, then stopped. This time I rushed toward the door and swung it wide.

There was nothing there.

"If you have something to say, say it!" I yelled up the stairs. "If there is something you need to do to me, then do it. Quit fucking around!"

It happened a third time, in the middle of the night. I was lying in bed half awake when I heard the *click* again, then a quiet creak of the door. I sat up in my bed and looked around the corner through the doorway. The door was open about a foot. I quickly got up, closed it, then ran back to my bed and spent the next hour staring at the door to my room, waiting for Her to walk through.

Since I'd left Timken Mercy, I hadn't told Laura or anyone else about seeing Little Girl again in my dreams. I think Laura, along with everyone who knew about Her, assumed that I had hallucinated Her or made Her up. To them, Little Girl was something left in the past. Admitting I was seeing Her was admitting that I had not left the hospital magically transformed. It was admitting that my troubles were far from over.

One night Laura and I headed out to the gas well. I was bitching about my parents and T.J. Maxx and rules and prescription drugs and anything else that I felt was oppressing me.

"Why are you so concerned with bending yourself in knots to please all these people?" she blurted out in the middle of one of my tirades.

"I don't know," I said. "I guess I just want to do the right thing. Right? Isn't that what I'm supposed to be doing?"

"Fuck the right thing," she said. "You need to spend less time worrying about what's right and start thinking more about what's true."

"What's that supposed to mean?" I said.

"It means be true to yourself and you can't go wrong," she said. "If you worry about doing the right thing all the time, you'll just try to make everyone happy, and that's impossible. Just find out what is true and real; then you'll know what to do."

"Oh, come on. From you, that is the biggest crock of shit I've ever heard," I said.

"What do you mean?"

"I mean, how can you be so pious about truth when you never give anybody the truth? I mean, what do you do when we aren't hanging out? What is your life like? Who are your friends? What is the fucking deal with you and college for this fall? We've spent half our free nights together for the past year and a half, and I couldn't answer one of those questions. Why? Because you keep everything hidden."

Pause.

"You aren't truthful," I continued. "All you are is evasive and vague."

"You wouldn't understand," she said.

"Try me," I said.

"Actually, I wanted to let you know . . . I'm leaving in a few weeks."

"Where?"

"Baruch College . . . City University of New York."

"New York? *You* are going to New York City?"

"Yeah."

I couldn't tell if I was shocked or angry or both. Deciding to go to college in New York City was not something you did on a few days' notice. It was apparent to me that she had been planning this for months yet had chosen to keep it a secret. Whether she'd kept quiet because she was unsure what she wanted to do or because she was afraid to tell me didn't matter. It was lame. I wanted her to know that.

"Really? Who do you know in New York City?"

"I don't know anyone in New York City."

I decided to fill her in on New York City (a place that I had not been to either). I talked about crime and grit and danger and the loneliness of being in a city with millions of strangers. She never said a word. She didn't argue back. She just sat there and took it from me.

"I'm sorry you are so disappointed" was the only thing she said.

Laura gathered her things and started back toward the car, silently informing me that it was time to take her home.

We spent most of the drive not saying anything. As we turned off Route 62 toward her house, I said softly, "I guess I'm hurt that you're leaving. But I'm more upset that you didn't tell me."

"Um, less than a month ago you were hanging out with a guy who thought he was Jesus," she said. "I figured this could wait."

I wanted to ask her why she hadn't brought it up the month before that—or the month before that—but let it go. I was tired. I needed to get back to my parents' house. I didn't want to make it into a fight or act like an asshole. Saving the conversation for another night meant another day or two of pretending like I'd heard her wrong. Another day or two of pretending it wasn't real.

A few days later Laura showed up at my front door unannounced in the middle of the afternoon. No mention of where she had been, why she was stopping by, or how she'd gotten there. No car, no friend dropping her off. No reason to be anywhere near my house.

"What are you up to?" she asked when I answered the door.

"Just stuff," I answered.

"Can stuff wait for a bit while we go do something?"

Since neither of us had a car, we just walked to the park up the street from my house and sat on the swings.

The day after Laura's announcement, I had had a talk with my parents. Moving to Kent was no longer an aspiration; it had to be a reality. I didn't care what I had to do to make it happen. Cut my hair, go to church, wash the cars every day, wear a tie, sing hymns around the house—done. I would do it. If she was leaving, I figured, then I was, too. It's harder to be left behind when you're running away as well.

Sitting on the swing, I told her about my Kent plans, still slipping in occasional but regular passive-aggressive snipes at New York and the idea of her moving there for school. Taking the subway was dangerous. You couldn't trust anyone. In New York there were cockroaches the size of your foot. She really never had much to say in response. She just didn't let it bother her; she let me get it off my chest.

"I have a gift for you," she said with a coy smile.

"A gift?"

"Yeah, something from me to you," she said, reaching into her bag and pulling out one of her notebooks. Inside the front cover was a torn piece of paper, which she picked up, looked at for a moment, then handed to me.

It was a piece of blue-lined graph paper, probably three inches square. On it she'd written in thin pencil:

> *Teacher*
> *bring me to heaven*
> *or leave me alone.*
> *Why make me work so hard*
> *when everything's spread around*
> *open, like forest's poison oak*
> > *turned red*
> *empty sleeping bags hanging from*
> > *a dead branch.*

I looked at it for a moment.

I asked her where it came from. She just stared with a slight smile emerging at the corners of her mouth.

"You don't know?" I asked.

She puckered her lips slightly.

I continued with more questions: Did she write it? Who else wrote it? What was it called? What does it mean? Who was the Teacher? Who was taking whom to heaven? What did that part mean? I dissected the poem with questions, but Laura just stood there staring back at me, giving no indication that she planned to answer anything. She just let her smile grow slightly larger with each question.

"I don't want to seem ungrateful, but I don't get it," I said. "Why are you giving me some mysterious poem, yet not telling me what it is or who wrote it or what it means?"

"Just think about it for a while," she said. "You'll eventually figure it out."

"But what's it about?"

Laura seemed to struggle a bit, not wanting to give anything away.

"It could be about us, I guess," she finally blurted out. "Well," she quickly continued, as if to pedal back. "It's from me to you. Let's leave it at that."

I read it over again.

"How is this about us?" I asked. "I mean, who is who in this, and who is doing what, with what, where?"

"Just think about it for a while," she repeated.

"Is this some kind of joke or something?" I asked. "Are you serious about this?"

She paused.

"No, it isn't a joke," she said.

As we sat on the swing set talking for another hour or so, I was doing exactly as she suggested. In fact, I did little else but think about the Mystery Poem. As Laura talked about some book she had just finished, I was trying to decipher what she was trying to tell me, and why now.

After she went home, I pulled out the Mystery Poem and read it again.

Part of me wondered if the protagonist's asking to "bring me to heaven" was her way of telling me that she cared about me—or wanted to. Part of me wondered if "or leave me alone" was her way of telling me that she was giving up, tired of waiting for me to become something I wasn't. Part of me wondered if "why make me work so hard" was her way of telling me she believed in me, but waiting for me to get my shit together was hard. Part of me wondered if this was her way of telling me she was frustrated. Perhaps the reference to empty sleeping bags on a dead branch indicated what she felt the future held for her—or me—if either of us stayed here in Canton. Maybe she was using the poem to say she loved me. Maybe she didn't want to be friends anymore. Maybe she was trying to tell me all these things. As I pondered each, I ran through our entire history together, trying to find a way to make connections. The words of the Mystery Poem seemed like they could potentially express any or all or none of these.

I folded up the Mystery Poem and put it into my pocket.

• • •

In between bites of an open-faced turkey sandwich during our last post–*Rocky Horror* diner visit, Jamie the corset boy declared that all music began and ended with Bauhaus. Vikki laughed and nodded in agreement. It was the kind of thing you say to be provocative in the midst of a provocative conversation with the hope that no one asks you to explain yourself.

"What about Tones on Tail? Have you heard of them?" Laura asked.

"Of course I have," Jamie dramatically snapped back.

"Well, Eric saw them play in Cleveland." She then looked at me like I was supposed to say something.

"What?" I said.

"Tell him about the show," she said.

"You were there, too. Why are you asking me to tell him?"

Laura told a girl from Mansfield that I had just finished reading *Animal Farm* (which she had loaned me). When she overheard this older guy named Tom talking about the movie *Eraserhead* (which Laura and I had seen together at least three times), she tried to get me to share some of my observations. It was like Laura was trying to turn herself into the Eric PR Department.

I realized what was going on. She was matchmaking. Laura was trying to find someone—or some people—to replace her in my life. She wanted to find people to help take care of me after she left. She was trying to help me find my tribe. To find a group of people I'd fit in with. She didn't want me to be alone.

I had been dreading this night all week. Not simply because Laura was leaving for New York in a few days, but because she was handling this night exactly like I feared she would: by not telling anyone anything.

After breakfast in the diner that morning, everyone gathered in the parking lot to say goodbye and good night. It was late August, and everything was cool, crisp, and moist with dew. Laura didn't tell any of our crew that she wouldn't be back again. She just said goodbye to them like it was any other Saturday that summer. So typical, I remember thinking. She just flits away without telling anyone the truth, then leaves me to come back the following week and explain everything she should have said before. When we'd driven up earlier that evening, I'd asked her if she planned to tell anyone that she was leaving. She didn't respond directly, just saying something about wanting to enjoy the moment.

"Well, while you're enjoying your moment," I said, "you should realize that you are pretty much lying to everyone by not being honest with them."

"How is that not being honest?" she protested. "I haven't told anyone anything that isn't true."

"But you haven't told the truth," I said. "Which, trust me, is worse."

When we got into the car at the end of the night, she pulled out a bottle of wine that I didn't even know she'd been carrying around all night. She started taking drinks from it, occasionally passing it over to me. As we were just about to get off the highway, she told me that she wanted to go out to the gas well before we went home.

"You should keep hanging out with those guys," she said. "They are good people. Fun."

"Maybe," I said.

We were quiet for a few minutes as the rising sun began to brighten and color the horizon.

"I was reading this article that was talking about New York clubs," I said as I spread the green felted blanket out over the gas-well gravel. "You know, they charge you *five dollars* for a beer there?"

"Yeah, so?"

"So, I hope you weren't planning to drink beer in clubs. There is no way you could ever afford that."

"Eric, you need to stop it," she said. "Because you just go on and on because you think it's important to tell me stuff like that, and it isn't. It's small to do that, smaller than you."

She took a long pull off the bottle.

"I still just don't get it," I said, plopping down on the blanket.

"Why do you have to *get* anything?" she said. "It's what's happening. That's all."

She lay down on the blanket and curled up next to me. I was staring up at the sky trying to make out the fading stars.

At some point, I felt her kiss my cheek and move closer to me. Then she started to kiss me on the mouth and pull me on top of her. She ran her fingers through my hair as we kissed.

"I want you to make love with me," she said.

"What?"

"I want you to make love with me," she said.

My heart started pounding in my chest, my fingers started shaking.

I wrapped my arm around her and started kissing her. I pulled away for a moment and looked at her eyes. A moment later she slowly opened hers and had trouble focusing, then her eyes rolled half back into her head before she told me to kiss her again.

I sighed and rolled over.

"What's wrong?" she said.

"I can't do this," I said. "You're drunk."

"So?"

"No, it isn't right."

"I thought you'd . . ."

"I do, but it's not the way I . . . we can't."

She could barely sit herself up. "But I want to," she said.

"How do I know that?" I said. This wasn't the way I'd thought it would be. Everything was wrong.

She sighed and lay back down on the blanket. The sun was about ready to peek above the horizon.

"Do you want to go home now?" I asked eventually.

"Yeah."

We were already supposed to get together the following night—our last time together before she left. In a rare moment of advance planning, Laura had set aside this night among the packing and preparation and family dinners and other farewells. When I asked what she wanted to do, she suggested we go out to the gas well one last time. We even swung by Lake O'Dea on the way, for old time's sake.

We lazily chatted as we drove out. The sun was close to setting. I badly wanted to bring up the night before but had no idea how. At a quiet point, I just let it spill out.

"Do you remember what happened last night? What you said?" I asked.

"What's that?"

"At the gas well? You really don't remember?"

Laura looked out the passenger window and stared at the buildings rolling past. "I was a little drunk, I think," she said.

"Do you want me to tell you?"

"Go on."

"We started kissing and you said you wanted to make love."

Laura's eyes got huge.

"You don't remember this?"

"Umm . . . no," she said, returning her eyes out the window.

"Oh."

From there, everything was idle chatting, as if nothing had happened or was happening. We watched the sun go down and just sat next to the gas well talking, with the car windows rolled down, playing tapes loud enough so we could hear. Inside, I wanted to scream. I wanted to yell that I felt like she was deserting me. Inside, I was still reeling from the night before. I wanted to pull my hair out and kick and scream so loud because I just felt like she wasn't willing to hear me otherwise. I just tried to push it all out in a big sighing breath.

"I'm really going to miss you," I finally said.

She smiled. "Let's not," she said.

"Let's not . . . what?"

"Let's not talk about this," she said. "Let's just leave it with you knowing that I am always there for you. You can call or see me anytime you need to. All you have to do is give the word."

"So if I tell you that I need you, you'll come back from New York?"

"If need be, yeah."

"Well, what if I told you I needed you right now," I said. "Would you stay and not leave?"

She sighed and looked away.

"Let's not . . . okay?"

"Okay," I said. "How about you just spill the beans about the Poem instead?"

She just shot me a stare.

I walked over to the car to light a cigarette on the car lighter.

"Oh, by the way," I said. "Here's your book back."

I pulled her feathered copy of *Slaughterhouse-Five* out of the car.

"Did you enjoy it?" she asked.

"Yeah, I . . . no. To be honest with you, I never even opened it."

"Oh," she said. "Well, you can keep it if you want . . ."

I had no interest in reading it. Since she'd given it to me, I'd become a bit perplexed by her insistence that I read *Slaughterhouse-Five*. It had become somewhat like the Mystery Poem to me. She wouldn't tell me *why* she had wanted me to read it, but she really, really wanted me to read it. She had asked about it several times. To me, not reading it had become my own little passive-aggressive touché fuck-you. If she wouldn't give me the satisfaction of knowing why it was so important, then I wouldn't give her the satisfaction of reading it. In fact, I avoided the book for years afterward, under some false idea that it still mattered.

"I doubt I'll have time to read it," I added. "I have my own life to get on with, right?"

I handed the book to her. Sticking out of the top of its pages was an envelope. The envelope contained a letter I'd written earlier that day. I was hoping she'd notice it but not right away. Maybe when she got home and put the book away, she'd see it there and wonder what it was.

We both knew it was time to go.

"Goodbye, old gas well," she said, reaching out to pet the corroded steel. "May you pump lots and lots of gas and have a happy life."

She got into the car and we started back toward her house.

About halfway there, she reached over and took my hand, holding it for the rest of the drive.

When I parked the car across from her parents' house, I turned to her. "Look—" I said.

"No . . . don't," she said, putting her finger across my lips. She kissed me, then held me close. "Don't say anything. Not a word. Please, let's just not do this."

Not do what? I thought. Leave? Be apart? Fight? Stop being friends? Amen, sister, I thought. I'm right with you.

Then I realized that what she didn't want to do was say goodbye. What she didn't want to have to deal with was the truth: This was the end of us. Maybe not forever, but at least for now. She didn't want to say how we felt. She didn't want to heal anything or hear any apologies. She just wanted it to be done.

I nodded to show I understood. She kissed my forehead and then touched it to hers.

Then she opened the car door, picked up her bag and the copy of *Slaughterhouse-Five* wrapped around the letter I'd hoped she'd notice, and left.

In the letter, I told her, again, how hurt I was by her leaving. I told her how, to me, the Mystery Poem was the epitome of our relationship. I told her how frustrating it was that she always kept me at a distance, cloaking herself in deliberate ambiguity and vagueness, and never considered letting me get as close to her as she insisted on being to me.

I thanked her for being my friend through the past year. I told her that no one had stuck with me except her and that I'd never forget that.

Then I told her that I loved her.

I told her that I didn't need her to love me back. I told her that there was nothing we needed to do about it. I just wanted her to know that I felt that way. I told her that just saying that was good enough. I knew we would always be friends, no matter what happened.

I asked her to forgive me for not being a better person. I told her that I was glad I made her a little happy and how much I wished I could have made her happier. I apologized for being so much work. I told her that I knew she'd always be there for me. And I told her that I knew she would do well at school and have wonderful experiences in New York, things I could never even dream of.

I'd written the letter earlier that afternoon, but I'd known since she told me she was leaving that I'd have to confess all this to her. Almost every night I'd promised myself I'd do it, but I always chickened out. I'm not sure if it was because I thought she'd laugh at me, or be scared of me, or maybe I was actually scared that she'd tell me, just before leaving for New York, that she loved me too. There was no doubt in my mind that she loved me in some manner. I guess my biggest fear was that the way she loved me was far different from the way I felt for her.

The thought of letting her know I'd written a letter was terrifying. So I'd hidden it in her book. But not too well, I hoped.

The next day I stayed near the phone all day. I allowed myself to hope that she'd notice the envelope, get curious about it, read the letter, call me immediately, and cancel her plans to leave for New York—or at least delay them so we could have another chance to talk.

By around seven that evening, about twelve hours before she was supposed to leave, I still hadn't heard from her. I was pacing the floor in the makeshift bedroom in my parents' house, telling myself the envelope in the book was such a stupid idea. She was so busy getting ready to leave that she probably put the book on a shelf without even noticing. I had to go over there. I had to come clean and share my feelings. I'd open the letter and read it to her myself. She always wanted the truth, and I'd never forgive myself if I didn't tell it to her.

Her mother answered the door and said that Laura was out for the evening. "She's out with a group of friends," she said.

"Oh, right, yeah . . . right. They all went out tonight," I said, pretending that I knew this. "I think I know where they're heading. I'll go meet them there." It was probably some of her friends from school. People I probably knew as well, but people who had never even seen Laura and me together, let alone people who would think to include me in anything they had planned. They were her real friends, I thought.

I thanked Mrs. Patterson and headed back to the car.

A week later, I'd receive a postcard from Laura with a painted street scene in New York on one side, and on the other, "Here. No time to write. I'm sorry."

A few days after that, I'd walk into Dr. Chang's office and place all my medications on his desk, leaving them there after telling him we would never be seeing each other again.

"If you do this," he'd warn me as I got up to leave, "you will live a life of misery."

Soon after that I'd simply stop going to my appointments with Blumfield. He'd leave one message inquiring if I was planning to come back. I'd never hear from or see him again. A week after that, my dad would help me move into my dorm room at Kent State. Then I'd start my new life. A clean slate.

I believe I was motivated to move on, to get away from the last lifelines to my past, because I felt like I had something to prove. I was angry and hurt. The last thing I wanted was for Laura to come home and find me in the same place I was in when she left. I felt a compulsion to do things with my life that she couldn't have conceived for me. That compulsion drove me, and still drives me, to never be satisfied or accept expectations. Laura had done so much for me over the previous months, but it took the anger that she inspired in me to truly push me forward.

On that night, as I walked from her parents' house to the car, the idea of life without Laura had stopped being theoretical and became real. It wasn't something that was about to happen. It had already started happening. Without even realizing it, I was already in the middle of it.

I was already haunted by the memory of our friendship. The ghost of her was already vivid in my mind.

• • • •

Even though Kent State University was only thirty miles from Canton, it felt like a different planet. There were a few kids from my high school who went to Kent as well, but I was about as uninterested in them as they were in me, so I just started my life over again, from scratch.

Despite the freedom to start over, I really had no clue of where I wanted to go or what I wanted to do there. I was content to just *begin*. My new, fresh life really wasn't that different from my old one, minus the substance abuse and dead children following me around.

After I moved to Kent, my Little Girl dreams and feelings seemed to come to an end, much like they began: slowly, in fits and starts and pieces and fragments. Then they weren't there anymore. I really hadn't noticed this happening at the time. I was in a new place, around new people, and living a new life. For the most part, I was just happy not to have to deal with it; I wasn't terribly concerned with why. I was ready to move on.

I would, occasionally, reflect on what had happened, seeing if time and distance provided any insight. They didn't. But I didn't want to press my luck either. This is what really led me to the fear of ghosts that stayed with me throughout my life.

While Little Girl no longer seemed part of my life, ghosts, in general, seemed to sneak in to take Her place. I was so worried about provoking Her presence that I would end up avoiding unfamiliar or spooky-feeling places where I would be alone or in the dark. I'd also stay away from closed doors. Evading any potential Little Girl–friendly location eventually evolved into going out of my way to dodge anything even remotely rumored to involve ghosts. I would walk blocks out of my way to steer clear of a house that looked or felt particularly spooky. I'd suddenly change the topic or walk out of the room during the occasional late-night ghost story exchanged during the last smoldering embers of a party. I begged off watching ghost movies—even stupid stuff like *Poltergeist* or *Ghostbusters* would cause me to suddenly find something else to do somewhere else.

Whenever I was around a creepy or supposedly haunted place, I'd get this slightly sick, overwhelmed feeling. Then I'd try "calling out" to the ghost. Sometimes it made me feel better; sometimes I just lay, sat, or stood there in terror until I could get away.

Once I got settled into school, I signed up for a shift at the college radio station, WKSR, which was a step up from WKSC but not that much of a step up. It was an AM station, but it was carrier-current (which meant that it had about a dozen small transmitters stashed around the dorms on campus, each with a range of about thirty feet). But WKSR had a staff of hipsters and its own record collection (which the staff pilfered on an almost daily basis) and new record service from record labels (which the staff also routinely stole, often before they'd even been removed from their shipping packages).

I took classes—and actually attended them—and did a

modicum of the required work. I got a part-time job painting lines on the football fields (which felt like a tremendous step up from cleaning toilets). I lived in the dorms and seemed to take pretty quickly to college life. I even made some friends.

Most of my friends were musicians and artists—or, more specifically, students who liked to think of themselves as musicians and artists. The big difference was that none of them sold drugs—or really took drugs, for that matter. Music was the currency in this crowd, so there were a lot of bands formed and disbanded, sometimes in the course of the same evening. We'd be sitting around, bored and watching television, when someone would say something like "Hey, we should start a band where we dress in Viking costumes and all our songs are about cheese."

Then someone else would pipe in: "Yeah, we could call ourselves Omelet du Fromage."

A few weeks later Omelet du Fromage would be rocking Kent, Ohio.

There was a never-ending stream of these bands. If we weren't playing heavy metal while wearing wizard costumes, we were covering Barry Manilow songs in our underwear or playing funked-up children's songs by candlelight. We thought that the abstruseness would delight our small audiences. More often than not, the novelty wore off by the third song. After some initial smiles and giggles, even our closest friends would start shifting around in their seats, staring at the signage on the walls, or picking at the worn laminate on the tabletops.

My first introduction into this world was also my first "serious" (read: actual) band, called Not Made With Hands, started with John, a guy I befriended in a film class. Shortly after we started practicing, we somehow managed to talk our way into opening for a touring band in town for a night. It was our first gig. I was a nervous mess.

By the time we were supposed to start, I was sweating, shaking, stammering, and feeling nauseous. Right before we went on, our drummer, Adam, handed me a tambourine and told me that it might help. The second I walked onstage, I started banging the tambourine. Of course, I had forgotten that I had a beer bottle in my other hand and ended up spraying beer all over the stage. John took this as a cue and started up our first song.

Our set got better from there but not that much better. It felt a lot like having sex for the first time. By the time I got my sea legs, it was over. We'd played eight songs in thirty minutes, but to me, it felt like the whole thing was over in about twelve seconds. I was tired, sweaty, confused, humiliated—and I couldn't wait to do it again.

But, like 99.9 percent of bands, Not Made With Hands eventually imploded, a year later. It was never meant to go anywhere, which is exactly where it went. Playing music would be part of my life in fits and spurts. At the time, I thought every project was amazing and a gift to the world. Years later, I'd realize that none of my bands and musical efforts were really very remarkable at all, but that didn't matter. There is no sensation in the world like playing music, loud music. Slamming your hands down on a guitar and hearing it emit noise. Singing out into a microphone was almost like a religious experience and orgasm wrapped into one. I've found many other ways to capture that joy, but at the time I couldn't imagine anything making me any happier than playing in bands.

I only saw Laura once during my reimmersion into the world at large. Since the first postcard, I had received only a few cryptic letters from her in New York, talking mostly about the job she'd gotten at a bookstore and a few concerts she'd seen. In all fairness, I only stayed at that first dorm for a semester and moved without telling her. Every holiday or break, we'd try talking on the phone or make some effort to connect while we were both in Canton. The conversations were always weird—there was always a lot of uncomfortable silence. I'd always have some excuse for not trying harder to see her: *She* owed *me* a letter; I had tried to call *her* during the last break, so it was now her turn. We spoke on the phone briefly on Christmas, but we both were heading back out of town the next day. Next time, we promised each other. Next time.

On one hand I was desperate to see her; on the other I was desperate to avoid it.

Talking with her, writing to her, receiving something from her, or even thinking about her, frankly, hurt. It hurt more than not hearing from her. Seeing her scratchy handwriting or hearing her voice made me think about how much I missed her. How periodically lost I felt without my best friend. Even hearing a great new band bummed me out, because my in-stinctual reaction was to want to tell her about it.

She and Cassandra (the girl who had called to get me to talk to Laura when she first returned from Finland) came to a Not Made With Hands show that coincided with a trip home from New York. By that time, our occasional phone calls were be-coming less tense, less as if we had something to prove to each other. We planned on hanging out beforehand, but Cassandra and Laura were hours late. They showed up just as we started. I could see them walk in and sit. Because of the stage lights blaring into my face, I could only see her outline, but I knew it was her. As we played, I just looked at her, trying to pick up any possible detail. They stayed for about half our set. Then the two of them walked up to the stage between songs and said they had to leave. Laura had to get back to New York the next morning.

Her hair was long, grown out past her shoulders. It was covered with a bandana and hung straight down her back. Her face looked exactly the same. Whatever had happened to her since moving to New York, she wasn't showing it in her eyes. She was just as beautiful, just as reserved. Standing at the foot of the stage, she was less than two feet from me, yet felt so distant. That's really all I remember about the encounter: her stepping out of the shadows to say hello and goodbye.

It was the last time I'd ever see her.

A short time later I was moving from one shithole college house to another shithole college house when I came across a manila envelope marked "Laura." It contained most of the let-ters, cards, pictures, and scraps of paper she'd given me during our friendship. The only thing missing from that envelope was the Mystery Poem. It had disappeared during some previous move, covered and forgotten under some other debris and clutter from my life. It was just one of those things that always seems to be around until one day you notice it's not—and you have no idea when the last time you saw it was. Yet I remembered it vividly. I could quote it verbatim, having committed it to memory while reading it over and over. I still had no idea what it meant.

"Just think about it for a while. You'll eventually figure it out."

Someday it would dawn on me—or I'd just wait until we were friends again and pester her into telling me. A moment would come and all the pieces would fit into place. But when that would be was her choice, wasn't it? Not mine. She'd gone to New York and pretty much forgotten about me. Despite her promises to the contrary that night at the gas well, she was gone.

The whole envelope went into the trash.

Over the following year, I was still struggling to figure out who the new me was going to be. I started drinking again, though it never came close to what I had been doing in Canton. I was still playing in bands, hoping to become a rock star. But just in case that didn't work out, I decided to major in political science. I was fascinated by public-opinion research and polling, understanding the difference between what people say and what they mean. I'd gotten a summer job working at the local public radio station and found a terrible attic room in a house for the summer. I had some friends. I pursued some girls with occasional bits of luck. I had a cat that I took care of. It wasn't an ideal life, but it was something. Something that felt like a start.

. . .

Clearing. Picnic table. Wolf costume. Woods. Little Girl in a Blue Dress. Gibberish.

I was sitting upright in my bed, covered in sweat, not from the dream but from the temperature in my bedroom. It was the midst of a muggy heat wave. I had a tiny fan in the small window at the end of the alcove, which just moved the hot air around inside the attic.

Where the fuck did that come from? I wondered.

I was in that disoriented not-sure-if-you're-still-dreaming-or-not state as I looked around the room, completely unsure of what was or wasn't really there.

"I'm going to close my eyes," I said into the hopefully empty darkness. "And if there is a ghost here, I will see it when I open them again."

I closed my eyes tight, then quickly opened them.

Motionless darkness. Nothing.

I needed to get out of the house. I needed to go for a walk.

It was the first Little Girl dream I'd had in a long time. I hadn't even thought about Her for months.

The house where I lived was just two blocks from the main strip in Kent—if a guitar store, four bars, a deli, and a butcher shop constituted a main strip. It was just before 1 A.M., so I figured there was a fair chance that at least a few of my friends would be stumbling from one dive bar to another.

As I headed around the corner onto Franklin Avenue, I saw a group of four or five people walking toward me.

One of them was Cassandra.

As her friends waited in a drunken state of impatience, Cassandra and I exchanged hugs and phone numbers. We were both a bit in shock to see each other. How weird, we both commented. How strange it is that we'd both be randomly walking down the street and run into each other, especially when she didn't even live here. I was just going for a walk, I said. At one A.M.?, she asked, chuckling. Yes, at one A.M. We both laughed, while her friends looked more annoyed. They wanted to go to the bars, not stand around and watch us be blown away by our strange coincidental meeting.

A few days later I called Cassandra. I hadn't given any more thought to our chance meeting, or its timing, or even the Little Girl dream that preceded it. It just seemed like an unexpected but still kind of normal set of occurrences. Whenever I tell anyone this story, that series of events is what I always feel I have to explain. No Little Girl dreams for more than a year— then suddenly, I have one. Then in the middle of that night I decide to dress and go for a walk. Then I run into an old friend who just happens to be in town barhopping, and we make plans to talk. Frankly, if I was listening to someone else tell this story, I'd find it hard to believe that things lined up so neatly. But they did. While it is hard to think that they might be connected, it is even harder to think that they aren't.

When I called, Cassandra and I spent about thirty minutes talking about her life at college, her new boyfriend, and odds and ends of family news. I told her about life in Kent and my budding music career.

"When was the last time I saw you?" I asked.

"I think it was when Laura and I came to see your band," she answered. I had actually been avoiding mentioning Laura during the call. I didn't want Cassandra to think I was pumping her for information, nor was I sure I really wanted to hear whatever she had to say about Laura.

Then Cassandra was quiet for a moment.

"I wanted to ask you something before we hang up," she said.

"Okay."

"I wanted to ask you how you are doing with this Laura stuff," she said.

Pause.

"What Laura stuff?"

Pause.

"The situation with Laura," she stammered.

"What situation with Laura?" I asked.

"Oh my God," she said. "You don't know?"

Pause.

"Don't know what?"

"Oh my, you don't know, do you?" she said. "Why didn't someone tell you?"

Cassandra became very flustered, half thinking out loud what to do, half trying to avoid saying anything at all. She refused to explain further, her voiced filled with increasing panic.

"What situation?" I yelled at her.

"I can't tell you," she said. "Not like this, not over the phone."

"Listen," I said. "If you don't tell me now, I'm going to get in the car and drive to your fucking front door and make you tell me to my fucking face. What is going on?!"

I could hear Cassandra exhale into the phone.

Fewer things are messier than learning about a tragic death after everyone else. They've just started to recover from their grief. They are able to talk about the deceased without losing composure. In short, they are moving on. Then you show up. You are back at square one. You are in shock. You are a blubbering souvenir of the pain and loss they are struggling to climb above.

Old friends who were normally reticent to talk to me in the first place were even more so now. A few phone calls were returned, a few details confirmed, a few new tidbits added to the mix. Most people I got hold of were willing to discuss things they'd heard. Almost no one wanted to talk about how they felt.

I'd managed to piece together some things.

Laura had attended Baruch as she'd planned, but it hadn't gone well. She didn't like the school, she didn't like the students, she didn't like the roach-infested rat hole they'd given her to call home. She eventually transferred to Hunter College and also took a few classes at Columbia before taking a semester off. Eventually, she decided to leave New York and return to Canton.

She'd gotten a job as a waitress and started taking classes at Kent Stark. In the four months that she'd lived in Canton, she'd let most of her friends know she had moved back, except one. Me.

One spring afternoon she rode her bike to the drugstore. As she was leaving, she crossed the intersection of Twenty-fifth Street and Fulton Avenue. She was wearing headphones and listening to her Walkman. She rode her bike into a through lane, was hit by a car and knocked down into the road. She died almost instantly of a head injury.

Laura died on a Thursday and was buried on a Saturday. None of my friends seemed to know or remember exactly where she was buried. Eventually, I figured out that it was the Evergreen Memorial Gardens, very close to where the Putt-O-Links had been. I'd heard that there was no marker to go by, so I asked the caretaker for some help locating her. After following his instructions, I came to a neat box of turned earth cut into the grass. I sat down in front of it. I said I was so sorry.

I was sorry for what happened. I was sorry for being such an ass. I just kept repeating it over and over again.

"Say, ah . . . that isn't your friend," the caretaker eventually called out. "She's one row back and a few spots to the left."

I looked over. There was another neatly cut rectangle of dirt.

I moved over to Laura's grave.

"I really don't feel like starting over," I said. "I'm sure you heard everything I told the other dead person."

After staring at the dirt silently for a moment, I broke out crying.

There was no marker. No flowers. Nothing. It would be a few years before a headstone was placed there. I visited a few times and kept wondering why nothing was there. Part of me questioned whether this was perhaps a big mistake. Maybe Laura wasn't dead at all. Maybe this was someone else they confused with Laura. I kept waiting for her to show up and explain how it had all been a big misunderstanding.

I'd like to tell you there's more to this part of the story, but there really isn't. It, like all death, was a sudden, harsh ending. There was no final climax, no big lesson or moral—it just ended there.

The only thing I clearly remember feeling was that I knew, even then, that I had come to another turning point in my life. I realized that I could use this as a reasonable excuse to do just about anything I wanted: completely freak out, be inspired to greatness, start taking drugs, live as a hermit in the back woods of Oregon—you name it, I had the perfect rationale.

Several years later, my friend Barry died. He passed away on his couch in an apartment in Columbus, Ohio. Several months earlier, for no apparent reason, Barry had abruptly walked out of his job and slowly started to cut himself off from his friends.

And then one day I got a call, and he was dead. He'd just died—no obvious cause. While we'd theorized that it may have been drugs or AIDS, no one quite knew for sure. The only sure thing was that Barry, for some reason, had decided to stop living, then went and sat in his apartment until he got what he wished for. I was sad to lose Barry, of course, but then—and many times since—I've thought about how close I came to ending up the same way myself. One of those times was standing there in Evergreen Memorial Gardens.

In the moments that I wasn't overwhelmed with grief at Laura's death, I felt confusion and anger. Why had she never let me know she'd moved back to Canton? She was living there for months with me less than forty minutes away and never made an effort to let me know. I was mad because I missed her, but also because I'd worked so hard to build a life that would, someday, be worth her approval. Now that day was never going to come. Not only would we never get a chance to completely reconcile, but she would never see what happened to me. That I turned out okay after all.

Over the years, this has always been the part of this story I've struggled with most—wanting to understand why she never did anything—not a card, not a phone call, not a word passed through a friend. Was it out of anger? Out of spite? Was she embarrassed? Did she think I'd tell her that I knew all along that things wouldn't work out in New York the way she thought? Was she waiting for something to happen or fall into place first? Even now I'm dumbstruck thinking about how much cleaner both our lives would have been with just one evening spent winding through the back roads surrounding Canton.

I stood staring at the loose, turned dirt above her grave. The person I'd wanted so much to be close to, and had missed so terribly over the previous two years, was right there. She'd always be right there. There was only a few feet of dirt separating us.

For some reason, I took a step forward so that I could stand on top of the dirt of her grave. I don't know why, but it felt like I'd be closer to her if I was right there over her. Almost as soon as I'd placed both my feet on top of the turned soil, I started to sink. It felt like quicksand. It seemed in an instant I was in past my ankles. I scrambled, falling on my back in the soft grass. I hastily brushed myself off and headed for my car, leaving two fresh shoe prints at the foot of Laura's grave.

NOW

Mansfield Reformatory is bigger than I had imagined.

In fact, it's fucking huge. It is more than a quarter million square feet, divided into two main wings, each containing cell blocks six stories high. Prisons like Mansfield were designed to dehumanize and humble their residents with imposing scale and grandness. Mansfield's size, plus its towering Romanesque façade, makes it a pretty stunning place. You've probably seen Mansfield Reformatory before, as it's regularly used as a movie set. *The Shawshank Redemption* was filmed here, as were parts of *Air Force One* and *Tango & Cash,* as well as music videos for everyone from Lil Wayne to Marilyn Manson.

I've known about Mansfield for most of my life, though I've never been here before. It's about an hour west of Canton. Far enough away that curiosity about the place, as intense as it was, still wasn't enough to get me to venture over here.

Mansfield, also known as the Ohio State Reformatory, was Ohio's primary prison from the 1890s until the 1970s, when it was slowly put out of use. More than two hundred people died here—from execution, murder, and suicide—while it was a functioning correctional facility. It was such a terrible, inhumane place that calls for its closure started as early as 1930.

Since the last prisoner was moved out in 1990, the place has been pretty much abandoned. Today Mansfield is something between a historic ruin and an EPA Superfund site in the making. Lead paint peels off every surface that isn't corroded; walls and ceilings are falling apart or completely missing; and asbestos and plaster dust are everywhere. Then there's the broken rusty metal, missing guardrails, exposed wiring, doors off their hinges, loose stairs, and so on.

I'm walking through the deserted prison in the bright light of a sunny afternoon. Seeing it by day, I just can't imagine that you could take in all the grandness of the place exploring alone in the pitch blackness with a three-watt flashlight. But that's exactly what I intend to do in a few hours.

What makes Mansfield truly notorious is its reputation for the paranormal. The place is rumored to be filled to its sizeable brim with very serious bad mojo. Unlike other haunted sites, where people feel cold breezes or light touches, or see a floating head or something, Mansfield hosts interactions with the dead that are on a different level. The living are grabbed, punched, shoved, and pushed. Things are thrown and slammed.

A bald, muscular, and mildly intimidating man, Scott Sukel, is showing me around. In something between bureaucratic malfeasance and sheer stupidity, they actually allow people to come in here. Since 1995, a preservation group has maintained the site and conducts tours.

"Yeah, the worst thing I've ever experienced here was about two years ago," Scott says. "I was taking a few people through the administration building and I got punched in the left kidney, which left a bruise for three days. I was standing here and everything was pretty quiet and normal, then I got this 'Oh, shit' feeling—you know, like something bad is going to happen—then *bam*. I ended up on my knees on the floor.

That's when I realized that I needed to stop being a tour guide and start trying to figure out how to get these people out of here safely, without them panicking."

That incident happened during one of Scott's ghost hunts in the prison. Even crazier than letting people inside Mansfield Reformatory during the day is that several times a year Scott and his crew escort people into the building at night. Everyone meets on the front steps at 8 P.M. Then all have to sign one of the most complete and comprehensive liability waivers you'll ever see in your life. Then Scott's crew gives folks a quick orientation tour to help get everyone adjusted. Then they turn off the lights. Then it slowly gets dark. Then the group is free to roam the entire prison structure, almost completely unrestricted, until dawn.

Of all the haunted places I've read about or encountered, Mansfield is by far the place that people are least skeptical about. Given all the horrible things that have happened here and all the terrible people who have passed in and out of its gates, I think people are just willing to accept that fucked-up paranormalness would naturally happen here, if anywhere. In fact, I don't ever recall encountering anyone who has stepped forward and said there isn't some kind of lingering presence here.

If there are ghosts anywhere, this seems like the place to find one.

At this moment, Mansfield isn't feeling as foreboding as it rightly should be. I'm distracted by another presence. Mansfield is less than an hour away from Canton. The place that holds clues to so many of my unanswered questions. Clues that could turn into answers if I could just muster the courage to go there and seek them out.

My family doesn't live in Canton anymore. They live about halfway between here and Canton, yet I didn't even tell them

I was making the seven-hour drive to visit the reformatory. Laura's family still resides there, or so I've heard from some people I've spoken to. I'd never been able to figure out how to approach them about Laura, what became of her after she left for college, and to start filling in the voids of my understanding about what happened and why. I'd also heard that Laura's mother was sick with cancer and did not have long to live, so I knew not only that I had to be in touch with them but that it had to be soon.

While I seem to have found the courage to go traipsing around the country scaring myself looking for ghosts, I had a far harder time forcing myself to go to my hometown, to look up a phone number in the phone book, to call, to reach out in any way.

To me, the grand towers of Mansfield are like giant compass needles pointing toward the ghosts I really need to be chasing, inviting me to clear away the fear between me and what I really need to confront but couldn't or wouldn't.

Since I began this journey, I've started to feel less like a writer and more like a detective: searching for clues, following leads, and ferreting out details among a mass of twisted and confused memories. Throughout my experience as a journalist, I've had to root out truth, uncover facts, and sort through contradictions. I never thought that my most evasive subject would be myself.

It's a weird feeling, contacting people from your past, asking for their help to remember things—often very uncomfortable or unpleasant things—about, well, about you. Whenever I first spoke to someone, I'd almost feel compelled to let them know, subtly, that I wasn't crazy. I'd talk about my interests or my job—you know, things that normal people talk about. Once that was established, I'd pretty much lay out my quest, all the nonsense I'd believed back then, and the fact that everyone involved was either dead, couldn't remember it, or didn't want to. Then I'd weakly smile and hope they still thought I wasn't crazy. .

At one point I even tried to find Dr. Blumfield, but to no avail. From the hospital records, I learned his first name: Haywood. You'd think with a name like that—especially for someone who hangs a shingle as a therapist—he'd be easy to find. But outside of those hospital records, I could find no references to him, then or now. Even looking back to the directories from those years, I couldn't find a telephone listing.

But reaching out to the Pattersons had always seemed absolutely necessary, yet absolutely impossible.

Walking through the decrepit hallways of Mansfield Reformatory provides a distraction, or at least a delay. A spooky, frightening, and kind of fucked-up delay.

"Yeah, you spend enough time in here, you'll see it all," Scott says as we make our way through the west cell block. "On any given night we'll see a full-body apparition, hear voices screaming 'Get out' or 'Stay with us,' cell doors slam open and shut, and sometimes you'll get smells, like roses."

Apparently one of the former wardens' wives—a wife who was accidentally killed here when a loaded revolver fell off a closet shelf—loved flowers. She's supposedly a regular presence in the residential areas. Sometimes she is seen, sometimes she is heard singing, sometimes visitors just smell floral perfume or roses.

"Yeah . . . we'll make sure you get to have an experience tonight," he adds. "And who knows, we might be able to keep you from getting raped."

Despite my mixed feelings about being in Mansfield, being raped was definitely not on my to-do list for the evening.

As nighttime approaches and the rest of the prison explorers assemble on the front steps, Scott and I discuss my plans for the evening. I came alone and plan to explore the prison on my own or tagging along with others. If it gets late in the night and I haven't had a satisfactory "experience," then he'll send out some of his crew to, as he puts it, "stir some stuff up."

As the orientation tours wrap up, Scott takes a long look out the windows lining the back of the building. The sun is setting.

"Looks like it's time," he says as he starts to head down the hallway to kill all the lights. "Here's hoping you have a very interesting night tonight."

A few weeks before coming to Mansfield, I finally worked up the courage to do something else completely scary and uncertain: Write a letter.

"Dear Mr. and Mrs. Patterson," I wrote. "I'm sure my name is one you haven't heard or thought of in quite some time. I was good friends with your daughter Laura before she passed away."

Approaching the Pattersons to try to understand more about their deceased daughter troubled me greatly. During her life, I had very little exposure to her family, mostly by her choice. I once asked Laura what her family thought of her taking off several nights a week with someone they hardly knew.

"I think they're just happy that I have a friend" was her reply.

After learning that someone named Patterson still lived at her old house east of Canton—and had the same phone number I used to call two decades ago to speak with Laura—I talked myself into thinking that writing a letter would be a better approach. It was definitely a better approach for me, but I rationalized it would be better for them, too. That is, if they answered it.

Several of my friends cautioned me against approaching the Pattersons via letter.

"Letters are too easy to ignore," my friend David offered. "They'll get it, read it, think about calling you, and then never do it. Could you blame them?"

David's advice, along with that of several others I talked to about this: Call. Just pick up the phone and call them. That seemed crazy to me. Imagine sitting at home one night watching TV when the phone rings and some stranger from your dead daughter's past is on the other end, full of questions. Even if I just called to reintroduce myself to them, it still felt like I'd be showing up out of nowhere to pull a scab off an old and deep wound. Laura's death wasn't the only tragedy the Pattersons had experienced, as Laura's younger brother had shot himself several years after she died. I just couldn't imagine I would be a welcome complication to a long and twisted series of painful events.

Writing the Pattersons felt strange for a bunch of other reasons, too. Like the fact that I'd never contacted them after Laura's death. Having learned about Laura's death in such an awkward manner—and two months after the fact—made talking to anyone about it difficult. At first I'd thought about visiting. Then I thought it was too late to visit and that I should call. Then I thought it was too late to call and I should write a letter. Then twenty years seemed to slip in between my good intentions.

I kept thinking about what their reaction would be to receiving a letter from me now. So I sat down one evening, banged out the letter in ten minutes, and walked it down to the mailbox before I had a chance to change my mind. I figured it would take a few days to reach them, a few days for them to process it, a few days to decide how to respond, and then we'd see what happened. If I don't hear anything in a few weeks, I'll follow up with a phone call, I told myself. "Give it some time" was my latest excuse for doing nothing.

But tonight I don't have to worry about any of this, I reason. There are other ghosts to chase.

From my informal tally of fellow expeditioners I run across in the hallways during my first few hours in the reformatory, there is one report of footsteps followed by human growling coming from a far room in the east wing's infirmary, one butt-grabbing on a staircase in the warden's residence, one sighting of a phantom guard sitting in Central Processing (which turned out to be a napping member of Scott's crew), and one incident of an explorer smelling garbage, which may have been actual garbage (as compared with paranormal garbage). Other than those, not much beyond a few heebie-jeebies. Nothing is happening in my presence that can't be easily explained.

Most people are exploring the prison with the groups they'd come in with. A group will wander through a section of the building, someone will think that he hears/feels/sees something and point it out to the rest of the group, then everyone else in the group investigates the area for a few moments before losing interest and moving along. With the exception of a pizza break around 11 P.M., the groups pretty much repeat this process over and over again for the first five hours.

Scott is unimpressed with my lack of interactions with Mansfield's spirit population, so he tells me to follow him. Seven flights of stairs later we're in the attic above the west cell block retrieving a digital recorder that Scott placed hoping to capture some EVPs.

"So I left this here on the voice-activation setting using this prototype mike I got last week," Scott says. "No one was up here, yet it recorded . . . thirty minutes of . . . something. Let me show you why I like to record up here." He uses his flashlight to lead me through a small hallway off to the side of the staircase where he placed the EVP recording. "There used to be three more stories up here. You can see the marks on the wall there that show each level. Right? Now, walk through here."

We walk through a small opening into a large area that I could tell, even in the dark, goes up much higher than the room we just left. Scott stands still and points his flashlight straight toward the ceiling.

"Now look up," he says.

I shine my flashlight up to meet my gaze. I see three nooses hanging from the rafters directly above us. We're standing at the bottom of the old prison gallows. Three old, slowly rotting pieces of rope, moving slightly in the air we kicked up by opening the doors. We just stand there for a few moments, watching them sway.

It's weird and it's chilling, but it still doesn't explain the fact that the EVP recorder captured thirty minutes of clanking noises. Could they have been made by a ghost? Sure. They also could have been made by a raccoon or the building roof cooling off after a warm day or someone who snuck up here to mess with the recording.

As I stand there watching the nooses sway in the light of our flashlights, my mind drifts to Canton again. I can just go over there in the morning, I tell myself. I can just leave here, sleep for a few hours, and then go. I'm not entirely sure what I plan to do once I get there—show up at the Pattersons' front door, march up to the edge of Lake O'Dea. As compelled as I feel to do it, it seems like a dramatic and ridiculous thing to do. Arguably, spending the night in Mansfield Reformatory is equally ridiculous, but still. The more time I spend in Mansfield not seeing any ghosts, the more I feel compelled to bring this journey to a close. *I wrote a letter,* I say to myself. *Just give it a bit more time.*

Scott drops me with the "three ladies," as he keeps referring to them—his best ghost provokers.

Cheryl is kind of the "hype man" of the crew, trying to work up both the spirits and those trying to communicate with them in order to facilitate some kind of something. She's accompanied by Tiffini, who is carrying around a set of dowsing rods and a combo digital EMF meter/thermometer, and Amy, who has a rigged portable radio known as a "Radio Shack hack" that she's using to try to capture live EVPs. Amy's radio has been altered so that it constantly scans frequencies on the AM band. It pauses for half a second on a frequency before jumping ahead to the next. Whenever it briefly stops on a frequency, you hear a short burst of noise. Sometimes it's static, sometimes it's the audio of a radio station, and sometimes, the crew believes, you can make out the voice of a nearby ghost.

We head to the first-floor staircase in the administration building. The four of us sit on two benches lining the hallway, with the grand staircase rising up at the end of the hall. Supposedly if you sit in this hallway in the pitch dark, you will see full-body apparitions walk down the stairs from the floor above.

Before turning on any of the equipment, we decide to just hang out on the benches for a bit and watch the stairs. It's amazing how easily pitch black plays tricks on your eyes. Once or twice a minute, my mind places a swirl of pale motion at the top of the stairs, momentarily convincing me that I'm seeing something materialize and come toward us.

Amy leans against the wall and turns the EVP radio up to its loudest setting. We all gather around her in a circle, straining to hear the tinny bursts of static and noise.

"Zero-point-zero," Tiffini calls out. This is her way of saying that the EMF meter is picking up exactly nothing. No electromagnetic anything, spiritual or otherwise.

"Okay, are you listening to me? I want you to answer me, now!" Cheryl commands. She's trying to "get tough" with the ghosts, figuring that some orders barked by *a woman* will get them worked up. We'd moved up a floor in the administration building, at the end of a windowless hallway connecting the administration building to the prison cell blocks behind them. We came here because the One Who Answers in Threes told us to.

The location is very familiar in a weird way. In *The Shawshank Redemption,* there's a scene where Tim Robbins's character locks himself into an office and plays an opera record over the prison PA. The guards have to break a window in order to get in and stop him. As we stand in the dark trying to insult a ghost into communicating with us, we're standing in the room where that scene was filmed.

Amy asks if there is someone here whom the spirits want to talk to.

Suddenly, we start hearing a lot of loud sounds emitting from the radio.

Fft-fft-fft-fft-hmmmm-fft-fft-fft-heeaam-fft-fft-fft-fft-hhmmmm-fft-fft-fft-fft-hyyyyymm.

"It said 'him,'" Amy says, raising her eyes to me, the only male (okay, living male) anywhere in the administration wing. "It wants to talk to you."

Tiffini busts out her dowsing rods. Almost as soon as she has them in position, the left one starts to shake and tremble.

"Show me what 'yes' looks like?" she says.

Almost immediately, the dowsing rods swing across each other, forming an *X*, then go back to their normal position, pointing perpendicular from Tiffini's chest.

"Okay, very good," Tiffini says. "Now, can you show me what 'no' looks like?"

Again, almost immediately, the rods swing outward, both pointing as far away from each other as possible.

Tiffini asks if it would like to communicate with us, if it would like us to move to another area of the building, and if the second floor would be a better location. After each question, the dowsing rods cross themselves, then return to their normal position, meaning yes.

"Are you the warden?" Tiffini asks.

The rods cross and then straighten once, twice, and a third time.

This perks Tiffini up considerably.

"Are you Warden Glattke?" she asks.

Again, the rods cross and straighten, three times.

"Uh-oh," Tiffini says. "I think it's him again. He answered three times."

After a momentary pause where I realize that the women all know what Tiffini is talking about, I bite.

"Umm, who is he?" I ask. "The 'three' thing."

"Oh, he is a mischievous one who likes to play around and lie a lot," Tiffini replies. Whenever they ask this spirit questions, he answers three times. So they call him the One Who Answers in Threes.

This seems reasonable.

So, at his request, we came upstairs. Once there, the One

Who Answers in Threes tells us he was the warden, and that he was the warden's wife, and that he was murdered here, and that he was a prisoner, and a bunch of other things. Basically, the One Who Answers in Threes answers yes to everything. Well, almost everything.

I ask if I can try. Tiffini tries to mute my expectations, as I am untrained in how to use the dowsing rods. Plus, who knows if I have the ability to summon spirits?

After I'm given a brief tutorial on how to hold them, the rods are completely still. My hands are out in front of me, positioned almost like I am about to throw a punch but with my fingers loose and relaxed. The rods are resting on the outside of my index fingers.

"Do you want us to leave?" Tiffini scolds the One Who Answers in Threes. "Because if you keep playing around, we'll walk right out of here."

The dowsing rods quickly whip outward and back three times.

"No."

I didn't move at all. I didn't move the rods. My eyes dart around, looking to see if there is something that would make a breeze to move them. But if there was a breeze, wouldn't I feel it against my hand too?

My skepticism melts away. I feel my stomach fill with adrenaline. At the very first sign of something I can't easily explain, I'm back at square one. I notice the rods beginning to shake. Except this time I know what's causing it.

I am beginning to tremble.

"Oh! I think we've got something here," Tiffini says, bringing her EMF meter up to her face. "Zero-point-four . . . zero-point-five."

Cheryl starts to bark out commands to the One Who Answers in Threes, indicating that the answers should be sent through Amy's EVP radio. Amy squats against the wall in almost a fetal position to concentrate. She turns her headphones up so loud we can easily hear them throughout the hallway.

Fft-fft-fft-fft-fft-fft.

"Now you are going to answer me," Cheryl calls out. "Is your spirit bound here, or did you come here recently?"

Fft-fft-neeer-fft-fft-fft-fft.

"New!" Amy shouts out.

"Does that mean he's . . . oh, zero-point-seven, zero-point-eight."

The three ladies seem to get quite excited. I stand next to them, now clenching the dowsing rods tight so that they can no longer move. Even in the dark, Tiffini notices my grip on them, shakes her head, takes them from my hands, and places them in the front pocket of her hoodie.

"Tell me when you came here," Cheryl says sternly.

Fft-fft-fft-fft-fred-fft-fft.

"Friday?" Amy offers.

"When did you arrive in town?" Cheryl asks me.

"Yesterday," I answer. "Friday."

Fft-fft-fft-fft-fft-fft-fft-heeaam-fft-fft-fft-fft.

"It said 'him' again," calls Amy, quickly looking up at me before returning her concentration to the radio noise. "You should have him ask the questions."

It still doesn't sound like anything consistent, just random syllables from a scanning radio. Still, my mouth is completely dry.

"One-point-two . . . One-point-three!" Tiffini exclaims. "Temperature is still going way down. Sixty-two-point-six . . . sixty-one-point-seven!"

The hallway feels noticeably cooler. Cheryl looks at me.

"You ask questions," she says. "And don't be afraid to provoke him."

"Okay," I answer.

We all stand still for a few moments.

I feel something new and unexpected.

I suddenly want to believe this is real.

I want to accept that we are talking to a ghost.

I want to let go of every bit of skepticism I have.

I am completely terrified and I want to believe.

I have no idea what to ask.

"Okay," I yell out. "So . . . I'm here. I'm listening. If you have anything to say, I'm all ears."

"One-point-three," Tiffini yells.

Fft-fft-see-fft-fft-fft-hee-tuu-fft-fft-fft-ur-mmm-fft-fft-fft.

I take a step back from the others.

"One-point-seven. Temperature sixty degrees," Tiffini calls out.

Fft-fft-fft-fft-fft-fft.

"One-point-eight."

"Do you know anything about a Little Girl?" I ask.

I feel completely foolish saying this out loud. The ladies have no idea what I'm talking about, and I immediately cringe, thinking of what must be going through their minds.

Come on, I think. *Just tell me something so I can end this.*

Fft-fft-fft-fft-fft-fft.

"A Little Girl in a Blue Dress. Do you have anything to tell me? Was She real?" I call out.

At that moment I wonder: What if I actually get a response? I mean, I've been struggling to make any sense out of this for more than twenty years. Of course, I've never given this any consideration or thought at all before this point, but what do I plan to do with my answer?

Fft-fft-fft-unnn-fft-fft-ger-fft.

"Anger," Amy calls out.

"Is that supposed to be an answer?" I call out.

"One-point-two . . . zero-point-nine," Tiffini says.

The three of them look at one another.

Fft-fft-fft-fft-fft-fft.

"Zero-point-four," Tiffini reports, moving the meter around the air trying to get a different reading.

Fft-fft-fft-fft-fft-fft.

"Zero-point-zero."

Fft-fft-fft-fft-fft-fft-fft-fft-fft-fft-fft-fft-fft-fft-fft-fft-fft-fft.

After a few moments of listening to the burst of static from the radio, Cheryl steps toward me. "I think he's gone," she says.

I pause and step back from the others. Everyone is quiet.

I'm feeling something else now, that feeling you get when you realize you've been cheated. That epiphany of being scammed or robbed. I don't blame the three of them.

I blame myself.

The ghost isn't gone. He was never there.

I know this, but still, I was right there. I felt foolish. No one pushed me into believing. Even after all I'd thought and experienced, I went there so willingly.

The ladies begin to pack up their gear. It's 4 A.M. You can start to see an outline of color on the horizon. The evening is almost over. I am completely exhausted and still have a seven-hour drive home in front of me.

Instead of bringing me to any conclusion, my night in Mansfield Reformatory has just left me more uncertain. I know I need to come back to Ohio soon. It's time to face some real ghosts.

About a week after returning from Mansfield Reformatory, I received a Facebook message from someone named Jason Patterson. It was Laura's youngest brother. The last time I had seen Jason, he was about seven years old, sitting with his parents on the couch watching television with a coloring book in his lap. Now about thirty, he was the family's only surviving child. His parents had received my letter, then mentioned it on the phone to Jason. I got the distinct impression that Jason was intended (by himself or his parents) to be the gatekeeper. His responsibility was to check me out.

It seemed that Jason, who was ten when Laura died, had started his own quest to learn more about his sister. She seemed as enigmatic a presence in his life as she was in mine. Jason and I helped each other, shared stories, and started connecting each other with friends we knew how to find. Over the next few months, a small network of people emerged—other friends, Laura's boyfriend at the time of her death, and her parents—people reconnecting to talk about a young life we all missed so badly.

I eventually worked up the nerve to ask Jason if their family still had her copy of *Slaughterhouse-Five,* and if so, would they be able to look inside it for me to see if there was an envelope. I felt completely ridiculous asking, partly because I feared the answer and partly because it felt like a potentially semi-creepy thing to ask. Part of me hoped that Jason or his parents would still have it sitting on a shelf in their living room. Then they could pull it down and easily determine if there was a letter nested inside. If it was there, unopened, that meant that Laura had never seen my letter and probably never knew (for sure) how I felt. If the book was there but the letter wasn't, then it was reasonable to assume she had found the letter and, thus, read it.

Jason and his mother looked, but the book wasn't around anymore, nor was it in any of the remaining boxes of Laura's things. I don't know why I was surprised to learn this. I'm not sure I could put my hands on any given possession I owned twenty-five years ago. At the time, I surrounded myself with trappings I considered absolutely essential to the life I led: books, magazines, tapes, albums, clothes, et cetera. They defined me. Yet I probably couldn't fill a shoe box with the things that have stayed in my life since then. Tapes and albums were replaced by CDs, which, in turn, were replaced by binary computer files. Clothes were worn out or became dated. Books were loaned, stolen, lost, forgotten, or sold for rent money. I guess they were, in hindsight, the most meaningless parts of me.

As I connected with the Pattersons and others who'd passed in and out of Laura's life, I had to let go of any notion that Laura and my relationship was in any way a unique one for her. I didn't want to, but I kept finding a web of people throughout her life, men and women, with whom she had similar deep, intimate, and intense one-on-one friendships. Yet, just like me, no one knew much about anyone else. Every single one of them admitted that when they first heard from me (and why I was contacting them), they initially felt a bit threatened. They all thought their relationship with her was unique and were a bit jealous to hear they weren't the only one. I have to admit I felt the same way about them. Laura was my best friend; she was a lot of other people's best friend as well.

I think that was Laura's gift. She was a mysterious girl who had an amazing talent for making you feel like the most inter-esting and important thing in the world to her. You just natu-rally assumed that you were as special to her as she made you feel.

I learned a lot of other things about Laura as well. I learned how badly New York hadn't ended up the way she'd planned.

When she moved to New York, she changed her name. For no clear reason, she started going by her middle name, Lee. When I spoke to anyone who'd met her after she left Ohio for college, they always referred to her as Lee and found it kind of silly that people from Ohio know her as Laura. She got a job at a bookstore and started assembling a new life. But school was hard, New York was overwhelming, and she seemed to be-come a magnet for dark people and dark situations.

After Laura had dropped out of school entirely, her mother got a call from her roommate. Laura had been living in some crappy apartment with a woman and her child, who noticed that Laura hadn't been home in a few days. No one knew where she was. Her things were still in the apartment. She had simply vanished. A few days later Laura's mother got a phone call. The other end of the line was silent, then the phone was hung up. Laura's mother managed to get the number of the caller, somewhere in New Orleans, and called back. She asked if Laura was there. The voice who answered said there was no one by that name there. A few hours later, Laura called.

From talking to people who were in and out of Laura's life at this time, I gathered that she worked very hard to hide what happened to her in New Orleans. Laura knew no one in New Orleans, had never been there before, and had no apparent connection there at all. One day she had simply gotten it into her mind to go and was gone. She seemed to have befriended a group of homeless kids and gotten immediately caught up in the drama that surrounds homeless kids. Different people heard different versions of different stories, but some people thought there may have been drugs involved and some run-ins with police. A few suggested that Laura had been assaulted during her time there, which just drove her further underground.

After several attempts, Laura's mother convinced her to leave New Orleans and come home. Laura agreed, on the condition that her family not ask why she had gone to Louisiana or what she did there. Once she got back to Canton, she seemed fine—until it was time to return to New York.

On the way to the airport, Laura started crying that she didn't want to go back. They turned around and went home to Canton. Laura and her dad did drive to New York a few weeks later to retrieve her things, but otherwise she never returned to her life there. She got a job as a waitress in Canton and started looking for an apartment.

While learning all this deepened my understanding of her and what she went through in the time after our friendship, it felt so foreign to hear these things, which were so unlike the Laura I knew. I still can't decide if this bothers me because her life headed in a direction that was so different from what I expected or because I have locked into my head a vision of her that can't be changed or grow into something different. I can't imagine I will ever be able to fully reconcile the two.

All this new information provided no insight about our relationship, how she had felt about me, or what kind of significance I had to her. Outside of a single birthday card, none of the letters or scribbling I gave her have survived.

One of her best friends throughout her life, a girl named Kris, wrote me a letter after a long phone call, a pile of emails back and forth, and reading some of my reflections on Laura. She told me something I heard regularly from people and had to admit to myself. Despite her thirst for life and singular personality, Laura was an insecure kid. Though she may have looked and acted a bit different, she wasn't all that different from other eighteen-year-old girls. The big difference was that Laura decided not to settle. She cast herself out into the ocean but had trouble keeping afloat.

"It's so clear to me how much you meant to her," Kris wrote. "I believe she gave you her all as a friend, but not more, because that was what she had to give at that point. I feel strongly that because you and your friendship meant so much to her, she valued you too much to delve into territory where she did not have the confidence to handle. When you really care about someone, it's too scary to embark on a path that screams out danger the way intimacy does. It was because she loved you that she couldn't go there with you."

While Laura was back in Canton, Kris was camping with a boyfriend in California. One evening she had a terrible dream (which she does not remember) and woke up worried about Laura. Even though it was the middle of the night, Kris was so freaked that she went to a pay phone and called Laura back in

Ohio. They talked for a few hours, the conversation ending with Kris apologizing for calling so late.

"You never need to apologize for that," Laura told her. "I love you. You need to remember that I am always here. Always here for you whenever you need me."

The next morning Laura was on her way home from the drugstore and was killed.

When I spoke or corresponded with Jason and the others, I kept hearing references to Other Laura. I'd come to learn that Laura Patterson had a deep friendship with a girl named Laura at the same time she was friends with me. Not at relatively the same time, but at *exactly the same time*. When I spoke to Other Laura, we realized that we would often be hanging out with Laura Patterson on the same night. Other Laura spoke about Laura Patterson showing up at her house late at night with some clove cigarettes and wine—clove cigarettes and wine she'd taken from me when I dropped her off. Laura Patterson and Other Laura would go see concerts together, drive off to remote places to talk for hours, and treat each other like best friends. And yet Laura Patterson had never said a word to either of us about the other one. Until I contacted her, we were complete strangers.

"I remember one night we were in the Flats in Cleveland before a 7 Seconds concert," Other Laura told me. "She liked going around there. We were walking around some old useless warehouses, then we came across a brick wall where someone had spray painted IF YOU CAN'T COPE, USE THE ROPE. Hanging in front of the wall was a noose, suspended under an overpass."

The noose was high off the ground, but not that high. Laura and Other Laura were a little drunk at the time but figured they could reach it.

"I think the conversation went, 'You probably couldn't hang yourself in that, could you?' 'You probably couldn't die here, could you?' 'Let's try it,'" Other Laura told me.

Eventually, Other Laura ended up on Laura Patterson's shoulders putting her head inside the noose, just for kicks. The noose looked like it was long enough for Other Laura to reach the ground, so Laura Patterson started to step away and let go of Other Laura.

The noose wasn't long enough to reach the ground.

It quickly tightened around Other Laura's neck. She called out to Laura Patterson for help, and Laura quickly put herself under Other Laura to support her weight.

Other Laura struggled with the noose. The rope, thick with hardened grime, wouldn't loosen. Laura Patterson happened to have a pocketknife and gave it to Other Laura. The pocketknife was about as effective as a toothpick would be for cutting a steak.

"And the more I struggled with the noose," she said, "the tighter and tighter it became. I was choking and struggling and thrashing around. Laura was holding on to my legs and trying to prop me up on her shoulders."

The Lauras had no idea what to do. Laura Patterson was struggling to hold Other Laura up. Both were at the point of exhaustion. The noose was in a small open area surrounded by abandoned buildings in a neighborhood of abandoned buildings. There was no one around. No way to call for help.

"I kept telling Laura that it was okay. I told her, 'You have to just let go. You aren't strong enough,'" Other Laura told me. "She refused. She told me that she wouldn't let go. That she'd never let go."

Eventually, Other Laura forced the noose open just enough to pull it over her face, causing lacerations and burns over her cheeks and ears and even pulling some skin off. They both fell to the ground. They cried and laughed and held each other. They sat there smoking and talking and trying to recover. Then, with Other Laura still bleeding from the rope burns, they decided to go ahead and see the show anyhow.

While listening to her tell the story, I could practically see it playing out in my mind. I knew those warehouses—the same ones that Laura and I had visited. I could see the rope, I could see them horsing around. I could see them getting into trouble. I could see their gratitude at finding a way out. Had I heard this story when it happened, I probably would have seen it as a metaphor for Laura's strength, pushing herself to the point of exhaustion and refusing to let go of her friend. But hearing it now, I see it with another, darker dimension. Knowing more about the complexity of her later life, I can't help but wonder about what she'd do if it had been *her* neck that ended up in that noose. I'm not sure she'd have struggled so much.

"That was the moment," Other Laura recalled. "I knew. I just knew I loved her and I knew that she was the best friend I'd ever have. I know it sounds so bullshit and cinematic, but it was probably the most real moment of my entire life."

● ● ●

A few years ago, not long before my dinner with my friend
Matt, with most of this story uncomfortably stuffed into the
corners of my head and almost-but-never-really forgotten, I
moved to Washington, D.C. I was upstairs in my loft unpacking boxes of books. Or at least I was *supposed* to be unpacking.
As is usual when I'm unpacking, I was lazily browsing and
reminiscing as opposed to putting any effort into systemati-
cally removing and locating the items I was supposed to be
paying attention to in the first place.

I was thumbing through some of my surviving old notebooks and journals when I saw a stray piece of paper flip out of
the box and flutter to the floor next to my foot. I wasn't sure
why, but my attention kept returning to that fallen piece of
paper. Then it dawned on me.

It was the Mystery Poem.

I'm not entirely sure where it had come from, but it had
obviously been stashed inside one of those old journals, where
it had stayed safely hidden from me for close to twenty years.
If I had had it along the way, I'm sure there were various times
that I would have shredded and burned it, used it to console

myself in my grief or to try to make sense of my past. Instead, it had sat unintentionally nestled between some pages of bad poetry I'd written. It had managed to remain undetected all this time, until I was ready to deal with it.

I sat on the floor of the loft for an hour just staring at this tiny scrap of paper and reading it over and over again.

> *Teacher*
> *bring me to heaven*
> *or leave me alone.*
> *Why make me work so hard*
> *when everything's spread around*
> *open, like forest's poison oak*
> > *turned red*
> *empty sleeping bags hanging from*
> > *a dead branch.*

I'd remembered it almost perfectly.

It seemed more dramatic and melancholy than I remembered. It felt more antagonistic than I remembered—like the writer was blaming the Teacher for whatever situation they were in.

But what did it mean? Was I supposed to be the Teacher? Or was that Laura?

Reading it felt like being back at square one. I had no clue what it meant. I had no clue what it was. I had no clue why she had given it to me. I had no clue why she had insisted on not answering my questions.

"Just think about it for a while. You'll eventually figure it out."

The Mystery Poem was the only relic of Laura's and my friendship. I had no photos, no letters, no cards. This was all that was left. Yet, twenty years later I still felt clueless, dense, and like I was missing something frustratingly obvious.

Over the years I had made various stabs at trying to root out its origins. With the evolution of the Internet, I'd periodically Googled parts of the Mystery Poem. I'd pretty much given up, assuming that Laura had written it herself. With it sitting there in my hands, I decided to try one more time. I entered "teacher bring me to heaven" and started combing through the W.A.S.P. lyrics and early home-school education materials that littered the results. On the second or third page, I noticed the phrase "or leave me alone" in the search results quote. The site was in German but contained the first three lines of the poem and a reference to a book by Allen Ginsberg called *Sad Dust Glories*.

A week later a used chapbook arrived in the mail. It was a very rare collection of poems that Allen Ginsberg had written during the summer of 1974. After combing through the book, I found it. The Mystery Poem was actually a stanza, the second stanza of a long poem, one of three in the chapbook, a poem called "To The Dead."

I slumped against the wall as I read the first lines of the poem.

> *You were here in earth—in cities*
> *Now you are not.*
> *Where are you?*
> *Bones in the ground,*
>   *thoughts in my mind.*

What was this? I thought. My first reaction was that it seemed better suited for Laura than for me. In fact, it was perfectly suited for Laura. It made a knot form in my stomach.

Then came the stanza I'd been carrying in my head for twenty years.

I stopped reading.

This was *really* making far more sense as something I would say to Laura, rather than she to me. It was also a prophecy. She was in cities, then she was gone. Bones in the ground. Dead branches. But there was no way she could have ever known where I'd be when I'd figure out where the poem was from—no way she could possibly know what would happen to us both in between.

But she didn't say it was about her from my perspective. She specifically said the poem, or rather the stanza, was just "from me to you"—which really told me nothing.

From there, the parallels kind of fell off a cliff. The poem rambles on about pine trees, Buddhism, and sleeping with young boys. It doesn't even end with a lingering deep thought—it just ends.

It didn't seem to answer much. This poem was about Allen Ginsberg, not Eric Nuzum, and not Laura Patterson. Like everything about Laura, the more I learned just made things less certain, made me feel farther away rather than closer.

••••

"Hello, I'm sure this will probably rank as one of the most unusual letters you'll ever receive," I wrote. "My name is Eric Nuzum. I grew up in your house. While I lived in your house—and this is the unusual part—I thought your attic was haunted."

Over an afternoon cocktail on my front porch, my neighbor summed up what everyone I'd told about my final ghost hunt was thinking but wouldn't say: "They are never going to answer that letter," he said. "And if they did, they're never going to let you into their house."

It did seem like a bit much. Not only the whole backstory but also my request. I asked if I could come visit, go back up into the attic, and see if I could figure out if I was right or not.

Yet three weeks later I'm walking up the driveway of the house that I grew up in—someone else's house.

My parents sold the house in the late eighties to a couple who did extensive renovations to the place, almost doubling its size. That isn't supposed to happen, is it? Aren't our previous homes and schools and workplaces supposed to simply freeze in time when we're done with them? They are supposed to be kept as sacred relics of our life there. We're allowed to change and grow; those places are not. If we ever see them again, even decades later, the first thing we do is focus on the differences.

I have no idea what the owners of the house are expecting when they open the door. Less than a week after sending the letter I got a voice mail from a guy named Tony, who owns the house today. The message simply said that I was welcome to come by whenever I wished. Tony said he found my letter intriguing, then he paused before saying softly, "Considering what we've experienced in the house, I have no problem believing your story is true."

I'd kept the descriptions in my letter deliberately vague. When I returned his call, I got a bit more specific. I told him about the thuds coming from the attic.

"Yup, we've heard that too."

I told him about the feeling that someone was on the other side of the door or watching me.

"Yup, that's happened a bunch of times," he replied. "Sometimes I get the feeling that someone is looking over my shoulder. And no matter which direction I face, I can't shake the feeling. When it happens, it's, like, everywhere."

I couched my story by saying that I was a young kid at the time and a bit on the fucked-up side.

"Listen, I'm fifty-eight years old," he interrupted. "And I'll tell you, I've never experienced anything like this, any other place, at all."

After Tony and his wife answer the door, there are some awkward but genuinely friendly greetings. I can't help but feel overwhelmed by how familiar yet disjointed the place feels. The entrance hallway is supposed to be lined with photos of my family, not some woodland paintings and pictures of strangers. The whole place is carpeted, covering up the beautiful original hardwood floors underneath. The walls are the wrong color. I compliment them on the addition and renovation work, but inside I'm a bit shocked and hurt. This house was my family's home. By changing so much of it, these people were saying that its previous manifestation wasn't good enough.

"Well, would you like to see the upstairs, then?" Tony says.

"Yeah, sure," I say, waiting for him to lead the way.

Despite the number of changes to the house, the doorway to the attic is exactly the same. Same finish. Same door handle. In fact, when he opens the door, it is like stepping back in time.

The last time I was up these stairs was the morning I went to Timken Mercy. I start to feel a little sick. It's fear building up in the pit of my stomach.

Tony stands aside and waves his arm in front of the open stairway. "After you," he says.

As I reach the top of the stairs, I can't help but wonder if this is unwise. Despite all the work I've done to confront my fears and memories, being here sets me right back to where I was at the beginning of my journey. What if She's here? What if She can follow me back out, hitch a ride, and hang around my house in Washington?

As I silently walk around my old purple bedroom, now a tasteful shade of blue, Tony starts talking about the experiences he's had in the house. The door to the spare room in the back of the attic stands open, but I can't walk anywhere near it.

"Yeah, we used to hear lots of noise from up here," he says. "That was probably the bats."

"What's that?" I ask. "Bats?"

"Yeah. We found a lot of bats living in the chimney. They'd made their way into the walls as well. We could hear scratching."

"But that doesn't fit," I say. "I heard thuds. Heavy, thick thuds. Bats don't make thud sounds."

"Well, we heard bats up here. They were everywhere when we bought the place."

Whenever people buy a house, they convince themselves that the previous owners were crazy idiots with no taste and questionable home-remodeling and maintenance skills. I realize that, to Tony, we were those crazy idiots, allowing bats to take up residence in our chimney. I just let it go.

Tony shares details of his other spooky encounters in the house, but they don't match my own. Most of his experiences happened in their bedroom, which is in the new addition to the house, which wasn't even built when Little Girl was haunting me here. And he always feels like there's something in the room with him, even telling me that, on several occasions, he feels something sit on the bed while he lies there.

"But up here," I say. "Have you ever felt or experienced anything up here in the attic?"

"Here? No. This was the kids' playroom. We turned this into a big fort when the kids were young," he says. "This was always a happy place. It was really neat."

Tony keeps talking about his experiences, but they feel more and more tangential to me. Whether it's supernatural phenomena or an active imagination, it becomes apparent that his experiences—real or otherwise—are his experiences. They have nothing to do with me.

I finally work up the nerve to walk toward the spare room.

As I step inside and stand there, it is completely foreign to me. It shouldn't be. Outside of a coat of paint, new windows, and carpet, it is exactly the same room. I turn to Tony. "It's so different than I remember" is all I can think to say.

He agrees, yes, it is. That was a long time ago, he adds with a chuckle.

It was. Though it is perfectly preserved in my head, that place doesn't exist anymore. If it was an evil place or a place with bad mojo and history, the only place that badness existed was in my memory. To cleanse it, all I have to do is let it go.

I pause for a moment after realizing that what I'm really feeling is nothing. If anything, I guess I feel . . . alone. There is no ghost hiding up here. There is nothing up here to be scared of. Whatever was here at one time has moved on, probably long ago. I should move on as well. None of it is still here. The only place it existed was inside me.

"You know, at the time I lived up here, I had a friend who died," I say.

Tony looks a little confused.

"Was she the one who you thought haunted here?" he asks.

"No," I say, adding a smile to demonstrate that I am, in fact, not crazy. "She haunts somewhere else."

"Well," he says, shuffling a bit uncomfortably. "Have you found what you were looking for?"

"Thank you for doing this, but I'm not sure it was ever here," I say, turning to head down the stairs.

• • • • •

So, after all this, do I believe in ghosts?

If by ghosts you mean cloudy spectral things that float around a room, say "Boo," and then vaporize into thin air, then no. I don't believe in that.

After spending many hours in some of the most notorious haunted locations I could find, I've been brought to the inevitable conclusion that I don't believe that *places* are haunted, but I do believe *people* are haunted. People carry around the ghosts of their pasts, the people they've known, the world they've experienced. Most of the time, we never notice they are there. If there are any ghosts in my life, I no longer would count the Little Girl in a Blue Dress among them. Am I haunted by Laura? Yes. Am I haunted by the other loss I've experienced? Again, yes. Yes I am.

All this ties to a question I've had for years: Why do almost all ghost stories involve a spook that comes out only at night? Every time I ask this of a ghost hunter or paranormal expert, I get the same answer. They note that people have ghost experiences during the day all the time; they are just far less common. But at night, the world quiets, slows down, and goes dim. The noises, trappings, and energy of the daytime fade into darkness. All we are left with is ourselves and the things we carry around with us all the time: memories, thoughts, and experiences. During our everyday lives, we are too distracted. For all we know, ghosts could be everywhere and we are too frantic with our daylight lives to notice. But when we're alone at night, our senses can focus on different things: sounds we'd otherwise miss, images or motion that wouldn't stand out in the middle of the afternoon.

When the world fades away, we are left in the darkness with ourselves and the things we carry with us. But are they paranormal presences? Ghosts? Spirits? Specters? Phantoms? Poltergeists? I don't think it matters what we call them. To those who experience them, they are real.

But do *I* believe? Do I believe that what happened in those dreams and in that attic was real?

I think I've come to a place of peace with that question. My answer would be that this quest has convinced me less and less that these questions really matter. This quest started off trying to prove whether ghosts were real or not, but it ended up being about casting them off, being done with them, coming to a place where I am ready to let them go.

The Little Girl in a Blue Dress had some meaning in my life regardless of whether or not She was real. She was a provocateur, a guardian angel, or perhaps a messenger. In the end, whether She was a ghost, a drug-induced hallucination, a lost soul, or a complete illusion really doesn't make a whole lot of difference. While a definitive answer has eluded me, I've come to realize that the answer doesn't have a lot of bearing on my life.

Throughout the course of this quest, I found myself becoming increasingly comfortable with the "haunted" places and things I was experiencing. While I never once encountered definitive evidence to prove anything one way or another, I encountered plenty of potentially freak-out-inducing phenomena. I've since watched other people shudder and squirm when I share stories I learned along the way, and I realize that they didn't really bother me so much.

In fact, up until the other night, I would have told you that I had made tremendous progress in dealing with my fear. That changed during a dinner with my aunt, uncle, and cousins. They asked me about my ghost adventures, so I told a few stories about Lily Dale and Mansfield Reformatory and so on. They squirmed and laughed and shook their heads. Then my cousin's boyfriend, Jerry, who'd been quiet the entire time, spoke up. "You know, I've had a fair amount of ghost stuff happen."

Jerry once had a job as a maintenance worker at a state park in New Jersey, which entailed periodically staying overnight in some old buildings on the grounds. Along the beach were two old, abandoned lifesaving stations that were used to provide medical attention to those injured on shore or at sea. It also once served as a temporary morgue for drowned swimmers and shipwreck victims.

"We'd hear stuff all the time down there," he said. "Children laughing, crying, all kinds of stuff, and nobody was around. We'd hear these voices, then go look to see if somebody was there, and it would be empty."

The house he stayed in had previously belonged to an old lady who sold her property to the state. Jerry and his co-workers all believed that the old woman's ghost was still hanging around the place to keep an eye on things.

"It was so common that I'd just talk to her whenever I'd hear her moving things around," he said. "I'd say things like, 'It's just me, Jerry,' or 'I'm just getting something to eat.'"

Jerry told of a time he was downstairs and heard feet dragging across the floor above. He went upstairs and saw nothing. Once he went back downstairs, it started up again—the sound of shoes dragging across a sand-covered floor. He yelled upstairs to keep it down, and everything suddenly got quiet.

All of us were absolutely silent as Jerry told his stories. Afterward, others around the table started talking about their own experiences. My older cousin remembered repeatedly smelling Bobalu's favorite perfume long after she died. My aunt talked about watching the motion detectors on her security system trip repeatedly while she heard strange noises.

I took it all in stride. But then later that night I had terrible dreams of being trapped inside an old house with a collection of odd shadows and voices lingering around the corners. After barely sleeping, I realized that I might not have come very far at all. Ghost stories can still send me into a tailspin, often when I least expect it.

Ultimately, what this quest has reinforced is that I am a huge believer in fate.

I feel that everything happens for a reason. I think that all things are interconnected and even the smallest gesture serves a larger purpose. I believe a tiny event in one life can ripple through the lives of others, growing more significant with each progressive wave. Everything that rises must converge. Nothing cheesy like butterfly wings eventually creating hurricanes, but something more simple and human.

The big problem is, and always has been, that I don't know what that reason is. I don't know why I had the experiences I had. I don't know why I made the choices I made. I don't know what the Mystery Poem was supposed to mean. I don't know why I am alive and Laura is not.

I guess, if anything, I've come to realize that it is okay not to have all the answers right away. It's okay to never have the answers. Because life isn't neat and binary and clean; life is messy, troubled, and leaves ghosts in its wake.

I'd like to tell you that I survived these events in my younger life without repercussions, but in truth I've suffered some long-term cognitive effects: an inability to recall lists, remember names and events, and, occasionally, to pronounce words. But I still consider myself lucky.

I'd like to tell you that this story has a happy ending, but there really is no ending.

I'd like to tell you that I have always been well behaved, but that isn't true.

I'd like to tell you that my life was carefree and painless after that time, but I can't.

I'd like to tell you that the relationships with my family have always been good, but they haven't.

I'd like to tell you that I never again used alcohol or drugs to deaden pain, but I can't do that either.

What I can say is this: Remember that feeling I described when Laura got into my car after returning from Finland? About ten years later, I felt it a second time. I had just started working at a public radio station in Ohio. I was walking quickly around a corner and came about two inches from plowing into the most beautiful woman I had ever seen. She had dark red lips and deep brown hair and looked more than a bit annoyed that I'd almost knocked her over. I just stood there speechless, staring at her. I felt numb and everything was still, as if time had stopped just so I could drink in that moment. I stumbled out an apology and stepped aside. It took me another nine years, but I eventually talked her into marrying me. We recently welcomed a son into our lives.

As for Laura's and my friendship, I think the best way to

explain it is to share how I've come to feel about the Mystery Poem. As much as I've struggled with the poem's meaning over the years, I think I've finally figured something out.

Whatever "gift" was inherent in Laura giving me the poem, it wasn't the words or their meaning. The gift wasn't the ideas and emotion it contained.

The gift was the poem itself.

The gift was being angry at Laura.

The gift was losing the poem.

The gift was keeping it in my mind for more than twenty years.

The gift was finding the Mystery Poem once again, by mistake.

The gift was wanting to know more.

The gift was wanting to understand my fear and struggling to face it.

I never told anyone this at the time, but I carried the Mystery Poem with me on all my ghost-hunting adventures. It was in the trunk of our rented Mustang as we cruised up and down Clinton Road. I'd pull it out of my suitcase while in Lily Dale in the evenings. I carried it in my pocket across the battlefields of Gettysburg and through the prison cells of the Mansfield Reformatory. I even had it with me when I climbed the stairs to my parents' old attic. All that time I was hoping that some bizarre something would happen that would stir a revelation inside me and its meaning would suddenly become clear.

"Just think about it for a while. You'll eventually figure it out."

The thirty-four words of the Mystery Poem don't need to mean anything.

The gift was the poem itself.

There is no possible way that Laura could ever know where

that piece of paper would take me. There is no possible way she'd ever know how right she was, or how long it would take, or what I'd have to go through in order to understand.

Laura was just a girl. A girl who died too young.

I'm still here. And it's my job to make the best of it.

My original plan was to burn the Mystery Poem during my final ghost hunt or perhaps hide it somewhere in some supposedly haunted place where no one would ever find it. What good is it if I'm not willing to set it on fire? Then, to me, it would just be a memory—a symbol. However, I've decided to hold on to it for a while longer, keep it safe from my sometimes questionable decision making.

"Just think about it for a while. You'll eventually figure it out."

I park the car at our usual spot at the end of the road near Lake O'Dea and face the front toward the lake as the moon sways and shimmies against the rippling water.

As we settle in, I get out and lie back on the hood of the car, listening as Laura explains some theory. I feel the heat from the car engine warm my back.

"What I'm saying is . . . so . . . we think our lives move along some kind of linear path through time, right?"

"Okay," I say.

"One thing happens, then another, then another," she continues. "Day after week after month after year. Right? So do you think time itself moves along a linear path, or we just think it does? I mean, what if it doesn't? What if everything is just scrambled up or it all happens in a flash and it just takes us years to soak it all in?"

"So what you're saying is that maybe the past isn't the past, because it may be happening right now?" I ask.

"Or maybe even that the past hasn't happened yet," she says. "Maybe it is all just one big moment; everything happens at once."

"Hmmm, that's interesting. I have no idea," I reply. I really don't care about time; I just like listening to her talk.

I close my eyes and inhale deeply through my nose.

The cold October air fills my lungs. It is energizing. It makes me feel alive.

I let out a deep sigh. "I love the fall," I say, interrupting her.

"Well, good for you," she says, continuing where she left off, joining me on the hood of the car. "Then that means nothing is old, nothing is new, nothing ever goes away. That there is no past, no future, only right now."

She rests her head on my arm.

I feel calm and relaxed.

I feel like everything is just as it should be.

I feel like anything is possible.

Teacher
bring me to whatever
or leave me alone
why make me work so hard
when everything's spread around
open, like forest's poison oak
· turned red
EMPTY SLEEPING BAGS HANGING from
a dead branch